FREYA STARK

The Valleys of the Assassins

and Other Persian Travels

INTRODUCED BY MONISHA RAJESH

JOHN MURRAY

First published in Great Britain in 1936 by John Murray (Publishers)
An Hachette UK company

This edition first published in 2021

1

B format ISBN 978-1-529-37977-8
eBook ISBN 978-1-529-37976-1

Typeset in Adobe Garamond by Hewer Text UK Ltd, Edinburgh
Printed and bound in Great Britain by Clays Ltd, Elcograf S.p.A.

John Murray policy is to use papers that are natural, renewable and
recyclable products and made from wood grown in sustainable forests.
The logging and manufacturing processes are expected to conform
to the environmental regulations of the country of origin.

John Murray (Publishers)
Carmelite House
50 Victoria Embankment
London EC4Y 0DZ

www.johnmurraypress.co.uk

Contents

Part One: Luristan

Part Two: Mazanderan

Introduction

Freya Stark was one of a kind. Fearless, determined, and largely dependent on her wits, she weaponised these qualities to explore some of the Middle East's most inhospitable regions with aplomb. Unlike her peers – both male and female – who often exploited aristocratic connections or relied on family wealth, guides and luxuries to conduct their expeditions, Stark usually set off against official advice, atop a mule, wearing little more than cotton shoes, a darned skirt and a smile to disarm her opponents. While absorbed in her tales, it's easy to forget that she was travelling in the 1930s, so casual is her retelling of being mauled by dogs, and fainting from malaria in a part of the world where less than a handful of Europeans had ever travelled, let alone a single white woman with no clear incentive.

Judged by today's standards, her jaunts into the tribal regions of Persia would put most contemporary travel writers to shame. 'Jaunts' might sound diminishing when taking into consideration the scope and scale of Stark's achievements, but as the author herself declared, 'I must admit for my own part I travelled single-mindedly for fun. I learned my scanty Arabic for fun, and a little Persian – and then went for the same reason to look for the Assassin castles and the Luristan bronzes in the manner here related.' Which begs the question: what on earth would her travels have revealed had she set out with great intentions?

THE VALLEYS OF THE ASSASSINS

On her ninth birthday, Stark received a copy of the *Arabian Nights* from an aunt, a book that inspired a lifetime of travel, with the exception of a short period during which she was married. However, after separating from her husband she returned to her one true love and began travelling again. In 1934 she published her first book, *The Valleys of the Assassins*, the story of an ambitious treasure hunt in Luristan, followed by an attempt to discover the stronghold of the Assassins in Alamut, a Persian sect that had 'treated murder as the suffragette did the hunger strike and turned it into an avowed political weapon'. This became the first of twelve volumes of travel writing that vaulted her to the high ranks of a society that had once excluded her. On the book's publication she became a celebrated geographer, explorer and cartographer, sending the maps she had drawn of the uncharted region to the Royal Geographical Society.

As a fellow woman travel writer, it's hard not to imagine how one might have felt in Stark's shoes, arriving from her then-home in Baghdad to travel alone through Persia. That said, although she certainly arrives on her own, Stark is never without company, often to her dismay. Before departing for Harsin, she is told that the head of police himself will accompany her along the road. Wonderful, a more timid traveller might feel. But Stark's frustration is relatable to the travel writer who knows very well the need to blend into the background in order to takes notes, observe customs and eavesdrop with ease, while also hoping not to be 'deported or interned as a vagrant'. Typically, she's quick to recognise a possible advantage, and wonders if she might be able to 'persuade him in the looting of a grave or two'.

Now here's where things become tricky. In our post-pandemic world, we will all have to become more mindful about how we travel: climate change is a serious and unavoidable issue, as is the nature of how we engage with our surroundings. Decolonising travel is high on the agenda, so how do we as twenty-first century readers reconcile this pioneering adventure alongside the blunt fact that Stark is ransacking graves in a foreign country? While she admits 'I knew what I was doing went directly against this law', she justifies her actions by asserting that theft is rampant and that her actions aren't going to cause problems for her Persian assistants who believe she has permission from Teheran. In a genre long dominated by European explorers, Stark can't be blamed uniquely for her often overt displays of entitlement as she passes through these regions with an almost inherent understanding that she will be well received, assisted and granted access with her British passport. One can't help but wonder how the same tribespeople would have been treated in England should they have arrived to pilfer skulls from ancient tombs. Would they too have been offered a house of their choice with the residents put out for the night and their only food devoured? It's a privilege that even the modern-day Western traveller takes for granted, not realising the hoops and hurdles that citizens of most other countries have to jump through and overcome to travel.

In his *New York Times* book review, published in November 1934, Charles G. Poore noted that Stark is 'given to salty commentaries', many of which are descriptions of the very people who are assisting her journey and hosting her in their homes, 'sinister-looking villains', their roving eyes 'shrewd', 'cunning' or 'sly'. But these, while unacceptable today, can be forgiven as a relic of their time. Invariably these salty comments come at moments of frustration when Stark is either being held up by the hapless Shah Riza saying his prayers in her Burberry coat, or overhearing her plans being deliberately scuppered. As the journey goes on, her characters appear 'charming and kind' with 'bright dancing eyes', which suggest Stark is finding herself more at home in her surroundings, and she marks the end of the book with a beautiful and poignant gesture in a garden surrounded by flowers.

Throughout her life, Stark wrestled with her own womanhood, preferring to stay in the company of men while tossing off dismissive comments about the ignorance of women and their whining, and notes in this unfortunately timeless line, 'The great and almost only comfort about being a woman is that one can always pretend to be more stupid than one is and no one is surprised.' It's this very comfort that serves to underpin hairy moments in her travels where most men would have come undone. While researching my own books, I have often spent many a train journey smiling vacantly, struggling against every instinct to admonish the bombastic, but choosing instead to lap up their unfiltered conversation for my notes. Although Stark is well-equipped to disarm men who present an obstacle, it's her interactions with the women and children she encounters that are the most touching and revealing. Quick to produce quinine and any other form of equipment to remedy their ails, Stark finds herself bedding down with harems where she deftly observes the dynamics of the wives' relationships with one another that defy the usual stereotypes about submissive Middle Eastern women. It's here that Stark is at her most tender and humane, fighting back the urge to impose her own morals when faced with child brides, and hungry children watching her finish their last morsels.

Towards the end of the book, it becomes clear that Stark is most at home in the wild, free from restraints and left to roam at will. Tetchy and bothered when things don't go to plan, her tone instantly lifts when she finds herself in the heart of natural beauty, so much so that one can almost hear her smile through her descriptions. 'The valley was now full of loveliness. A last faint sense of daylight lingered in its lower reaches. The moon flooding the sky with gentle waves of light. Here was more than beauty. We were remote. No map had yet printed its name for the eyes of strangers. A sense of quiet life, unchanging, centuries old and forgotten held our pilgrim souls in peace.' It's also telling that she excelled in cartography, given the extraordinary detail with which she documents and explains what she sees, conveying a deep insight into how her mind worked. She likens mountain ridges to the lines on a fever chart and names every hamlet, village, town, mountain, plant and tree that she spots. From the colours of the walnut trees lining the banks of black rivers, to willow trees drooping over fields of daisies, she's constantly scanning and forming pictures in her mind's eye. However, it's in her search for peace that she reveals her soul, and when she finds it, one can feel the explosion of romantic love for the landscape, and her solitude within it. It's almost as if she knew, ninety years ago, that tourism would become a blight on the natural world, noting that, 'to go to the lonely and majestic places of the world for poor motives, to turn them to cheap advertisement or flashy journalism, jars like a spiritual form of prostitution on your true lover of the hills.' And with that, she sits in the sun, resting her eyes in the sight of the hills, willing her reader to do the same.

Monisha Rajesh, 2021

A Note on the Text

In looking back into the past to rediscover, and republish, out-of-print travel books, we have inevitably come across terminology that might not be used today. We made the decision not to change Stark's original words, but rather to acknowledge that language and attitudes have moved on since the time of writing.

The Valleys of the Assassins

Preface

An imaginative aunt who, for my ninth birthday, sent a copy of the *Arabian Nights*, was, I suppose, the original cause of trouble.

Unfostered and unnoticed, the little flame so kindled fed secretly on dreams. Chance, such as the existence of a Syrian missionary near my home, nourished it; and Fate, with long months of illness and leisure, blew it to a blaze bright enough to light my way through labyrinths of Arabic, and eventually to land me on the coast of Syria at the end of 1927.

Here, I thought, all difficulty was over: I had now but to look around me, to learn, and to enjoy.

And so it would have been had not those twin Virtues so fatal to the *joie de vivre* of our civilized West, the sense of responsibility and the illusion, dear to well-regulated minds, that every action must have a purpose – had not these virtues of Responsibility and Purpose met me at every step with the embarrassing enquiry: '*Why* are you here alone?' and: '*What* do you intend to *do?*'

I may confess at once that I had never thought of why I came, far less of why I came alone: and as to what I was going to do – I saw no cause to trouble about a thing so nebulous beforehand. My sense of responsibility was in effect deficient, and purpose non-existent. When excessively badgered, the only explanation I could think of for being so unwantedly in Asia was an interest in Arabic grammar – a statement rarely accepted in that candid spirit in which I offered it to unconvinced enquirers.

I came to the conclusion that some more ascetic reason than mere enjoyment should be found if one wishes to travel in peace: to do things for fun smacks of levity, immorality almost, in our utilitarian world. And though personally I think the world is wrong, and I know in my heart of hearts that it is a most excellent reason to do things merely because one likes the doing of them, I would advise all those who wish to see unwrinkled brows in passport offices to start out ready labelled as entomologists, anthropologists, or whatever other -ology they think suitable and propitious.

But as this book is intended for the Public, and is therefore necessarily truthful, I must admit that for my own part I travelled single-mindedly for fun. I learned my scanty Arabic for fun, and a little Persian – and then went for the same reason to look for the Assassin castles and the Luristan bronzes in the manner here related. And here I would like to thank the much-tried, frequently accused, and not unreasonably perplexed officials who came across me, for much indulgence, not always unmixed with disapproval, but invariably kind.

I have given events and impressions as they occurred, as accurately as I could. This I am particularly anxious to say in regard to the Treasure Hunt in Luristan, which might otherwise be suspected of fantasy by readers unacquainted with lands so sensational: the only alteration made there is to disguise the situation of the treasure map and cave.

I have many to remember who were good to me in my journeying, British, Arabic, and Persian, whose presence lives in the enchanted frame of days and whose kindnesses are beyond the possibility of recording.

FREYA STARK,
Villa Freia
Asolo
Italy

Part One

Luristan

I

A Fortnight in N.W. Luristan

In the wastes of civilisation, Luristan is still an enchanted name. Its streams are dotted blue lines on the map and the position of its hills a matter of taste. It is still a country for the explorer.

> He finds out what he cannot do
> And then he goes and does it.

I did not do it, for I penetrated only a very little way. But I spent a fortnight in that part of the country where one is less frequently murdered, and I saw the Lurs in their own medieval garb – the white tight-waisted coat with sleeves hanging in points from the elbow and white felt caps over the curls that hide their ears. As the aim of the Persian government is to have them all dressed *à la Ferangi* in a year's time, with peaked *képis* and the Shah's portrait stamped on the lining, it is worth while perhaps to give a picture of them as far as possible before too much tidiness spoils them.

Behold then *Hajji* and me, climbing on very scraggy ponies up to the Varazan Pass. Behind us is the town of Nihavend and the nearer mound of Gian where French archæologists give kind hospitality and press Bovril and ham into one's saddle-bags – the latter not to be touched, alas! because of religion, which is always interfering with the pleasant conduct of life. *Hajji* looks gloomy.

Friends have told him he is going to be killed. Lessening under our feet, the grassy slopes of Kuh Garu shut in Luristan as with a wall. This climbing into a country which is not considered safe is exhilarating, though no sense of peril is possible in so bright sunlight, such radiant solitude, such breadth of mountain ranges under the pale October sky. As a matter of fact, it is only the other three passes over Kuh Garu which are presumed to be held by robbers at this moment: our Varazan has been in the hands of government for the last six weeks. It is as well to know this before-hand; otherwise one might take the garrison for bandits instead of policemen. They come tumbling out of a round stone tower, their guns polished and clean among the *débris* of the rest of their attire. They take a toll of eight krans (1s. 5d.) for every pack animal across the pass. When the robbers held it, they took only seven-pence more, and might have gone on making a regular income for a long time if they had not lost their tempers one day with two merchants who thought to bargain fivepence off the tariff and whose death caused a stoppage in the charcoal trade which comes out of Luristan by Kuh Garu; whereupon government dislodged the bandits, handed over ten guns to some Lurs of Khava who are on the side of law and order for the time being, and left the pass and its revenue in their hands.

These volunteers were friendly people, delighted with conver-sation and chivalrous enough to forgo their eight krans in honour of their first *Ferangi* from the plain.

They brought little glasses of tea into the sunshine, spread a felt rug, and began to talk about the present security of Persia with the enthusiasm which is general there among the poorer sort. One of them had a wounded leg which I doctored with brandy, while the chief of the post, pushing his long hair out of his eyes and leaning on his gun, slowly read the address on my letter of introduction to the Governor at Alishtar. This letter was an 'Open Sesame': its quite insignificant contents were luckily sealed up, but the name on the envelope had already served to get me through the entanglements of the Nihavend police: its mere production gave the impression that I travelled with the authority of governments behind me and when I handed it to anyone, I tried to cultivate a manner to correspond. I had another letter to the brother of the Keeper of the Varazan, which produced more friendliness and promise of a night's lodging in the plain of Khava below. The Ten sat in a row looking at me: so did two menials who, they explained, came to do the sweeping, though there was nothing to show for such domestic efforts among the rocks. As the caravans of tribesmen climbed up to the pass, one of our group would stroll across to waylay them and exact the toll: the small black oxen, scarce visible between enormous sacks of goatwool filled with charcoal or grain, strayed on, surefooted, while the men stood counting out the money and brought news of the jungle or the town according as they came from south or north. Their road lay like a ribbon far below us across the plain of Khava whose southern edge, fringed with small pointed hills and further wave-like ridges, vanished into a gentle distance. Very few Europeans travel in this country. Sir A. T. Wilson has been there, and perhaps half a dozen more: and in 1836 Sir Henry Rawlinson marched his Persian regiment across it, locating in his mind as he went the vanished nations whose horses grazed over these open downs.

We parted from the garrison and proceeded with difficulty owing to the jagged steepness of the southern slope, which is scarce practicable for horses. The way from the pass runs down a stony cleft. The whole range is like a wave whose gentle slope we had been climbing from the Nihavend plain, and we now had the sheer side to negotiate: and as we slipped and stumbled among the sliding surfaces of the limestone, *Hajji* forgot that he had come to me pretending to know every inch of the road, and complained in a pathetic voice that this was no place for anyone but thieves.

It seemed right that the entrance to the forbidden country should not be too easy. Our expectation had been rising ever since Nihavend which, lying so close, yet speaks of Luristan as a region unknown, governed by laws and standards in which the peaceful townsmen have no part. Every day, from far in the southern jungles, the caravans of black oxen bring their loads of corn or charcoal across the mountain wall. The tribesmen, with uncombed hair and eyes frankly hostile, squat in groups of their own under the rampart of the old fortress and have no social dealings with the citizens. The guard on the Varazan, with its ragged clothes and shining gun-barrels, emphasized the point, as it were. When we came to them we reached the gate of a new country. No one travels here unless he has the freedom of the tribes or some other protection: there were no peasants or merchants among the climbers to the pass: only white-coated Lurs fixing us with suspicious, fearless eyes. They gave no greeting, but were ready enough, I found, to answer if one spoke to them.

And now, at a bend in our narrow gorge, the plain of Khava opened out below us, washing like a yellow wave to the rocks of Kuh Garu; dotted in an Arcadian way with black flocks and tents, and intersected from east to west by a grass-banked stream. Away on its southern side it was all pastoral solitude running to small hills; but in its centre were harvested fields of corn, tribesmen tilling, villages where the mountain sank into the plain, and mounds of buried cities here and there.

These must once have been populous places, with a beaten track winding over one of the easier passes from Nihavend or Harsin through the villages of Khava to Alishtar – mentioned in the fourteenth century as an important city – and so to Khurramabad and the eastern plains. Somewhere in this district the rebel Gautama is thought to have been vanquished by Darius: here possibly were the Nisaian pasture lands visited by Alexander on his way up into Persia, but famous for their horses under the Achæmenians long before him. One finds bronzes, flints, and earthenware in the lonely valleys. Wave after wave of people unnamed and unnumbered lose themselves here in unrecorded dimnesses of time.

This, however, was not what occupied our thoughts, but rather the problem of how to find our particular Lurs in a plain about ten miles by twenty in which no one knew the way. A weedy tall man with bushy eyebrows had come with us from Nihavend as a guide. He also, I soon discovered, had never been up before – and he was furthermore a wreck from opium, which takes people's legs more completely than beer: he would sit down at intervals looking like a traveller in the early stages of a Channel crossing, and refuse to take any interest in our hopes for lunch among friends.

We reached the area of cultivation, and, riding gently through ploughed fields and melon patches, finally came upon people who directed us to our Keram Ali Lurs at the mound of Qal'a Kafrash in the west, where a few mud houses and a row or two of black tents combine to make a village. The mound, about eighty feet high by eighty broad, rises with that artificial regularity of shape which shows the buried work of man all over Persia and Mesopotamia; it gives the feeling of a cemetery incredibly old to many a landscape there. The Lurs of Kafrash, however, were not oppressed by their antique surroundings: they were as cheerful a lot of villains as you could wish to meet, and delighted with us for being, as they said, brave enough to come among them. In the absence of the Khan, his wife ruled the house. She was a lovely woman with a very narrow long face and arched eyebrows – a beauty fierce and strange, but with the most roguish smile imaginable. Her dark hair, with gleams of henna in it, was curled in two long ringlets on each shoulder and crowned with an immense *sarband* or turban of coloured silks aslant over one eye, which gave an absurd mixture of rakishness and dignity to her appearance. She wore an old red velvet coat full at the waist, with tinsel edges, over a loose cotton gown of yellow printed flowers: and she walked like a queen. She ruled her household also like a queen, with none of the submissiveness of Persian women in general. She seated me beside her, tried my hat and examined as much of my clothing as she could get at, embraced me, told me that I was her sister, and allowed me to hold the baby in my arms. Cousins, uncles, brothers, and brothers-in-law meanwhile sat in a half-circle on the opposite side of the hearth, waiting for these female amenities to end. They had furtive, long faces, with eyes rather near together, but strong, big-boned and healthy. They thought nothing of the people of the plain. 'We smoke no opium here,' said they, glancing at my guide, who was just lifting a piece of lighted charcoal to his second pipe. *Hajji* too, who cannot conceal that he thinks a Persian town the only synonym for civilization, was being left in the cold as an alien. But I am a hill woman myself, and I travelled in Luristan for pleasure: they accepted me kindly.

When evening came, and the last mouthfuls of rice had been scooped off the round tray before us, they brought an enormous camp bed for me to sleep in, looted from the Russians. My host and his beautiful wife arranged themselves under a quilt in a corner of the room; and four brothers or cousins disposed themselves at my feet. As a last after-thought, they picked my shoes off the floor and put them under my mattress, for I had not yet learnt that one sleeps on all one possesses in Luristan.

Next morning might have been an autumn day in Scotland. A faint mist trailed in and out of the woollen roofs of the tents and along the ground, among sparse willow trees that followed the course of a little stream. While the women lighted the fire indoors, the men stood to get warm against a sheltered wall in the early sun. Mahmud, a shifty-eyed brother of our host, offered to take me over the pass to Alishtar. 'Your man from Nihavend will not be necessary,' said he. 'He can go home.'

Now I had been thinking this myself, but did not like the idea so well when presented by someone who might be planning unpleasantness. It meant risking a lonely pass in unprepossessing company with one's escort diminished by half, and *Hajji's* frightened looks, and the assembled tribesmen coldly taking note of them, made matters worse. I thought, however, that a man who smokes much opium is very little use in a crisis: and if the Lurs meant mischief they had every facility for carrying it out whatever our arrangements. I said I should be delighted, and tactfully added that I would remember the tribe's kindness to the Governor in Alishtar. *Hajji* tried some half-strangled remonstrance, cowed by the hostile eyes upon him. As for the guide from Nihavend, he burst into tears. 'A man like that would bring bad luck to anyone,' our new guide said as we watched him lope away across the fields.

We followed our track of the day before, along the Badavar River, by the village of Noah, through cultivated land: then turned south, where there are no villages, but rolling downs for miles, covered with thorny bushes of gum tragacanth which the Lurs collect and sell in the towns: every plant has a small pit dug round it, the stem is incised thrice a year at an interval of a week or so, and the gum oozes out ready to be sold. These pits make the most irritating country to ride over, as bad as a rabbity bit of Dartmoor.

As we were going along in pleasant loneliness, talking of this and that, with only here and there a shepherd and his flocks to break the long lines of curving empty land, I began to notice that we were not keeping to our intended direction of the Gatchkah Pass, where a police post guards the track to Alishtar.

'Why are we going so far south?' I asked.

'The Gatchkah is not safe to-day,' said Mahmud with one of his furtive glances. 'We are going round by a different way.'

'I thought there were police up there,' said I.

'So there are: but it is hilly country.' With which cryptic remark we had to be contented, and rode on in meditative silence, rather anxiously.

And now we came over a little ridge and saw before us a new settlement of tents and a few houses, the hamlet of Deh Kush. And a surprise was beyond: for there in absolute solitude wound a road, the unfinished motor road from Khurramabad to Harsin. Between us and it rode a policeman in pale-blue uniform.

He was more surprised than we were. He showed it more, at any rate, and came spluttering up to ask if I knew that I was in Luristan. I said that I not only knew it, but was on my way to call on the Governor: the famous letter was produced, with its usual impressive effect. It took a little time, however, to live down the shock of our appearance, and somebody had to be blamed. 'One can't travel like this in the middle of the wilderness,' said the policeman, turning on our guide. 'Why are you off the road?'

This question has never been solved. The man looked so guilty that I felt my worst suspicions confirmed, and only later, when I noticed how every Lur looks guilty when confronted with the Law, began to think that perhaps he was innocent after all.

Meanwhile we were not to be allowed to go on. We should

14

have lunch first, said the policeman, anxious *coûte que coûte* to make us do something we had not intended. It is tempting to give a soft answer when one knows that it will annoy, and we felt no great aversion to the idea of lunch. But partly so as to go on in the game of contradicting, and partly because it would be taken as a want of friendliness to the villagers, I refused to sit in solitude with my escort under a tree as arranged, and moved up into one of the tribesmen's tents instead.

Here as we crouched over the fire and watched a chicken turning like an heraldic animal on a spit, our feelings gradually softened. Our chance of making Alishtar that night was gone – but what is a day more or less on a journey? The policeman for his part had made us sit still when we wanted to go on, and could therefore feel authority safe in his hands. He began to look with appraising eyes at my aluminium water-bottle and to soliloquize on the usefulness of such objects to lonely guardians doomed to live far from their fellows in the hills. As for the Lurs, they drew gradually near to the one subject in which they are chiefly interested just now – and that is the subject of clothes.

They were given a year long ago to obtain European coat and trousers and a *Pahlevi* hat. No one had thought of doing so: fairy tales, which know human nature, always give a year and a day, and the hero does not begin to think about the matter till the last evening. Now a new message had come through from Teheran, and five days were to see Luristan dressed and shaved, long hair being considered incompatible with a civilized appearance. To procure a city suit in five days in the wilds of Luristan, is a joke only fit for *Punch* or the Persian government: the tribesmen gazed in unhappy perplexity while the policeman expounded.

'Do you think the *Ferangi* clothes keep rain and snow out as thoroughly as these felt coats?' I asked at last.

'Oh no,' said the policeman.

'I should think the *Pahlevi* hat would not last long in this climate either?'

'No time at all,' the tribesmen said in chorus, with obvious joy.

The policeman put down my water-bottle.

'It is an order from the Shah,' he observed with dignity; and suggested that it might be time to move on. The passes, he explained, were not so dangerous as before lunch: he did not think I need be escorted. If I used the water-bottle myself he would not dream of depriving me: he had not seriously thought of suggesting it. And would I tell the Governor how pleased I was with his services?

So we went on, keeping the Gatchkah and its hills well on our left, and making for the motor road, trodden, as far as one could see, only by the hooves of innumerable donkeys and mules. It is not yet completely finished, and the last and safest part of it, where cars do run between Kermenshah and Harsin, is apt to be raided now and then, and was so five days before I got there. Out here in the wilderness it seemed to sun itself in perfect peace, winding out of a rolling green country for sheep which rose to bolder hills and jungle patches in the south-western little-known valleys of Dilfan. As we rode through the quiet light of the afternoon, we saw no trace of human beings except the heaps of stones by the roadside and one white-clad shepherd with his flock on the slope of a hill.

This low, long ridge is called the Firuzabad Pass, and we knew we had crossed the watershed when we came to a little stream welling out from rocks on our left hand. The water was velvety and bright as a bird's eye, and ran down towards Alishtar; and we followed and came in the sunset to the opening of the plain and to a little colony of tents on its western edge.

Here under the open awning of the chief tent we waited while the Khan was told of our arrival. The Lurs, like the little girl with the curl, are very nice when they are nice, but when they are not they are horrid – and one rarely knows which it is going to be. There is an anxious interval when one comes to a strange tribe and waits to see. This anxiety is not confined to the stranger: I noticed that all my native guides shared it, and used to hasten to explain my presence with an *empressement* that could only be described as apologetic. On this occasion the explanation was accepted with reserve. The cunning little green eyes of our host wandered from me to my kit-bag with an obvious thought behind them, while he made no effort at conversation.

Time is the great factor on these occasions. We sat in silence and watched the twilight, while the smoke from its many tents floated like mist over the plain. Goats and ewes were coming to be milked; their shuffling feet and low half-bleatings filled the air with a sense of evening peace. A tree showed like lace against the distance, and the new road, going diagonally across to the gap of Khurramabad, lost itself in the dusk. Our horses crunched chopped straw out of the mud-built mangers close beside us – oats being mostly unobtainable in the country: they tossed their heads with a little jingle of bells now and then. And in the eastern sky the mountain of Alishtar and the range of Sefid Kuh were pencilled with so clear and pure an outline that the very sight of them filled the mind with quietness.

Whether it was the beauties of nature, or the more immediate prospect of supper, or just the fact that they were getting used to the sight of us, the Lurs gradually began to settle down for conversation with a show of friendly interest here and there. Unlike those of Qal'a Kafrash, these were real nomads who never live in houses. They are Mumivend. In summer they inhabit the fringe of Alishtar, in winter they move with all their tribe to their 'Garmsir', the warm valleys round Tarhan in the south-west. They were going to start in about a month's time, in November. The government is trying hard to make them build houses so as to keep them in one place, but they are unanimous in disliking the change, and say that to winter in the north means losing a lot of their stock: and as the government can penetrate only with an armed force south of Alishtar or Khava, the nomad will probably have his way for some little time yet.

I had a heap of straw put under my sleeping-sack that night and lay beneath the tent awning with the flocks and herds around me and Hajji by the horses close at hand.

Next morning we set off across the plain. On the far side, the Fort of Alishtar showed in a patch of trees. It is now the seat of law and order and the residence of the Governor of Northern Luristan; but three years ago it would have been impossible for a Persian policeman or indeed for any ordinary traveller to get within miles of it. Mir Ali Khan ruled there like a king. He held the whole of North Luristan, and harried Nihavend on one side and Khurramabad on the other, so that the plainsmen dared not sleep without their city walls. The Lurs were devoted to him: the Salsile, to which his own tribe of the Hasanavend belong, say even now that they number 20,000 fighting men, and many others joined forces with them: he fed, so they say, 300 guests daily at his table, and kept half a million tomans in gold together with his five wives in the castle. I met his sister-in-law at Alishtar, a young woman educated in Teheran with no sympathy for the tribes, and she told me her despair when they brought her to live up here, with no doctor to attend to her when she fell ill, with no one but the wild tribeswomen to talk to, and with no prospect of ever getting away.

The government finally decided to finish Mir Ali Khan. It sent an Armenian friend of his, called Sangari Garkhan, to join in some small expedition against a neighbouring potentate. The campaign was successful, and the two were riding back side by side over the Khurramabad Pass into Alishtar, when the Armenian suddenly turned on his ally: the government troops he had with him closed in and shackled Mir Ali Khan and hurried him off, before his men could rally, to Khurramabad, where he was instantly hanged. Meanwhile the Armenian entered the fort as a friend, took possession in the Shah's name, and proceeded to over-run and disarm the plains of Alishtar and Khava and to destroy any building that could ever be turned into a fortress. These ruins are still visible here and there. He was rewarded by being made Governor, but has since come to a bad and suitable end.

So our guide told us, as we jingled leisurely over the wide culti-vated plain, crossing branches of the Kahman stream at intervals and gradually drawing nearer to the hills of the eastern edge and the range where the Kahman rises 'in a grove of trees like Paradise', they say.

It was a warmer climate than Khava, with rice and opium poppies in the ground, and reeds in the water where a pale-yellow water-snake darted its head at us. In the stubble-fields grew quan-tities of small arum flowers, dark red and close to the ground; and after we had ridden an hour or so we came to the area of villages evidently very old, for there are tombstones here and there belong-ing to the early centuries of Islam – rectangular blocks of stone with a carved knob at each corner and a raised centre, covered and surrounded by script or ornamental arabesques. There are mounds, too, and a great mound and a village called Geraran, the largest in Alishtar, near the opening of the Kahman gorge on our left. Here, said our guide, the treasure of the Fire Worshippers was buried, though no one has found it yet.

Our guide was very friendly now, and sang in the Kurdish way, as they call it.

'Baina, baina,
Nazaram baina;
Agar dust nam diri
Shau neilim tanha.'

Baina, baina,
Look on me, baina;
If thou too lovest it
I shall not sleep alone.

or

'Kai lowa, lowa,
Murgakam lowa;
Jerkam arraye
Dusakam kowa.'

Kai lowa, lowa,
My bird lowa;
Because of my love
My liver is like a kabob.

At the end of each line the *Ai, ai, ai,* of the refrain, wild and shrill
with a high little sob at the end, was very like the yodelling of the
Alps but fiercer, as a purring tiger is like a cat.

When we reached Alishtar Fort, we alighted in the courtyard of
Kerim Khan, the brother of the Mir Ali who had been hanged.

We felt we were in a metropolis, for though it is a small hamlet,
the presence of the castle, the government and police, a school
with twelve scholars, and the beginning of a garage in view of the
future road, all make it busy.

Kerim Khan was at home, an engaging young man with his *Pahlevi* hat at a rakish angle: but the two ladies, his wife and mother-in-law, were having a bath, and repeated messages to ask for the key of the best room, and to say that we were hungry, appeared to have no effect at all: an answer would be sent that little Iran's face was just being soaped, or something of the kind. It was getting on for two o'clock and my host and I, both faint with hunger, sat opposite each other on a carpet in the second-best room, too languid to speak. Kerim would shake his head at intervals and ask me to observe how husbands are treated in Luristan: I would try to comfort him by remarking that such things are known also to happen elsewhere: and another message would be sent to the recalcitrant ladies, with no effect at all.

They finally appeared, about four o'clock, very fresh from their ablutions, and found us in a state of exhaustion disposed to accept any apology so long as it were followed by food: and the *pilau* was not long in coming. Kerim continued to mutter to himself between the mouthfuls of rice, but it was in the uncertain tones natural to one man when two determined females present a united front. The mother-in-law was really alarming: she looked like something between a frog and a grenadier and her manner revealed an independent income. She told me that her first husband used to beat her on the head before she got rid of him; I could not help feeling a secret admiration for anyone brave enough to do so. As for Kerim, he was as wax in her hands. He retired after lunch into the yard where the old Tartar had relegated his own mother among the servants. The two ladies sat on in the best room, one on each side of me, and explained how they were Christians in all but name. They hated Luristan, and hoped to wean Kerim from his delight in living with his own tribe on what was left of his land; they liked to live in a town, and had friends among the missionaries. 'They taught me that love is all that matters in the world,' said the mother-in-law, with her two grandchildren on her knee; 'and you cannot think how I love these children; all except that one over there,' she added, nodding towards the eldest little girl who sat neglected in one comer: 'I cannot bear her.'

This peculiar interpretation of Christian precept roused me to some mild protest; I think I said it was hard on the little third girl. A glassy look appeared in the lady's heavy-lidded eyes. 'That *is* love,' she remarked shortly;] 'it comes and goes as it wills.' And that was that.

As a Christian convert, the mother-in-law must have been distinctly embarrassing. I have never seen anyone with quite her uncompromising brutality. She had a pretty young stepdaughter of seventeen in the house, whom she had snatched from the school in Hamadan where the American Mission was educating her, and whom she now kept as a servant, never allowing her to come into the best room, to sit with us at meals, or to have any dealings at all with her own sort: no husband was going to be found for her, so that the child had nothing but a life of oppression and drudgery to look forward to, with no escape. She spoke good English, and told me her troubles that night when she took me down into the stable to have a hot bath; but I was never able to speak to her again, for the jealous old lady's eye was on us, and it would only have brought down more punishment upon her.

The mother-in-law had the virtues of her defects: I imagine that she had never in her life been afraid of anyone or anything. Some wild tribesmen murdered her factor on an estate near the Asadabad Pass, and the police gave it up as a bad job: but she herself crept out of her bedroom one night, left the light burning so that the villagers might not notice her absence, and went to search for the assassins in the hills. After five days she found them, got her own people to round them up, and handed them over to the authorities.

The two ladies were very kind to me, and it was restful to feel oneself in a perfectly safe place for a while, with the possibility too of getting a wash. By the evening, I knew all the society of Alishtar Fort. Kerim took me to call on the Governor in his castle, and I was received in a long audience chamber and introduced to the Chief of Police, a pleasant Nihavendi with delightful manners whom I was to get to know better later on. The Governor is also a Lur, from Dizful, with the good manners of the well-born Persian, but made rather melancholy by malaria, which is rampant near the rice-fields. He asked Kerim about me, in a sad and tired voice, and Kerim's sketch of my history, status, and future intentions, all made up on the spur of the moment, was a much more plausible affair than I could have managed for myself.

The castle is a mud-brick square with round towers and filled with buildings, where the Governor's apartments, the police quarters and prisons, the clerk's offices and the school, are all congregated. It looks neglected since the great days of Mir Ali Khan. In the long audience room the paint is peeling off the walls: they still have a dilapidated gaiety with hunting and battle scenes, ladies in coaches marooned in rushing streams, Persian officers in baggy trousers leaning on small cannon with field-glasses in their hands – the Victorian Age in Luristan, in fact, but with the sadness of decay about it all. Down below, in a half-circle round a melancholy table, sat the Governor and a dozen visitors or so. It was a silent gathering: the Governor was busy reading petitions, and only asked a question or two between one document and the next: he enquired if I could take his photograph: after another interval he got up, went to the side of the room, and stood there while two valets changed him into a pair of very elegant trousers: we all continued to sit in silence, our eyes fixed delicately either upon the floor or the ceiling. When the operation was completed, and a suitable coat had been added to the other garments, the Governor returned. With a noticeable increase of cheerfulness he informed me that he was ready for his picture, and we all removed to the courtyard, where I took him in an official attitude beside his fountain.

The second day of my stay was pleasant but uneventful.

We walked a mile or two northwards to the site of the vanished city which must have been the Alishtar mentioned by the four-teenth-century geographer Mustawfi. No buildings remain, but there are many of the stone tombstones which we had seen before, and shards of thirteenth to fifteenth century earthenware strewn about. All the people here spoke of an old minaret which seems to have resembled the one at Saveh, a round brick tower ornamented with raised scrolls and geometric patterns: the government troops levelled it to the ground three years ago when they feared a rising of the Lurs. Of the more ancient graves, for which Luristan is chiefly interesting, there was no trace so far east as Alishtar; they were to be found, I was told, in Dilfan.

My idea was to travel ostensibly westward to Harsin, but in reality to make a detour and look at these graves in Dilfan on my way. I had a shock therefore when Kerim told me that the authorities could not let me risk the journey alone, and that the Head of Police, the Sardari Naib Khan, would himself escort me along the new road. This came, I felt, of making myself too important: it is always a difficult matter to strike the correct balance, for one wants to have one's wishes attended to and if possible not to be either deported or interned as a vagrant, but on the other hand one also wishes to remain insignificant enough to be left alone. I thought, however, that if I waited till the Chief of Police were separated from his colleagues, I might stand a better chance with him, and perhaps even persuade him to help in the looting of a grave or two: there was, anyway, nothing for it but to accept their arrangement with as great an appearance of pleasure as I could.

I said farewell to Kerim Khan and his ladies next morning, and made westward again for the nomad land. We started alone: the Sardari Naib was to meet us at Deh Ram, an hour or so on our way.

When we got to this village there was no sign of him either there or on the plain behind us. I thought he could easily overtake our baggage animals, and decided to push on to the tents where we had lodged before, and so get across the flat ground while the day was not yet too hot. Both *Hajji* and the Lur had doubts about this plan and followed reluctantly: they did not think the Sardari would like those particular tents, whose loyalty appeared to be doubtful: but I was tired of watching my escort crumple up whenever we met anything in the shape of a policeman, and remarked that what was good enough for me was good enough for the Sardari, a monstrous heresy which reduced them to silence.

The day was fine: the light lay bright on the folds of the hills: the plain of Alishtar, like a shallow bowl with crested mountain rim on all but the western side, basked in sunshine and peace. The apricot garden round the fort dwindled to a small dark patch in the distance behind us. Villages grew scarce on either hand: the rice-fields changed to stretches of stubble or empty ground where sheep and black goats grazed. We were drawing near to the gentle western rise of the plain when, looking back, we saw the Sardari and an escort of five horsemen riding not in our direction at all but away from us northward towards the Gatchkah Pass and Khava.

Presently one small figure detached itself and came galloping towards us. It turned out to be a policeman almost incoherent with rage. He took no notice of me, women in Persia being considered so insignificant that their families and not they are responsible for any foolishness they manage to commit. My family for the time being were *Hajji* and the Lur, who bowed under the torrent without thinking to blame me, and began to pour fulsome apologies into the ear of the Law. We retraced our steps, and came with ruffled feelings to where the Chief of Police, with two more policemen, two small tribal headmen, and his Mirza or secretary carrying an enormous red account book, were all waiting for their lunch and for our truant selves in a colony of six or seven tents at the foot of the Gatchkah hills.

The Sardari Naib was not at all put out and welcomed me with great friendliness. Nevertheless, when I mentioned that Dilfan and not Khava was my objective, and that I had no wish to travel in the direction in which he was going, he was rather nonplussed. I spent the whole of lunch-time trying to convince him of the importance of prehistoric tombs, and felt more and more how prudent it had been to get him away from the official atmosphere of Alishtar Fort before tackling so difficult a subject. His natural amiability however, was on my side. He was a pleasant middle-aged man with fair features tanned by the sun and charming manners even to the poorest shepherds we met. By the time lunch was over, the aims of archæology appeared to interest him, and we had come to a compromise on both sides: I was to go with him across the Gatchkah and spend the night under police protection in Khava, and he would find someone to take me into the southern country next day.

To visit a camp with the Chief of Police was like disturbing an ant-hill, so great was the dislocation and agitation our arrival always caused: it was as if our appearance made the Lurs wonder which of their crimes had found them out. We were not liked, for wherever we went this matter of clothes was looked into, and someone would snatch the caps off the people's heads in honour of the new regulations: when we halted, a policeman sat in a tent close by and had in one Lur after another to cut off his hair. The poor people came back to our circle round the fire with sheepish looks, complaining of the cold on their ears and saying: '*Wallah*, this is civilization' – while the Sardari Naib, sitting cross-legged with his curved sword in his hands, would talk to the headman in the politest way, beginning: 'In the service of your Exaltedness let me explain, oh my soul,' and going on to specify how the Shah, like God on this earth, can order people to go about even naked, and there is nothing for it but to obey.

With great bustling and pomp therefore we started off at about two o'clock and rode up the stony way to the pass in single file. One man with a gun went ahead as scout and the rest of us followed in a body. The Mirza, his red account book under his arm, black goggles over his eyes, and two enormous pistols in his holsters, brought up the rear.

As we drew near the top, in a narrow defile, we met two muleteers striding down in an opposite direction. I had remained a hundred yards or so behind to take a compass bearing, and saw them coming along bareheaded, with black looks: their caps had been taken off and torn in two: and as they passed, muttering fiercely, one of the escort came riding back to see that I got safely by.

At the top of the steep and rocky climb a small tower guards the pass. On the other side the ground sinks away in grassy slopes to Khava and up again to the ridge of Kuh Garu. Stones of the causeway are visible here and there and the ruins of some old guardhouse.

The upper story of the little tower was roofed over with wool like a tent and reached by a ladder, and here the six police of the garrison live as best they can. They are not relieved at specific intervals, and may apparently remain indefinitely in the neighbourhood, although in winter the pass is closed and they descend to one of the villages below. There are six such posts, each with six men, dotted between Gatchkah and Tudaru in the west, and all their stores are supplied once a month from Khurramabad. The Fort of Alishtar is their centre. Here they collect the prisoners, of whom there is never any lack; on the morning we left, twenty were brought in with chains round their necks and feet and wrists. The percentage of brigands captured, however, appears to be very small: the country is fine for sniping and hiding, and the robber bands are usually made up of amateurs who take to the sport for a week or two and then disperse each to the protection of his own tribe before they are discovered. With all one's natural feeling for the tribesman, the Lur is so treacherous and cruel, and so unchivalrous in his crimes, that one's sympathy goes to the small handfuls of police who keep the country in some sort of order with such very scant means at their disposal. It is not their fault if the *effendis* of Teheran make them enforce absurd regulations about the people's clothes.

We came down into Khava in the sunset when the cliffs of Kuh Garu shine like opals in a light of their own. Mist lay in the hollows and the air was cold. In the village of Beira where we lodged, in the north-eastern part of the plain beside another ancient mound, the tribesmen had not yet moved from their tents into the winter houses, so that we had another evening in the open, roasting pleasantly round a fire of thorn bushes in the middle of the headman's tent, where his carpets were spread in our honour. One side was open: a long line of black oxen with felt

28

rugs on their backs blocked it and acted as a wind-screen: they chewed their feed gently through the night, while we slept as well as we could with rivulets of cold air creeping down our spines: now and then some tribesman, pirate-faced in the half-darkness, would rouse himself, heap an armful of thorns on the embers, and fill the tent with strange shadows and a fleeting warmth.

Here among the nomads even the universal Persian *samovar* has not yet found its way, and the water for tea was boiled in a beaked copper jug with the fire piled round so as almost to bury it. Water for washing one goes to look for in the landscape around, and as it was very cold and very public one washed rather little. The Lurs had no soap, but they were very particular to pour water over their hands before and after a meal, and used to warm the second water, so that it had some cleansing property: otherwise they neither wash nor pray, and seem to get on without either of these virtues. They are Shi'as. They give their money to any wandering rogue with a green sash or headband who declares himself to be of the Prophet's family: but they have none of the inhospitable bigotry of many Persian villagers, and are pleased to share their dish with the traveller; in fact one of the grievances against Jewish and Armenian traders who venture up here to deal in antiques, is that they refuse to eat or drink out of the tribesmen's bowls.

In the early morning we were very glad of our little glasses of hot tea. Our hosts chipped sugar from the cone and heaped it in with real generosity, for tea and sugar are the two luxuries among the Lurs. They never expected to be paid in any way. They may contemplate a raid on their guest's luggage while he sleeps, but that is another matter: it is the country's national pastime, with rules of its own: and who are we, after all, to demand consistency in morals!

As the sun climbed over Kuh Garu, I left Beira and the Sardari Naib, and set off with my original escort of two, to visit the Nurali Lurs of 'Abdul Khan in Dilfan. Though he was a friend of the Sardari's, and to be trusted, we were not to stay away more than a day before rejoining our police on the west of Khava in Chavari. As we left them all behind us, the spirits of Mahmud, my Lur guide, rose, and he yodelled in the freshness of the morning: but *Hajji* dragged behind with returning gloom.

We skirted the southern edge of Khava south of the great mound of Cheha Husein, and noticed for the first time the rolling breadth of the beautiful plain. The track from Arjine and the Jungle comes in here. Strings of black cattle were creeping along it under their sacks of charcoal; the men's white coats showed here and there, not tampered with as yet by the police. The men never gave a greeting of their own accord; but they smiled when spoken to, and seemed friendly in spite of their bad name. It takes them three days to make the charcoal, and four more to bring it from their homes to Nihavend: seven days in all, for which they get twelve krans, or 2s. 5d.

We were now among the shallow hills we had seen from the Varazan Pass, and we followed a trough among them between two low ranges: it is called the Valley of Gatchenah, and belongs to the Nuralis. At the entrance to the valley we crossed the new road, and saw the deserted beginnings of three or four hovels, represent-ing what the Persian newspapers describe as the 'Building of settled villages in Luristan'. We soon left these feeble efforts, and rode from group to group of black tents, busy with the winnow-ing of their corn. Stubble-fields covered the easy slopes: there were neither houses nor trees; but a delightful openness, a sense of remoteness and peace and the gaiety of harvest: the people were friendly on the way: the name of 'Abdul Khan worked like a passport: and as we went along, the women who carried flour to the tents, balancing it on their heads in small goatskins instead of sacks, would stop to exchange the frankest badinage with our guide, who was well known in the district.

There were a few ruins of buildings in the valley, put up they told me by 'Abdul Khan's father in the days before the Nuralis had been defeated by their enemy, the Emir Afshar from the south. 'Abdul Khan himself had to fly from him, and spent fifteen years in Nihavend, becoming civilized and incidentally learning how to smoke opium; and he has only been able to return to his own country last year with the support of the government troops: hence his loyalty. His splendour, however, is dimmed, and as we went along, our acquaintances by the way would shake their heads and tell us that we should have seen the Nuralis of Dilfan in the days of their greatness.

'Abdul Khan was settled near the end of the little valley where a willow tree or two break the line of the hills. The sun was sloping down into the afternoon when we arrived. We found him sitting on a mattress over a brazier in the dimness of his tent, a skeleton of a man with yellow parchment face wrecked by opium, but a pleasant and cordial host. In winter he reads Firdausi, and Persian translations of French novels, and he was immediately interested and sympathetic to my quest for prehistoric Lurish skulls.

The Valley of Gatchenah is lined from end to end with grave-yards of every date and description, and one need only explore a few hundred yards up either of its sides to find the looted and open remains of ancient tombs.

He himself had never done so illegal a thing as to open a grave, said 'Abdul Khan, picking at his opium pipe with a bronze bodkin two or three thousand years old, and looking at me with the calm innocence of a Persian telling lies. 'But as it is the wish of my friend, the Sardari Naib, that you should see one, I will set my tribe to hunt for you, and if God wills we may find something to-day or to-morrow.'

I said I would give three tomans to anyone who found a grave with the skull intact inside it. A wave of enthusiasm swept over the Nuralis. They scattered up every hillside within sight, in little parties led by men with long skewers, which they dug into the earth in an expert way to feel for the flat stones that roof the graves. It did not look as if it were their first effort of this kind. The graves are not usually more than two or three feet underground and seem to lie on the sides of low foothills near springs of water.

The earliest go far back to times when flints and rough earthenware alone were buried with the skeleton crouching in its narrow bed lined with stones: later come graves with flint and bronze together; and round graves where the dead were seated, surrounded with potteries and bronzes; and the *Lihaqs,* which really belong to central Luristan, in which, they told me, twenty skeletons or more are found together. I am not convinced whether this latter kind exist in Gatchenah or no: two of the tribesmen offered to show me some if I would ride back four miles, and we did so, trotting at a brisk pace over the empty downs, for the sun was very low. But when we reached the place, the *Lihaqs* had vanished: the stones which had been their penthouse roofs, and which my friends told me they had seen in position about a fortnight before, had been carried away, possibly for the new road and the landscape showed nothing but about thirty shapeless holes and some scattered boulders among which the sheep were picking their evening way home. As we rode back, and the valley lay shining before us with the mounds of its cemeteries, or habitations perhaps, plainly visible under the folds of the ground, the great age of the world seemed to be revealed with a sudden poignancy: here men had wandered for thousands of years, their origin and their end unknown. Their dead lie thicker than the living amid these hills.

The sun had set before we reached our tents, and we met the digging parties returning in a subdued vein, with their skewers and picks on their shoulders after an unsuccessful afternoon. They were going to try again next morning, and meanwhile scattered to their homes to collect bronzes to sell.

Sitting over 'Abdul Khan's brazier with the Nuralis around me, I now had a difficult time, for, with no experience to guide me, I had to estimate every object as it came along and strike a balance between my anxiety to secure it, the necessity of not spoiling my own market, the advisability of not showing that I had any money to speak of with me, and the fact that in truth I had very little. I knew nothing at all of the market price, though of course it must have been well known to the tribesmen themselves since the whole of Europe is now flooded with antiques from Luristan (many of them fakes). 'Abdul Khan, with most remarkable disinterestedness, now and then told me I was giving too much, and tossed me a dagger or a bowl for one shilling instead of two, to the disgust of whichever of his clansmen it happened to belong: no one, however, contradicted the chief, or would refuse to sell when he told them to do so.

When the last of the bronzes had been produced and disposed of, we made a circle round the fire by lantern-light, and talked of progress, the old days how bad and how pleasant, the new how good and how dull: and of the government, which demands so many children from each tribe to be sent to school in Khurramabad; and how the nephews of 'Abdul Khan, two cheerful chubby little boys sitting beside me, had wept so bitterly when they were included among these victims of education, that the tribe took pity on them and sent two other less important little boys in their stead.

We had another guest with us in the circle, a Muslim trader from Dizful, who was able to travel here by virtue of a Lurish wife of the Ittivend tribe south-west of us; he was on his way to see her and, I gathered, to collect bronzes, though he did not say so: but he questioned me suspiciously and was evidently very little pleased to see a European in his preserves. His oily manners made an unpleasing contrast with the friendly outspokenness of the tribesmen, and he would have done his best to prevent me from entering farther into the country if he could.

That night I slept in the ladies' tent, which was friendly, but handicapped by the want of a language, since they spoke no Persian and I no Lurish, or *Laki,* as the language is called in the north-west of Luristan. They wore *sarbands* or turbans even bigger than those of Alishtar and Khava, and as they moved about stiffly in their loose gowns and enormous head-dresses, it looked as if the figures of a pack of cards had come to life in the half-light of the tent.

These were far better tents than we had seen before, and the people lived in them all the year round. They were enclosed in a mud wall about five feet high which kept the wind out: inside it ran a screen of reeds woven in patterns with wool, and overlapping for five or six feet in the front of the tent so as to make a narrow corridor by way of a door. Saddle-bags, and *jajims* from Khurramabad, and rugs woven in central Luristan were stacked round the sides, and our sleeping-quilts were laid out for us in rows round the central hearth. I now took to these quilts without misgiving, for I found Luristan remarkably free from insects, and the nights were so cold that one was thankful for anything in the way of covering.

Next morning as I sat at breakfast, shouts and breathless messengers announced the discovery of my skull: we raced up the hillside and found an excited cluster of tribesmen round a grave. It was one of the earliest sort: the skeleton, nearly complete, lay on its right side, with its head to the south and its knees bent: there was nothing with it except a sharpened flint and three shards of the roughest earthenware. Close beside it, however, and in the same sort of grave, they had found some weeks before a beautiful jar with a brown flame pattern painted on it, exactly like the ware which was being dug out of the mound of Gian near Nihavend. I bought the jar, collected the skull – which broke into pieces in my hand and required careful packing – and came away none too pleased with the morning's result, for I had hoped for a grave of the Bronze Age, and it was now quite useless to expect the tribe to dig again. Their misgivings as to the permissibility of carrying away people's bones had been allayed by the fact that the skeleton had obviously not been laid in the direction of Mecca; but they were still nervous about the Persian law of antiquities, which has brought punishment for illicit dealing in bronzes on to several of the tribes. The government occasionally send spies and then get the chiefs to pay fines, and are really making praiseworthy efforts to save what is left of the graves in Luristan.

I knew that what I was doing went directly against this law: but there were some extenuating circumstances. The looting goes on all the time in a country which the police cannot possibly keep under observation: by the time that an organized expedition can face the risk of going there, very little will be left for anyone to find: I felt that one was justified in trying to discover as much as possible while one was on the spot. As for my Persian friends whose kindness was of such assistance, they had no responsibility in the matter, for it never entered their heads that I had not come with full powers from Teheran.

After lunch we took leave of 'Abdul Khan and started on our way to Chavari to rejoin our escort. Our Lur guide from Qal'a Kafrash had already left the day before: he took an affectionate farewell of me, but he carried off *Hajji's* sheepskin waistcoat as a souvenir without mentioning it.

'Abdul Khan gave me a new guide, a young man with a turban who rode his wild little pony like a centaur and dwelt lovingly on the days when Luristan still echoed with bullets. On the way down Gatchenah he asked me to turn aside to see a sick cousin of his in the tents of the Nuralis of Jusuf Khan, who lived a little way down the valley. This Jusuf had been a young leader beloved by all the northern Lurs: he was taken and executed in Hamadan; his followers, including my guide, lifted his body from the cemetery and brought it to Kermenshah, and then carried it with high wailing dirges four days' journey to its burial-place at Hulailan. Jusuf's brother is now chief of the clan.

He came forward to meet me, and led me into a tent where a dying man lay. The people of his tribe sat and stood around him, clamorous as soon as I came in: but the sick man was already far on his journey, looking out on to another world with the strange astonished glance of death. No crowd could penetrate into his solitude, nor did he change his gaze as I bathed his face and arms.

'Is there hope?' they asked, pressing round with their eager trustfulness which hurts so much because one cannot fulfil it. I was glad to come away into the open sunshine where the hills, in their slow steps of time, change more peacefully and imperceptibly than we do.

Our direction was north, across the low range behind which flows the Badavar River: but it is safer to keep in open country here, and our guide led us back to the plain of Khava near the mound of Cheha Husein. Thence, crossing the river and the road, we made north-westerly over the downs into Chavari, which is the north-west corner of the plain of Khava and runs up with a few villages to the foot of Kuh Garu. Deh Kabud, the largest and most westerly village, was the headquarters of our Sardari Naib, and I found him seated on the floor of an old circular guardhouse with holes on every side for shooting through, which made it very draughty. One climbed up by stone steps once evidently tomb-stones; and there was a little platform outside where six policemen waited in respectful attendance.

The Sardari made me very welcome: he had not expected to see me so soon, and had not thought to provide a lodging in the village. But he had a very good dinner cooking, and offered me half the floor to sleep on. It was hard and cold under my sheepskin sack; and what with the enthralled interest which the six police-men took in what little I did in the way of a toilette, and noises like rats running about and mingling with the harmony of the Sardari's snores – by the time morning came – I had no wish to spend many nights in a guardhouse.

A worse shock met me as I came down into the courtyard. The sergeant, on his face on a blue rug on the ground, was being basti-nadoed: one policeman sat on his ankles and another on his shoulders, and two more were hitting him alternately from either side with leather thongs. The Sardari sat close by on an overturned saddle, and called to me in a friendly way to come up too. The man, he said, had been stealing government cartridges. By this time I had come to the conclusion that he was not really being hurt, though calling lustily on one Imam after the other: perhaps privates are careful how they beat their own sergeants. When the Sardari had counted forty strokes, the two men got off their kicking superior, the executioners folded away their lashes, and the victim himself rose a little stiffly, but cheerfully, and saluted as if to suggest that bygones should be bygones.

We now prepared to separate again. I had, as I say, not found the right sort of skull in Dilfan. What I was looking for, was one of the graves in which men and horses are said to be buried together: they belonged to the Bronze Age and were said to have produced the beautiful bits and chariot trappings which caused the greatest interest in the Luristan finds of the last years.

Their date and origin are both unknown: and the very civilization to which they belong was unsuspected till a few odd bronzes were brought down by tribesmen to Kermenshah and roused the attention of archæologists. Perhaps they may explain the appearance of the horse in Persia, and may throw light on the mystery of its arrival there: perhaps they may prove a link between the pre-Sumerians and their unknown home. Meanwhile no one can investigate these problems because no one can stay for any time in that part of Luristan where the graves are. I had been told that I should find them in Alishtar or Khava, but this proved to be incorrect: they were along the valley of the Saidmarreh and its tributaries, in the country of the Ittivend, who have a peculiarly bad name among the tribes. The most northern centre for them is a valley called Sar-i Kashti, on a little tributary of the Giza Rud, and a long day's ride from Chavari.

Chavari touches the northern boundary of the Ittivends in Duliskan, and the Lurs thought there might be a chance of finding something there: it was easier also to present the matter to the Sardari in two stages rather than in one, and it is usually better not to worry people for permission to go into a country until one is so near the frontier that volunteers can be found to guide one across. So we arranged to go into Duliskan and rejoin our escort that same evening at Tudaru, the last garrison in the south-west. We would only risk the adventure of Sar-i Kashti, which was beyond the policed area, if nothing could be found to the north of it.

Chavari is the last of the settled country. The sites of its villages are probably very old, and it is largely inhabited by heretics, the unconscious remnant perhaps of a schism older than their own. These are Ali-Ilahis, and are supposed to be able to eat, or – according to the more scientifically minded – at least to sit in fire. They are not considered Muslim at all by the orthodox Lurs, who speak of them as unbelievers.

After leaving them, one still follows the southern slope of Kuh Garu and appears to be in the upper corner of Khava where it tilts away into shallow valleys that drain down into the Giza Rud; but it is not Khava, or Chavari: it is Duliskan; and these vague regions, enclosed in no visible boundary, in a country where there is not a house except for a few shanties built under government pressure by the *kadkhuda* of Tudaru, and only lived in when the police are looking – these names which seem to merge into each other so that there is hardly a fixed point in the landscape – are most difficult to the tidy mind of the geographer.

Duliskan, as I had imagined, had none of the graves I wanted; and its chief was away taking a holiday with his wife and family at an *Imamzadeh* just visible in a group of trees on the bare red flank of Kuh Garu. As there seemed nothing to be found here, I did not think it worth while to delay so as to visit him, but pushed on towards Tudaru which lies at thexs foot of a big mountain called Chia Dozdan, visible for many miles on every side.

As we approached, still riding across open downs covered with gum tragacanth, we gradually saw on our skyline the outline of Tang-i-Charash, the defile of the Giza Rud down which we were to venture on the morrow: the slopes of Sar-i Kashti also appeared, faint blue in the distance of the south.

Tudaru belongs to the Kakavend Lurs, who insert themselves here into the Ittivend country. They had their black tents by the edge of a reedy stream, with the crests of Gulanor and Chia Dozdan on either side of them. Their headman was a pleasant, friendly person, and entertained us in his new mud-roofed house, very dank and obviously never used except on these official occasions. A small son in a *Pahlevi* hat sat beside him, watching with anxious eyes while his latest toy, a beautiful bronze dagger dug up out of some-grave, was being offered to me; I had a pocket-knife, and we carried out a solemn exchange. The tribesmen came in in twos and threes, talking with quiet manners so different to the cringing politeness of the towns. The question of my journey to Sar-i Kashti was hanging in the balance. It was impossible to escort me there, as the police only ventured south of Tudaru in large bodies; ten of them had been killed in the defile a month before, and the Sardari was naturally not very anxious to let me go alone. On the other hand, I had all the tribesmen to support me; they said they could find a perfectly safe guide who knew the Ittivends; and presently brought along Keram Khan, a mild-looking Kakavend with an agreeable twinkle in his eye, and a nonchalant manner which made it seem ridiculous to worry about anything anywhere. He was dressed in a biscuit-coloured greatcoat of the 7th Royal Engineers, of which he was proud but a little reticent when I got him to let me examine the buttons and asked him how he had procured it: it was a present, said he, to the amusement of his friends: and added as an afterthought that it was only the people who wore Russian army coats who had stolen them.

After this we all took it for granted that I was going to Sar-i Kashti, and the Sardari said no more. He made me promise not to spend more than one night there: he would wait to hear of our safe emergence on to the Harsin track, which was to be our way back – and Keram was to send him news of it at once. At eight-thirty next morning I took a grateful farewell of him, waved to the assembled Kakavends of Tudaru, and started off down the defile of the Giza Rud.

This is called Tang-i-Charash, and is a narrow cut between Chia Dozdan (Hill of Thieves) on the west, and a group of hills beginning with Pir-i-Dozd (The Old Thief) and ending with Peri Kuh on the east. A green water runs through willows and spiky grasses at the bottom, and the Badavar River flows into it at the beginning of the defile.

Our path kept fairly high up on the slope of Chia Dozdan. We had low bushes of holm oak and beech around us, first signs of the jungle country in the south. Across the valley we could see another group of Kakavend tents with their black cattle grazing round them. A little procession was going down from them to the river, bearing a corpse which they washed in the running water with shrill lamenting cries. We were now in the place where the ten police had fought the brigands a month before and been killed: it was a sinister 'gate' into the Highlands.

Keram, however, rode on ahead, careless and unarmed, humming a little tune to himself, as though it were Richmond Park on a Sunday morning. The landscape looked peaceful, with round hills one behind the other basking in the sun. The valley opened to a broad green bottom of rice-fields where men were ploughing. It was warmer here than Khava or Duliskan: tamarisk bushes began to show among the willows. As far as we could see down the river track, where it ascends from the Saidmarreh in the south-west, caravans of charcoal-sellers were plodding up behind their small black oxen and enormous sacks: they rested in the shade of the rocks, and ate wild pears gathered in the jungle:

Keram told me that down the valley one soon comes to big trees, so thick that the sun never penetrates, where panthers are still to be found: and after the forest one comes out again into the open basins of Hulailan and Tarhan, where most of the ancient graves and bronzes are.

Even here we were in a country of graves. We passed a rifled cemetery by the side of the path, and tombs have been found all over the slopes of Chia Dozdan. Most of them in this region contain a jar with the skeleton inside; but there are also round graves, with bones of men and horses, so they say.

After about two hours we forded the Giza Rud, and turned south-eastward over grassy downs under the cliff of Peri Kuh, and then followed a stream called Kangaveri, which leads to Sar-i Kashti. Here also were graveyards scattered on the lower ledges of the hills, where the river flowed in loneliness. A few tamarisk bushes grew among the white stones of its bed, and flocks and herds of the Ittivend were grazing about it, with no human being in sight.

This is thoroughly risky country. A bullet may meet one round any corner. Keram, to whom our expedition was in the nature of a lark, rode on murmuring to himself at intervals: 'The hand of the Lady has shattered the Talisman of Luristan', and assured me that no European woman had ever been here before.

'Are there any police?' asked *Hajji*, who had been spoilt again by travelling with an escort.

'There were two; they have been shot,' said Keram carelessly, unconscious of the havoc he caused.

He was a charming man. I think he was never afraid, though the country seemed to be thick with relatives of people he had killed, and this was a serious drawback to his usefulness as a guide outside his own tribe. On the other hand, there is a certain advantage in travelling with someone who has a reputation for shooting rather than being shot: as Keram said, in a self-satisfied way, they might kill me, but they would know that, if I was with him, there would be unpleasantness afterwards.

He had a great sense of humour and was excellent at telling a story. He told me how he had been deprived of his gun for shooting the seven pet pigs of the Armenian Governor of Alishtar, the same who had betrayed Mir Ali Khan. The pigs were grazing near the castle, and Keram, like a good Muslim, never imagined that anyone would go to the trouble of keeping such animals; he amused himself by shooting six and laming the seventh. It limped back to the castle just as the Governor came out of the gate for his evening ride. 'What is this?' said the Governor. 'I shot six pigs in the wood,' Keram explained innocently. Whereupon his gun was taken from him, 'and since then,' said he, 'I have had to take to opium; my heart is so sad for the long days in the hills.'

It was the time for his pipe, and I offered to sit by the roadside and wait while he smoked it – a suggestion which evidently touched him, for he repeated it over and over again to his friends as an illustration of the *Akhlaq-i-shirin* or sweetness of character of women in Europe.

During the fighting last year he took sides with the government against Mehmed Ali Khan of Tarhan, and had a bad time. His enemies held the springs of water, and the Kakavend were also hard up for food. The Persians used aeroplanes to drop provisions, but unfortunately hit the wrong camps, so that Keram had the added annoyance of watching his enemies eat his food.

Now he is prosperous under government employ as a sort of liaison between the authorities and the tribesmen, but he is not very happy with it all. 'They have turned us into women: they have taken our guns,' says he.

'If I had brought a rifle,' I asked, 'I suppose I should have been robbed long ago?'

'Why yes,' said he. 'I should have stolen it myself.'

Stealing is the national art. The Lurs appear to pride themselves on it more than on anything else. In the days of the Crusades it is recorded that they were so expert in escalading walls that Saladin, thinking them a dangerous people, used to put them in the advance of his attacks so as to exterminate them if possible. When the Persian commander was up in Duliskan a year or two with 1,800 men, the Ittivends got through the lines at night and stole the clothes and weapons from his tent. The next night the guard was doubled, but they managed to get in and take the blanket off his bed and escape as he woke up. 'There is no one like us for stealing in the world,' said Keram.

I wondered how under these circumstances the Jewish merchants, who come for antiques as far as Sar-i Kashti and are known to carry money, manage to get over the passes at all. It appears that they pay a regular blackmail to the bandits in the shape of bullets and so buy their way through at the expense of other travellers.

Meanwhile, after four hours' ride from Tudaru, we were in Sar-i Kashti itself.

It is as vague and undefined a region as any other round about, and covers the northern side of a round heap of a hill called Bala Buzurg which fills up the landscape south of the Kangaveri and which Sir A. T. Wilson saw and mentions when he travelled from Khurramabad and had it on the west. It has a very holy *Imamzadeh* on its southern slope, and frequent bandits on the top near the passes. It forms, as it were, the boundary between the open downs and the jungle, though the older Ittivends remember thick trees north of it, in all the country of the Giza Rud up to Chia Dozdan, as recently as fifty years ago.

After nearly two hours' riding up the Kangaveri in absolute solitude, we came to a small mill built of boulders with no mortar, down by the water's edge: and here we saw the miller, a ragged Ittivend with four wild children round him, who got over his astonishment at the sight of us so far as to point out the way to the tents of Amanulla Khan, whom we were looking for, along a little tributary to the south. All this part of the valley is full of flint, pinkish and white in colour, cropping out through what looks like limestone: the presence of so much raw material for their instruments may have had something to do with the thick population of the region in the days before metals.

We climbed up the steep little stream towards the lower shoulders of Bala Buzurg, and after about twenty minutes came out into a green corrie full of stunted oak and beech-like bushes, and with two settlements of Ittivend tents at a small distance from each other.

Amanulla Khan was away; he had gone for five days to Alishtar to pay his taxes. It was most unfortunate, for there appeared to be no one left with any authority, and the tribesmen received us with far from welcoming looks. They spread a rug in the open guest room of the tent and sat round in a gloomy silence. Unlike my other guides, Keram made no attempt to explain me, but devoted himself to his belated opium, which I felt would make him quite useless if things became difficult as they appeared rapidly to be doing. He interrupted his puffing for a moment to tell me that they thought I was a spy; I smiled as best I could and devoted my attention to one of the fat Lurish babies who were always charming. Luckily at this moment the uncle of Amanulla Khan appeared from the next settlement; he looked a villain, but at least a cheerful one; he had a short, thick, red beard, and a roving eye which settled at frequent intervals on my luggage. I had brought very little with me – and nothing in the way of cloaks, bed, field-glasses, or weapons that might tempt a Lur: but even so I always felt there was a certain danger in the few possessions I carried, for there was no mistaking the looks that were cast upon them even among the friendly tribes. My hat was always a great attraction, being made of finer felt than any in Luristan, and I had several times to explain that it was a woman's hat and that men would be ashamed to be seen in it; whereupon it would regretfully be put down.

The uncle belonged to the Duliskan Ittivends and was in Sar-i Kashti only on a visit. He knew the Sardari Naib, and Keram showed himself less absorbed in opium than I had supposed and immediately began to tell him how the police of North Luristan were waiting anxiously for my reappearance on the safe side of the Giza Rud. The red-bearded uncle listened carefully, nodding now and then and asking questions in Laki which I could not follow. Tea appeared and the atmosphere grew a trifle more friendly. I cautiously approached the subject of graves. There were plenty of them, they all said, and dealers still came to buy in spite of the new laws. But they refused to dig for me in the absence of their chief. No woman, said they, had ever travelled in Luristan: they did not think I was a woman at all: and they had heard that the government sent spies who pretended to come for antiques: they would not go against the law. This pedantry, in a district which always shoots its policemen, seemed to me extreme, but there was nothing to be done about it. I could not wait five days for Amanulla Khan. After a great deal of persuasion, and signing a document in which I took the responsibility for whatever might happen, they said they would see if they could find anything in the cemetery at the back of the corrie, and we started off with picks and skewers and began to push them here and there among the bushes: but though we struck rock, and worked away with rising hopes, we only came upon two miserable boulders: and nothing I could say would make them try again. They told me that in any case the graves in which horses are buried are rare and not to be found in a day. The red-bearded uncle murmured privately to Keram that he owned a camp down in the Giza Rud where a new and unexplored cemetery was waiting to be looted, and he would take us there to-morrow. If he found me a grave of the kind I wanted, he should have my old fur coat, said I: and having ratified this treaty of alliance in low voices so that the other interested Powers might not hear, we returned to the tents to think about supper.

We had an impressive view to look out on. Our corrie formed a sort of ledge and the long red cliff of Peri Kuh stood up against us at the bottom of our glen across the Kangaveri: it shone like a church window in the sunset, framed in the dark woollen walls of the tent in which we sat. The other settlement showed on a lower spur, etched blackly against that brilliant background. And the valley below was filling with evening shadows.

It should have been a scene of peace. But though I could understand very little of what was being said around me, I knew both *Hajji* and Keram well enough to realize that neither of them was comfortable. Keram was smoking opium again in a pensive way, but he leaped up very suddenly when someone put a hand on his back; he sat down in a different place and began to say something at great length in a quiet voice like a speech in Parliament. The Ittivends listened with their eyes on the ground: they looked peculiarly unattractive, I thought; the red-bearded uncle also sat

47

with his eyes on the ground, plucking at his henna'd hairs; he gave Keram a bad, little, cunning glance now and then. An old woman came to sit beside me: she looked out over the valley with sad, tired eyes; she had a beautiful old profile: her son was in prison in Khurramabad and she was waiting to hear whether he was to be executed or no; continual violence, continual bloodshed – no wonder the old look tired and sad. Presently the man who had put his hand on Keram's back got up and strode away. Keram returned in a nonchalant manner to his opium. The Ittivends continued to sit in their depressing silence. But the feeling of tension was some-how removed. A remark was made here and there. The red-bearded uncle came up to me and began to cross-examine me on the inter-esting but inexplicable problem of why I was not married: and by the time supper was ready, we were far more friendly than we had been through the course of the day.

I heard next morning what the trouble had been. The man sitting next to Keram had once had a brother who had tried to shoot Keram on a mountain pass, and killed his horse: Keram, however, had got a shot in in time and killed the Ittivend. When he felt the brother's hand on his back, he thought he was going to be knifed, and leaped up as fast as he could. He then explained to his hosts that he did not like to dine with a man by whom he expected to be murdered, and would they kindly remove him. The Ittivends took no sides in the matter and waited till the man departed of his own accord and left us to eat our supper in peace.

All the same we spent an anxious night.

Keram did not think it advisable for me to sleep with the ladies and out of his reach. He arranged my sack at the back of the guest tent, with himself in a strategic position between me and the open side. My luggage he piled carefully under his own head and mine.

The horses were tethered close by and *Hajji* settled down beside them.

Distant fires of Ittivend camps twinkled in the shadows of the valley and the lower slopes: the cliffs of Peri Kuh rose flooded in moonlight from the darkness: there was an immense and beautiful silence. Just as I was dozing off, *Hajji* crept up, and whispered to me to sleep lightly, for there would be trouble in the night: I opened one eye to watch him creep back and sit, a wakeful and forlorn little figure, guarding his horses in the moonlight: and I heard no more till, somewhere about the middle of the night, the two men woke me with shouts which frightened away a woman who was creeping from under the back of the tent towards the luggage I was sleeping on.

I called on Amanulla Khan's two wives next morning. They lived in separate tents and had very little to do with each other, and were both equally beautiful in an imperial way; in the dim light they sat like idols, hung with many necklaces and bracelets, under the weight of their great turbans. The tents themselves were extremely bare. Amanulla's first wife apologized; their furnishings, said she, were locked away in Khurramabad, since they could not have kept them here 'in the land of thieves'. Robbery in Luristan is as much the topic of conversation as horses and hounds in a hunting county.

We took our leave, and were watched down the path with not too friendly looks. The red-bearded Duliskani met us at the lower tents, and walked on ahead with Keram, retracing yesterday's route along the Kangaveri. Keram was complaining of not having slept: *Hajji* had roused him at intervals all through the night to look at brigands in the moonlight on the opposite hill.

'There were none there, I suppose?' said I.

'There may have been some,' said Keram in his indifferent way. 'They moved into Bala Buzurg yesterday, so that they would have been ready for us to-day. But they were not doing anything last night.'

We found the red-bearded man's camp pitched in the broad stony bed of the Giza Rud, and were welcomed by the *kadkhuda* and a dozen tribesmen or so. They made us an omelette while we sat and discussed the matter of bronzes: but even their chief's authority could not persuade them to dig. Like the men at Sar-i Kashti, they refused to believe that I was a woman: they preferred to find their own loot in private, and sell to dealers at their leisure.

As we sat here at lunch two gipsy women passed by. They looked like Indians, and came with their soft barefoot walk up from the jungle. They are called 'Cauali', and wander all over this country, treated with friendly contempt by the Lurs, who number them among the unbelievers, and say that they will eat pig though they will not touch a cock. The Lurs complained – rather amusingly – that they are great thieves.

We parted from the red-bearded uncle with mutual disappointment, for as he was unable to provide a grave, I stuck to my fur coat. I gave him a silver pencil nevertheless, in spite of Keram, who hated to see things wasted on an Ittivend, and did his best to intercept it. His spirits rose as we left the rival country and rode up the Giza Rud towards the confines of our own tribe. We had been in danger all the time, he informed me: he did not mind, said he – I believe with perfect truth – 'but it was unpleasant not to have a gun'.

Before reaching the Tang-i-Charash defile, near sunset, we turned westward and found a small settlement of Kakavend at a place called Tarazak on the southern slope of Chia Dozdan. Here we were among friends again; they gathered round Keram, and said, *Bah, bah! ya Abbas! ya Husein!* to the story of his adventures and the still stranger novelty he had been introducing into the unviolated paths of Luristan. Keram, between one pipe of opium and another, gave himself the airs of a showman. We sat round a fire of roots piled up in our honour, and at last went to sleep with a pleasant feeling of security, scarcely disturbed by the collapse of the tent in the middle of the night when a horse pulled up some of the pegs.

Next day was to be my last in Luristan, and I left the remainder of my stores, some tea and sugar and a few biscuits, with the headman of Tarazak. Even among a quite unfriendly tribe it was always difficult to make them accept anything of this sort after the night's lodging: hospitality is given free, and it was never stinted. In spite of their bad reputation, I was sorry to leave the tribesmen and their mountains. No doubt, if they find a traveller on a pass, they will strip him and not trouble to find out what happens afterwards: they have an expressive way of sucking their forefinger and holding it up to illustrate the complete destitution in which one is left on these occasions: but in their tents they were mostly agreeable and friendly, great lovers of a joke, and very good at conversation: and it is pleasant now and then to go among people who carry their lives lightly, who do not give too much importance to this transitory world, and are not so taken up with the means of living that no thought and time is left over for the enjoyment of life itself.

Our last ride took us about three and a half hours over the south-west shoulder of Chia Dozdan to Harsin. It was easy going, by rounded slopes and gentle passes, with groups of trees here and there beside the rents in the hollows: the land in broad open lines rolled away into blue distances on the south.

It fell suddenly in a steep slope with sheer hill faces overhanging the great hollow of Harsin. As we looked down and saw the town and its gardens below us in the distance, Keram asked to be excused from going any farther: he would be shot if the Harsinis got him, said he. Already once he had nearly been caught by a party of them out hunting, when he was in a cave and they had seen the smoke of his fire: they were coming in to see who it might be when one of the party sneezed, and as no one will enter a strange place after so bad an omen, Keram was saved.

I asked him to explain the origin of his feud with a whole township.

'It was a fight,' said he, 'two years ago. I used to live in Harsin then, as I had married a Harsini woman and had a house there. One evening in the *chaikhana* there was an argument, and I shot someone dead. I was right, but perhaps I did not think before shooting. Anyway, when I had gone home to bed, those accursed Harsinis came round to my house and shouted out that they did not want tribesmen in their town and I was to leave. I got up on to the roof and said I would not leave. Then they began to shoot, and I shot back and hit some of them. Then they all surrounded the house, and I went into the upper room which had a small window good for firing from, and we kept at it till the morning and all through that day. The house had high walls so that the people could not get in anywhere; and I had a friend among them outside, and in the dusk he crept up and spoke to me, and I told him to go into the mountain and call the tribe. Meanwhile the Harsinis knew that I always smoked my pipe of opium in the evening, and counted on getting into the house when I had to stop firing. But my wife was a good woman: I put her at the window with the gun, and she continued to shoot while I smoked, and hit a man, she says. Anyway, we kept it up all that night as well, and next morning just at dawn, *tik tak,* we heard shots all around in the hills, and we knew that the Kakavends were coming. Our tribe numbered 8,000 fighting men then before these last year's wars. Well, the Harsinis also knew that the tribe was coming down upon them, and they scattered like rabbits. My wife saddled my horse, and I rode out alone to meet the tribe, and came back with them up here into the hills. And I have never been into Harsin since.'

'And what did you do with your wife?' said I. 'I hope you took her with you. She seems to have been a useful sort of person.'

'I sent for her afterwards,' said Keram. 'I have her still,' he added, as if it were a rather remarkable fact. 'I am fond of her. She is as good as a man.'

After this we parted. I gave Keram the fur coat which the Duliskan chief had not earned, besides what little spare cash was left me, and went down into the land of motor-cars, whence I telephoned for transport to Kermenshah. As for Keram, he turned back to Tudaru, where no doubt he is still regretting in his heart the amusing days when everyone had a gun in Luristan.

II

The Hidden Treasure

The Coolies of Baghdad

The handsomest people in Baghdad are the Lurs of Pusht-i-Kuh. They stride about among the sallow-faced city Shi'as in sturdy-nakedness, a sash round the waist keeping their rags together, a thick felt padded affair on their backs to carry loads, and their native felt cap surrounded by a wisp of turban. They crouch in groups against a sunny wall in winter, or sleep in the shade on the pavement, careless of the traffic around them, and speaking their own language among themselves: and you will think them the veriest beggars, until some day you happen to see them shaved and washed and in their holiday clothes, and hear that they belong to this tribe or that tribe in the mountainous region that touches Iraq's eastern border, and find that they are as proud, and have as much influence in their own lonely districts as any member of a county family in his.

They own three hostels, or *manzils*, in Baghdad, and they all come from the country which lies between the Khanikin-Kermenshah road in the north and Dizful in the south; they are nearly all coolies, and will carry incredible weights, packing-cases, or iron girders, walking barefoot and bent among the crowd.

Seven years ago these people were more or less independent under their Vali, and lived in a happy chaos unsafe for the casual traveller. The Vali had trouble and fled. Some of his sons revolted against him, and he and part of his family are now in exile in Iraq while the strong hand of Riza Shah is stretched over their country. But though the Pusht-i-Kuh is as safe as any so lonely region can be, and though it has great attractions – mountains and forest so near the flatness of the desert – it is not a summer resort for Baghdad citizens. It is still, indeed, as primitive as it must have been ten centuries ago or more.

Once a year the Lurs of Pusht-i-Kuh who work in the Baghdad custom house give a theatrical performance, and show to a small audience the life and traditions of their province. There are bandits in white, with faces bound up as for the toothache all except the eyes (the correct costume for a brigand in the East): there are songs on the high, sobbing note like yodelling of the Alps: there are the full black velvet coats with sash wrapped round them and a dagger in the front, and tasselled turbans: there are white felt coats and pointed caps, where the hair sticks out in half a circle below, worn by the shepherds. And the charm of the performance is that it is no mere tradition of the past, but is what anyone may see who will take the trouble to climb from the Iraq desert over the most desolate of mountain ranges, up into Pusht-i-Kuh.

Until a year ago this high and lonely region had no houses at all except a small erection here and there belonging to the Vali. Now the Persians are building up the capital of Husainabad, and four boulevards (unfinished), a group of government offices, and the motor road from Kermenshah begin to cast shadows of progress over the quite unwilling spirits of the inhabitants. These live in groups of tribal tents scattered thinly between steep ranges, and move from the central heights east or west as the case may be to warmer winter pastures. Travelling there, you would think that so they must have lived from the beginnings of time. But as a matter of fact the land is covered with ruins of villages and cities, probably from days when Lurish Atabeks built on sites laid out long before by their predecessors in the land, the Kurdish Hasanwayds from Sarmaj near Harsin, and the Sassanians before them.

Christians and Jews were settled in this country in very early days; and graves of far more ancient people lie beneath the ground that runs towards the rivers, graves marked with boulders embedded in earth and thorns, but still visible to the eye of the expert and of the tribesman.

The country is divided by the almost unbroken ridge of Kebir (or Kabir) Kuh, and beyond, south-eastward, flows the Saidmarreh River, which becomes, lower down in its better-known reaches, the Kerkha. It is a fine stream, green and deep. It flows through desolate hills that lie in rust-coloured ridges, like the upturned hulls of ships, in parallel ranges eastward. The eastern bank is Lakistan, a dangerous country, whence Bairanwand and Sagwand raiders cross the stream in summer ebb and pillage the tribesmen of the border.

I have been into the north of Lakistan, travelling into it from the plain of Nihavend: but it was surrounded by so careful a cordon of police, and was considered so undesirable for the traveller, that I thought the best chance of reaching the centre of the country would be through the solitudes of Pusht-i-Kuh, if one could cross them unhindered and unobserved. This would have proved a perfectly sound and successful theory if a buried treasure had not come to complicate my plans.

The Treasure

'As you *are* thinking of Luristan, would you like to hunt for a treasure?' said someone at a party one evening, a few days before I was to leave.

'I should love it,' said I, quite ignorant and reckless.

'Very good. I'll bring you the accomplice to-morrow morning.'

And so I got involved.

The accomplice was a young Lur of eighteen or so who had been taken in early days from his own place and civilized. The process, I thought, had not gone very deep; not much beyond 'arak and cigarettes, a European shirt without the collar, and a passionate desire for life in *Ferangistan* with a *Ferangi* wife whose exact nationality was to be determined later, when the treasure was found.

The treasure was in a cave in the hills.

Now no one has travelled at all in the Near East, especially since the revival of archæology, without hearing of buried treasures at every other step. The finding of a single gold coin, or a copper one for that matter if it looks like gold, will fill a whole district with rumours. So I was sceptical about the treasure. But as the tale unfolded itself and, like mummies in their funeral bands, facts began to emerge from wrappings of irrelevance, I began to see something more positive than the usual report, and finally came to agree with my friend at the party, and to think that 'there was something in it'.

The father of young Hasan, my accomplice, was the head, or one of the heads, of a small tribe tucked away in the folds of Kebir Kuh, in the country still marked on the maps as unsurveyed. Some years ago a tribesman had come to the boy with a story: he had been caught by a storm on the slopes of the mountain, had taken refuge in a cavern of which these limestone hills are full, had seen a glitter in its depths, and had found twenty cases of gold ornaments, daggers, coins and idols. He had taken what he could conceal beneath his *abba*, and handed half a dozen daggers and a handful of jewels to his young master. Hasan had never been there, but he knew the place: he had a map of it which he would show: and being ignorant of the value of the things, and afraid of the job of getting them out of Persia and Iraq all by himself, he wanted some British person he could trust to help him.

So far so good: but now came the complications. When the tribesman first brought his booty, Hasan had shown it, together with his map, to his dearest friend and schoolfellow, and had given it to him for safe keeping. The friend showed it to his father, an Arab of some position in the city of Mosul, and an ex-vizier. This man seized it, and not only now refused to give up what he had, but claimed a partnership in the remaining booty of the hills. He would do all he could, said Hasan, to intercept any effort to reach the place without his acquiescence, and would probably play false even if his acquiescence were obtained and a share promised him.

On the other hand, he could do nothing by himself, for he had not the friendship of the tribes and would not dare to venture into their country. His son was still Hasan's friend, and ready at any moment to steal the jewels from his own father's house so as to restore them to their rightful owner. Meanwhile the fact of their being in enemy hands prevented my seeing the things: the venture would be an absolute leap in the dark as far as the ultimate value of the stuff was concerned; the difficulties were obviously great since not only the Persian authorities but the tribesmen also were to be kept in ignorance, and the stuff, even when conveyed in secret across five days of solitary mountains, would then have to run the gauntlet of the wicked vizier in Iraq.

To counterbalance these perils there was, apart from the fascination of a treasure hunt in itself, the certain fact that much valuable stuff *has* been found in these regions; it gets smuggled across the border and bought by dealers, the traces of its origin are obliterated, and it loses all historic importance. The great treasure of Nihavend has been thus squandered in very recent years. To find and record anything in its own cave might be a matter of real value to the antiquarian.

I said I would do my best to reach the place, Hasan was to meet me there a day or two after my arrival, and we would carry off what we could, and then study the best way of approaching a museum and the Persian government. He was to provide a safe guide and a disguise in case it were necessary.

As the various interviews with the young Lur developed, my share in the undertaking appeared to grow larger and larger and less and less reassuring. He could evidently not be trusted to keep silence. The secrecy of the East is, I believe, a myth; far more typical is the case of that man who was so proud of having murdered his innkeeper's son that he could not help talking about it and himself giving himself away. So it would be, I felt convinced, with Hasan: and the enemy, sure enough, suspected something even before I started, and prevailed on the police to confiscate the boy's passport.

I decided to go, notwithstanding, and to get off as soon as possible. M., who was responsible for suggesting the escapade in the first place, was to do what he could to see, first, that the boy actually started after me, and second, that the vizier did nothing drastic to hinder us in my absence. We told Hasan, who was twisting his knuckles in an agony of nervousness, that we would rescue his passport and help him to start; he on his side was to stop intriguing and deal openly if that were in him. He was not to travel with me – a fact which relieved my mind, since he was wanted by the police for having stirred up rebellion and was also of an age for conscription. But he swore by all his gods that he would meet me in five days. He brought the map, a dirty little piece of paper with a pencilled oval on it to mark the gardens of the tribe: a path led into a valley and up again: it kept west along a ridge and, after two gullies, came to a third where, in a cave with five 'wan' trees before it, the treasure lay hid.

'You cannot mistake it,' said Hasan: 'and if I am not there, go and do what you can. But don't let the tribe notice that you are searching for anything in particular.'

This last condition, together with the sketchiness of the map, seemed to make the affair quite hopeless. But it was no bad thing to get an introduction to the tribe, and if nothing came of it I still hoped to be able to go on along my own projected way and discover ancient burial places in Tarhan.

The evening before I was to start, Hasan came once more with a gaudy and engaging garment covered with flowers which he said would make me inconspicuous in the Kurdish hills. I had spent five rupees on a pale-brown *abba* with gold at the neck, and a pair of cloth-soled *giva* shoes. I felt equipped for any emergency. Our luggage was light: no bed, but a sleeping-sack; a saddle-bag with clothes and medicines on one side and food, chiefly tea and sugar, on the other. Next morning Shah Riza, the guide, arrived, in a long yellow and white striped garment with a ragged grey jacket, and a blue turban wound round his untidy old head. He had no luggage at all.

Shah Riza is really a maker of quilts, but he looks like a philosopher, which, in his way, he is. His philosophy is one of passive resistance to the slings and arrows of fortune as they hurtle round him: he sits among them looking as if he thought of something else, but ready, in his quiet way, to make the most of any lull in the general perversity of things. As an attendant he left much to be desired – everything in fact if an attendant is supposed, as I take it, to attend. But he was a charming old man, and would sit for hours, while all was bustle around him, filling little tubes of paper with native tobacco, lost in what one might take to be the ultimate perfection of resignation, but which was really a happy daydream, far from the toilsome world in which I was looking for keys or dinner, or any of the other things he was supposed to see to.

His first ineptitude was to appear on the morning of departure without a passport. The expedition was postponed while I went to see if such a thing could be produced by the Persian legation. It would take a week, and then would still be very doubtful; there was a hesitating look about the Persian secretary, as he handled the Philosopher's portrait; passport or no passport, I thought the thing to do was to get away as soon as possible.

We packed a car and crossed the desert from Kut to Bedrah on the Persian border.

Crossing the Frontier

The great and almost only comfort about being a woman is that one can always pretend to be more stupid than one is and no one is surprised. When the police stopped our car at Bedrah and enquired where we were staying, the chauffeur, who did not know, told him to ask the lady.

'That is no good,' said the policeman. 'She's a woman.'

'Yes,' said the chauffeur, 'but she knows everything. She knows Arabic.'

The policeman asked me.

I had not the vaguest idea of where we were staying, and looked at him with a blank idiocy which he thought perfectly natural. The Philosopher thereupon roused himself, and explained that I was lodging in the empty house of the son of the Vali of Pusht-i-Kuh.

The police and I being both satisfied with this explanation, we drove up the gravelly river bed of Bedrah to palm gardens on the left, where the house and its little village are enclosed in mud walls and surrounded by trees. The chauffeur, with curiosity unsatisfied, left us, and rugs were spread and my luggage deposited in a little cobbled court with palm trees and a tank of water, where a band of Persian exiles, mostly relations of Shah Riza, soon gathered round us.

Here, owing to the fact that I had not yet discovered the depths of my Philosopher's incompetence, and still expected him to do things, we spent three weary days, relieved only by *The Pilgrim's Progress* which I happened to have with me and by visits from the village notables. It was a curious little society of *émigrés*, full of whispers and intrigues and illicit intercourse with those of the old *régime* in Pusht-i-Kuh. I soon saw that my friends, if ever I were discovered with them, would all be most decidedly and justifiably 'suspect' to any Persian authority.

As for crossing the border, with or without a passport, there seemed to be no difficulty. The thing was to be guided by some family connection who could be trusted not to give one away. The smuggling of cloth, tea and sugar is now so extensive and continuous that all the secret ways were well known and animals could easily be found. Shah Riza's cousin Mahmud would walk across to some friends of his just over the frontier line, and arrange it.

Meanwhile they sat plotting late into the night, plying poor Shah Riza with conflicting advice, so that he looked more like a philosopher than ever, bewildered among the diversities of truth. They squatted near the tank in the light of a lantern, Shah Riza in the middle with wild grey locks and a pained expression, looking from one to the other, while they told him that, whatever else he did without, a *Pahlevi* hat and a pair of trousers *must* be procured and worn by anyone who wanted to enter Persia.

On one side of him sat the Vali's steward, a young man with Rudolf Valentino looks, white teeth, soft brilliant eyes, a slim figure, and most untrustworthy expression, under a large turban. On the other side was the Philosopher's uncle, the village headman, a shrewd and wrinkled peasant face, benevolent while no one contradicted him. Mahmud the cousin sat a little aloof, with heavy sleepy eyes and drooping moustache, a regular Lur type, and with the air of one waiting to act while others did the talking.

There was a great deal of talking, and I began to feel very dubious about the whole adventure. Crime, I decided, is not amusing. Danger is interesting and necessary to the human spirit, but to do something that will be generally disapproved of, if found out, must be humiliating unless one is so hardened that other people's opinions can have no influence at all. Only a fanatic can be happily a criminal. I thought by contrast of the pleasant dangers of mountaineering, or of exploring when there is no secret motive to weigh upon you, and decided to leave hidden treasures alone for the future.

The guests had gone away, the Philosopher was already asleep, rolled in a quilt like a cocoon on the cobble stones, and Mahmud was busy with his toilet for the night. The most important part of this was the arrangement of his gun, which he loaded and then laid under a flap of his rug at the foot of a palm tree: another rug was put on top to serve him for a pillow: he unwound his turban and wound it up again more tightly but less ornamentally than for the day: took a drink from the goatskin hanging on a tree; and lay down to sleep.

Thieves were around after dates, which hung in moonlit clusters on the palm trees, and Mahmud would wake at the slightest noise and go prowling round. But as a matter of fact there was little enough chance of sleep for anyone, for the moon went into eclipse, and a beating of tins from every roof, a wailing of women and frenzy of dogs, and occasional high yelp of jackal made chaos of the night. I sat up at last and tried to explain the solar system to Shah Riza, who was smoking meditatively, squatting on his hams.

'They say,' said I non-committally, as befitted so unlikely a theory, 'that it is the shadow of our world which hides the moon.'

Even the Philosopher's mild abstraction was roused.

'That,' said he, 'is quite impossible. Anyone can see from here that it is an insect which eats the moon. It is alive. It has a spirit. It means war and trouble coming. But it is only a sign, and Allah will not allow it to go too far.'

As if in answer to his words, the moon, a red and sullen ember, began to reappear: the blackness of sky dissolved again slowly into luminous spaces: the rattle of tins subsided: and, leaving the matter of the solar system unsettled, we were able to sleep.

The fruit of the night's plotting showed itself in time by the arrival of a young smuggler from over the border. He wore woollen *givas*, a white woollen tunic to the knees, and a round felt cap on his head. He carried a stout stick with iron-shod knob in his hand, and he treated the question of policemen along the frontier as a matter of indifference.

'But if you would rather have a passport,' said he, 'I have a friend who can easily buy one. It makes an easier journey for the lady, if one is not afraid of the police.'

This seemed a reasonable suggestion, and cheap at the price.

'Let us by all means buy a passport,' said I. 'And let us be ready to start to-morrow morning.'

The getting of the mules, and finding of a second man called Alidad, a sinister-looking villain who kept his left eye closed, and remarked that 'to the British, money is like water', occupied the rest of the day. Shah Riza was left free to attend to the matter of his costume, which he postponed till we were just about to mount next morning, and then he kept us while he went to the bazaar in Bedrah, and returned after an hour or more with a small piece of black alpaca, about the size of two large handkerchiefs, which he thought hopefully might be turned into trousers en route. Doubtful, but anxious to start at all costs, we acquiesced. We made across the last strip of desert north-eastward for the hills.

A dust storm was brewing, and the first frontier post, square and desolate between two desert streams, had no sign of life about it. We hurried by, keeping to the shelter of the low banks of the Kunjan Cham, among tamarisk bushes, till we emerged in Persian land, in a hollow screened from sight, where our smuggler had his home in a small colony of leaf-thatched tents through which the dust was blowing. His father was chief of the tents, and welcomed us while the whole community joined in the plot.

'A passport,' they said, 'is always better than none, and so easy to get. But Shah Riza *must* have a *Pahlevi* hat and trousers.'

Shah Riza evidently thought that his social status was bound up in the long yellow gown, and looked melancholy over the change. He produced his black alpaca with a reluctant air, whereupon the assembled elders, who had their doubts but no expert knowledge, called upon the ladies of the tribe. These advanced in a band from the back of the tent, and contemplated the inadequate remnant with scorn. 'That will only make half,' said they. They knelt upon it and measured it out with the palms of their hands; they turned it this way and that; when all had tried in turn, they gave it up as hopeless, while Shah Riza sat on in sorrowful meditation.

I was beginning to wonder if we would ever get off at all, when a young man appeared and cast a spare and quite presentable pair of trousers down on the ground before us.

Even now the matter threatened shipwreck. The Philosopher was feeling the proffered object between finger and thumb and murmuring something about its insufficient beauty. But I had had enough of him and his clothes for the moment. I got up from the seclusion of the best carpet on which I sat, and advanced into the tribal circle, stooped over to examine the garment with care, and declared that I had never seen a better pair, nor one more suitable for Persian travel. The young man's supporters agreed in chorus. A *Pahlevi* hat was found and placed on the Philosopher's head, giving him an air of unsuitable levity. With a sigh he stood up, pulled a piece of stick out of the roof, wound a pink cord round it, and began to run it like a bodkin through the waist of his new costume. The passport alone remained to be settled.

How that was done I do not know. He and the smuggler went off together and returned after many hours, having bargained it down from twenty tomans to two (about 4*s.*). It was written on yellow paper, with five stamps, and appeared altogether an impressive document. The afternoon was late, and questions in any case are rarely advisable. We departed without more ado, and with the last sunlight upon us made through low scrub for the custom house.

Here we met the Chief of Customs taking the air, with a puppy on a long chain in his arms and his wife beside him. He was a pleasant, elderly man with pince-nez, and an air of settled comfort about him which looked strangely out of place in so lonely and windswept a spot.

'He is a great man. You had better get off the mule before you come up to him,' said Alidad, and evidently expected remonstrance when I rode on unconcerned. But the great man did not look at passports: he waved us on to his subordinates in the square building, who examined our moderate luggage with favour and let us through as night was falling.

We now had an hour and a half before us, and rode through the flat lands of the Gawi Rud under a dusty moon, until in the darkness we became aware of mounds covered with earth, which turned out to be winter provisions of straw for the cattle to feed on dotted in a row outside the camp. We rode through a fury of dogs to dim shapes of tents, and dismounted at the settlement of the Zardusht tribe at Mansurabad.

Waterless Hills

The dust-storm raged all through that night.

Tired out with the sound of talking, of which the day seemed to have been more full than usual, I left the Zardushtis early and took refuge in a mud-walled cubicle both from the tribesmen, who sat on their carpets outside in the moonlight, and from their women, of whom only two or three ventured from their own part of the tent to watch my evening toilet. When I had undressed and washed, and had tried, to their rather fearful delight, the effect of cold cream on the faces of two gay young brides, I was left in solitude and darkness, while the dust swished in showers through the dry leaves of the roof above my head. The slight mud wall, here in the waste of open spaces, turned into the very emblem of solidity; no comfortable safety of London houses, with shuttered curtained windows and draught-proof doors, has ever seemed to me so sheltering as those six feet of upright earth buffeted by the Arabian wind. Not the thing itself, but the sense of other and contrary things, makes reality.

In the very early morning I looked out, and saw what appeared to be three little mounds of reddish earth lying in front of my hut. These, in the strengthening light, resolved themselves into the sleeping forms of my retainers, obliterated under desert sand. In the fullness of time they stirred, crawled as from a chrysalis, shook out their turbans, and were ready for tea, which the ladies soon provided.

The wind still swished along, a noise of fine falling particles betraying its invisible presence. To wear a hat was out of the question. I enveloped myself in the brown *abba*, tightly pinned under the chin; climbed, and crouched with my back to the gale on the pack-mule; and we started for the Persian hills across another flat stretch of desert; Alidad, with one sinister eye shut, led the way and held my animal by a halter.

The weather, which hid the world from us, also hid us from the police: if there were any about, they lurked somewhere behind the curtain of dust which moved as we did. On our right hand we passed Qal'a Seifi, a dim huddle of dilapidated houses with a vague shadow of a man digging in a ditch, seen for a moment and lost. The desert rose and fell in small undulations imprisoned in mist, sprinkled with bushes of aghul and camelthorn, and the bitter colocynth along the ground.

Beside the wide dry bed of the Gawi Rud the last police post showed suddenly square and lonely: though we could easily have skirted it in our misty privacy, Alidad and the smuggler both rightly thought that a passport, when it exists at all, should be used as much as possible, and walked up boldly to a young man in blue uniform who was busy in the cooking of the garrison dinner.

These little posts are inhabited by six policemen, but most of them were out looking for smugglers with an admirable spirit of conscientious optimism. The young man with the fowl in his hand, glancing up to me and seeing a respectable brown *abba* draped over native saddle-bags, thought no more of the matter. It is only the unexpected that ever makes a customs officer think; avoid that and all is well. Passports, though unintelligible, are not unexpected, and their subtle international differences are not bothered about by the lower grades of investigators. My appearance was normal; my Frankish hat discreetly hidden on my lap; the policeman invited us to lunch, heard our excuses with a good grace, and waved us on. We went out into the loneliness again.

All that day we saw no other human being except, an hour or so on, one tall man, wild and poor and contented, with bushy eyebrows white with dust, and red rags held together by a blue sash. His thighs were naked, and he strode down with an air of strength and freedom through the inhospitable weather, beating a little donkey before him. After we left him, our path began to climb.

The old Vali used to have a winter house on the banks of the Gawi Rud, and we lunched amid its ruins and the ruins of a village spread around it. The Philosopher woke suddenly from the depths of his habitual meditations and informed me that he had lived here many years, and skipped about among the crumbled walls with an astonishing agility, pointing out this and that, with an almost indecent liveliness, as if an old stiff-jointed goat should gambol like a kid. The nearness of his hills and long-unvisited home gave Shah Riza these accesses of enthusiasm, when his eyes, slightly pulled up at the corners into most engaging wrinkles, danced with a smiling light so different from his own idea of correct behaviour for a religious and respectable maker of quilts.

In the quiet hour after food which should be filled with benevolence, he and Alidad fell upon some misunderstanding: Alidad came up to me as I dozed in the sun, and asked with an alarming solemnity if I would condescend to shake hands with him. This ceremony I performed in a mystified manner, waiting for the sequel, when the disquieting statement was made that Shah Riza was a bad man, but that he, Alidad, would see to it that I came to no harm. Having accepted this promise with a composure that had a rather chilling effect on the emotional atmosphere, I waited while a sack of straw for the horses' supper was collected from the deserted fields round about, and we then proceeded across a stony river bed north-westward, with a ravine below us on either hand, and high barren shapes of hills rising faintly out of the desert dust.

This way into Persia is scarcely used except by smugglers and is steep and impracticable for heavily laden animals. At the top of the high rampart is the pass of Gildar, between two rounded hills. Here towards evening we climbed, and looked on an inhospitable land, a tumult of strata and hollows. The level ridges, that had lain peacefully beneath some sea, were tossed up and thrown in unexpected angles, covered with black fossil shells that lay about the ground, and scored into barren valleys by waters that rush destructive in spring and die in summer, leaving here and there salt and undrinkable springs.

This country belongs to the Malikshahi Lurs, who from their colder heights descend on it in winter, when there is a thin coat of pasture for their flocks. But now it was deserted: only the smuggler, walking swiftly by night, crossed its unfriendly paths. As we rode with the evening sky deepening above us, looking round for a place to camp, I thought that I had never seen a land so derelict, an empty husk, its life long since departed. The slow death of the universe was born in upon me and made visible. Even the yellow grasses in the beds of dry gullies, that looked soft from far away, changed, as we approached, into desiccated beds of thorns.

As the darkness began to fall we turned aside into a fold of the land, under a high cliff ridge called Zamiyah Kuh, out of sight so as to leave the path clear through the night to the Malikshahi smugglers.

A cold wind came creeping, not the fierce batterer of the desert, but an insidious creature that chilled one to the bone. The Philosopher, with great resourcefulness, seized my spare Burberry and put it on. Alidad made a fire in a small gully. Shah Riza answered my enquiries as to food by the remark that we had lots of flour, and the muleteers, having unpacked and settled down, began to mix a few handfuls of it with water, to pat it into a disc about an inch thick, and put it under the embers to cook. Shah Riza, whose dealings with the Burberry had shown a touch of the Epicurean, must belong to the Stoics after all, I reflected, and began to hunt for sardines in my saddle-bags.

'Another time,' said I, 'a chicken, alive or dead, is to be carried with us into any desert.' The three men agreed that female fragility might reasonably require such knick-knacks. They cleared a small space near the fire for my sleeping-sack to lie evenly, settled them-selves on the other side, and we were soon engulfed in the high, thin, nightly silence of the hills.

The Law of Hospitality

The Philosopher had been rather perturbed by the fact that his mare, a vicious grey with a blind eye, slipped over the edge during our descent from Gildar. The edge was not quite sheer, and she slid on her four hooves with the smuggler hanging on behind, using the tail as a rudder: the operation came to an end at the bottom of a small ravine with no injury but some surprise to all concerned, and though the Philosopher had not been riding at the moment, the incident disturbed him: he started off next morning with a tinge of gloom in his meditations.

As we left our sleeping-place, a fine ibex stood above us on a crag, its horns lit by the rising sun.

We now rode easily, in a country where trees began to appear. They showed at first on the high skylines on either side of us, and gradually descended to where, through white and crumbly lime-stone soil, our path went along with small ups and downs. There was broom and tamarisk, thorn and oak, a small-leaved tree called *keikum*, and the wan or *tere-binth* with broad leaves, aromatically scented, and peacock blue berries good to eat. I looked on this tree with great interest, for the treasure cave was to be recognized partly by the wan trees at its entrance.

I made a mental note to know the wan again.

We began to meet people, Malikshahis dressed in felt, with turbans round their caps, and sashes and daggers worn outside their white *abbas*: their hair was long, unaffected as yet by the Dalilah of government which shears the Persian tribesmen's locks.

Policemen, our smuggler told me, practically never take this road. After about three hours we came to a small rise covered with cairns of stones, and knowing by these symbols that a holy place must be in sight, looked forward and saw the *Imamzadeh* of Pir Muhammad with four white minarets and two blue domes ahead of us in a hollow filled with rice-fields, brilliant green in the sun.

It was only nine in the morning, but Alidad had friends here, and there was no other encampment to be met with for the rest of the day. So we left the *Imamzadeh* on our right hand and turned to dismount at a group of oak-bough huts in ploughed land by the stream, and rested here for many hours while the chicken, now considered a necessary part of my menu, was being caught, decapitated, plucked, speared on a peeled stick, and finally roasted over the fire. Bread was made for us, and a lengthy negotiation for a new mule was started by Shah Riza, with an opening burst of eloquence on the sufferings caused by his mare: the Seyids of the *Imamzadeh*, who own the ground around, sat in a judicial circle: a brown mule was finally produced with a new muleteer: and after parting regretfully with our smuggler, we eventually got away at one-thirty, wading up the limpid waters of the stream.

The whole country of Pusht-i-Kuh is divided by a long and high range, running north-west and south-east like a wall: its two chief peaks, called Walantar* and Warzarine, are a little lower and a little higher than 9,000 feet respectively, but it is not their height so much as the general unbroken massiveness of the ridge, keeping to about 7,000 or 8,000 feet for many miles with never a break worth speaking of, which gives its prestige to the range. Its far snows are seen from the desert of Iraq on a clear winter day,

* Or Waland Tar.

and for many months when the snow lies, the Malikshahi on one side, and the Bedrei on the other cannot meet – a difficulty which, judging from what they say one of the other, cannot distress them

For this great mountain we were making, winding now in a corridor of rocks and shadows up the canyon of the Pir Muhammad stream. Maidenhair grew in the clefts. Above, high up, leaning into the sky, were trees. Two women stood and called down from the edge, their heavy turbans and loose sleeves etched and fore-shortened against the blue like some Venetian ceiling. And as we crossed at intervals among the white boulders, we looked into clear water with fish in it, whisking transparent tails.

The Pir Muhammad would have led us all the way to the foot of the Great Mountain, but most of the defiles through which these torrents wind are too difficult even for Lurish paths, and we soon had to turn aside and climb on to the shoulders of the hills. They were tumbled in strata wilder than any we had seen before, but yet with a curious regularity, as if titanic hands had laid the blocks of stone in even courses, tilted and twisted for some incred-ible architecture. The trees among the rocks gave them beauty: and presently we left the lower chaos, and came to smooth hill-sides, with oaks not thickly planted, but each one separate in its own shadow on the bare white gravel of the soil. Here was no habitation, but a friendly peace: and woodcutters in white tunics driving asses now and then upon the road: and in the fall of the evening we came down by one shoulder after the other, till we saw a plain below us and the Great Mountain like a curtain beyond it in the dusk.

Black tents in groups of two and three, very small in their lone-liness, showed in cultivated patches down below. We did not go so far, but coming by a small spring on the hillside, found there three young and pretty women stooping over goatskins to fill them with water, and eager, when they saw we were travellers, to invite us to the poorness of their tents close by.

It was a small colony of four tents, the first of the Arkwaz land, and there was no chieftain to entertain us. The people were so poor that they had neither meat nor fowl nor eggs, milk, rice, tea, nor sugar: nothing in fact but the essential bag of flour and a tiny patch of tomatoes and cucumbers, of which they proceeded to pick every one with the noble hospitality of their code.

There were three charming women. I left the men outside and came to them by the fire, out of the night wind. An older woman, with a sweet and gay face, was mistress of the tent; it was her daughter, and a daughter-in-law, and a friend, who had brought us in, and showed us off as a delightful find picked up by rare good fortune. I soon discovered that I carried a kind of radiance about me, a magic not my own, derived from the city of Baghdad from where I came. The two young women had spent a few months there when their husbands worked as coolies, and the memory lived with them in a glorified vision. They stroked my city clothes with a wistfulness pathetic to see.

'*Kahraba*', electricity! I lit my torch and they murmured the word as if it held a whole heartful of longings. The worship of the East for mechanical things seems to us deplorable and shallow; but seen here against so naked a background, the glamour of the machine, of something that gives comfort without effort in a place where bare necessities themselves are precarious, and every moment of ease comes as a boon and a miracle; seen here by the fire in the tent that swayed in the cold night, the light that sprang at will from the palm of my hand did indeed hold a divinity about it – a Promethean quality as of lightning snatched from heaven and made gentle and submissive to the uses of man. So their eyes saw it, more truly, perhaps, than ours, who buy the thing as soul-less glass and wire.

I watched the beauty of the two girls – a fine beauty of an old race, with small hands and thin lips and long oval faces. On their heads they wore little skull caps embroidered with beads round which they wound the voluminous dark turban. There were beads round their ankles too, where the scarlet trousers were fastened tightly and ended in a woollen fringe over the little bare heels. This is a good and decent costume for women who sit about on the ground all the time. Over it they wore loose gowns of printed cotton, like the flowery affair I carried in my saddle-bag. The daughter of the house had a velvet coat too, full skirted and left open in the front. She had a turquoise and gold ring in her nose, over the tattoo mark on her lip; her hands and feet were tattooed with thin blue branches of palm leaf, not unbecoming; and on her wrists she wore heavy silver bangles which flashed in the firelight as she kneaded the dough for our supper.

I wondered if among their poets, who still sing in the old manner about the things they know, there is not someone who has told the splendour of his beloved's hands with their silver brace-lets, as she tosses the bread from one to the other with swift and lovely movement in this most beautiful of household tasks. When the flour was kneaded, a sort of convex shield of metal called the *saj* was laid above the flames, the pancakes of dough were thrown upon it one at a time, and the bread, warm and rather sodden, was ready in a minute or so.

But this was not all our supper. The tomatoes were cooking in a pot while our hunger in the meanwhile was being stayed with raw cucumbers. Our meal was evidently looked on in the nature of a banquet. Every now and then the mother of the family gave it a stir, tasted it, and nodded with an appreciation beyond mere powers of speech. Four little boys, subdued with expectation, sat in a silent row, while a smaller infant amused himself with two lambs, tied up in the tent near the fire out of the way of wolves, and evidently used to being treated as members of the family. The little daughter, the prettiest woman's eldest child, busied herself with household jobs, knowing well that her chance of the feast was remote.

And presently the dinner was cooked: the tomatoes were poured out steaming: they had dwindled, alas, and now only just looked presentable on three small pewter plates, one for me, one for the Philosopher, and one for the two muleteers. Such as they were, they were put before us, while the family looked on in admirable silence: only one boy, unable as yet quite to control his feelings, followed the plates with his eyes: his tears rose slowly, the corners of his little mouth turned down. His mother, ashamed, gave him a small slap and then, surreptitiously, offered him her fingers to lick, on which some savour of tomato still lingered.

I myself was hungry enough to have demolished all three dishes at once with the greatest ease; but who could withstand so heart-rending a spectacle? To say anything was impossible: our hostess would have been humiliated beyond words: but one could leave part of the dinner on one's plate. I pretended to be satisfied half-way through the microscopic meal, and the four little boys lapped up what remained. As for the daughter, she had learnt already what is what in this world. She neither got nor expected a share.

The Great Mountain

The dawn crept dove-coloured over the solitary landscape, subduing the high ridge before us to a uniform shadowy gentleness; even as the mind of men, growing in wisdom, may yet subdue and smooth away by very excess of light the obstacles before it.

Our obstacle was also our goal, the high wall where he who mapped for the Survey of India had stopped in 1923, beyond which, unsurveyed, lay Shah Riza's house and the treasure. I looked at it across the plain still dun in morning shadow, where the black tents in their small and even rows showed no sign of rising smoke or life awakening. I wondered by which of the little nicks against the sky, all running a more or less even line, our way would lie.

Even Shah Riza was ready to start, his prayers having taken him less time than usual. He was wrapped in my Burberry, to which he now clung day and night, inspiring that respectable garment with an appearance of jauntiness quite foreign to its nature. The sight of him and it together roused in me an unreasonable silent fury. Why should Shah Riza snatch my clothes without even asking by your leave? When I made a feeble attempt to retrieve it, all he had said was: 'And am I to die of cold?' Which is, I believe, known technically as a rhetorical question.

The forces of communism show themselves in an uncontrovertible manner when the forces of nature are with them. Given a sufficiently cold night and two overcoats, one human being obviously cannot claim more than one of these: the laws of property go by the board. This I was prepared to concede with a good grace; but it was a different matter to see the Philosopher in the warm sunlight by day still clinging to my favourite wrap with the obvious assumption that a holy man ought to be well dressed. Shah

Riza gave himself great airs of holiness: he was always saying his prayers when there was work to be done: it made him the most respectable sort of chaperon one could possibly desire, and there his chief usefulness ended.

I did not mind his prayers, though he chose the place nearest the fire to say them in, and caused us all great inconvenience: what I resented was the assumption that holiness is a virtue that other people should be glad to pay for, instead of being a private affair between yourself and you. In this opinion, however, I was alone. Shah Riza's holiness was an asset recognized by all. He used it to domineer in a mild way at every evening gathering, and when I asked him to arrange my sleeping-sack, or find the medicine box, or tackle any mundane chore, he would announce that he was just about to say his prayers, and relegate me and my importunities to an inferior plane.

This morning, however, we started early. The ladies woke up in darkness to bake our bread: the embers of the fire, which had died down in the tent through the night, were piled with fresh oak branches to fight the chill that comes before daybreak: and at five-thirty, with the light increasing, as if it were thrown in giant handfuls from behind the mountain rim into the upper air, we set off downhill to the plain.

The sun came towards us and the long shadows shrank as we advanced. Below, in small hollows on our right hand, the infant waters of the Pir Muhammad stream, which we met again above its skirted defile, shone with a peaceful early morning brightness. Shepherds from the tents were taking out their flocks, that walked in long files before them, with pattering feet like a summer shower.

The Great Mountain has, as it were, an outwork of low foot-hills wooded with oak. These trees have bigger leaves than ours, of a dull green without much life in it, and bigger acorns, too, with large frilly cups and pointed fruit, just beginning to turn yellow. In a bad year, when want of rain has killed the harvests, the Lurs make flour of these acorns, letting them first soak in water for three days to 'take out the heaviness'. They roast them in ashes also, and eat them whole like chestnuts. But they say that many pains and illnesses follow on this diet. The oak leaves, as well as roofing the summer tents, are regularly used as fodder for the flocks in the dry season. They clothed the foothills thickly, growing to a good size on either side, while we kept out in the open and followed a torrent bed of white stones that ran straight and wide like an avenue towards the mountain.

The harmony of the morning hour, if such a thing really exists, was shattered as far as we were concerned by the discovery that, with an uninhabited day before us, no one had remembered the chicken. Shah Riza, whose job it was, allowed my reproaches to slide off him absent-mindedly until Alidad gave some small opening for blame by not producing an Arkwaz tent where one was promised; whereupon the whole weight of the probably foodless day was shifted on to him with a promptitude creditable to the Philosopher's resourcefulness.

Alidad took the matter amiss: he walked along with his one eye shut, boiling for a quarrel; while Shah Riza, enthroned on the pack-mule some little way behind, talked to his cigarette in a voice of remonstrance, lamenting the hungry hours that lay before the lady. The new muleteer meanwhile dashed hither and thither among the little dells, looking for a last habitation before the empty hills began, where a chicken might be captured; and, as it happened, we came upon one black tent round a corner, and finally carried off a raucous cockerel with yellow eyes, and set him on our saddle-bow for the sum of fivepence.

We now began to climb, attacking the mountain without any sort of diplomacy, to where limestone needles took off from beds of scree. The path zig-zagged with a scrunch of loose stones among which shell fossils were still visible. Oak trees grew rarer, interspersed more and more with *keikum* which turns red in autumn, with wan trees and gigantic bushes of gum tragacanth that spread like shallow Japanese umbrellas close to the ground. The hard structure of the range grew visible: it leaped up against the blue sky in rocky fluted ribs, like the manifold sheaves of late Gothic pillars surrounding the rounded high summit called Walantar with a palisade of spikes.

The path was so steep that even the lightly laden mules had to be disburdened of our weight. In little over two hours we climbed 2,000 feet.

'This bitterness, this roughness, for the sons of Adam,' said the new muleteer, as he followed me.

Below, untidy as a sea with cross currents, lay the lower hills, vanishing into the western desert dust.

Except for the joyousness of height, the view had no great beauty, for the distant oak trees give a spotty look of smallpox to the whole, and take away the play of light and shadow, and Kebir Kuh, alone in all this region, has the true mountain structure. But when we reached the round and stony backbone at 8,300 feet, we looked out on a nobler view, over the unmapped country whose even ridges ran like a shoal of swimming whales, all in the same direction, through waves of woods in shadow that sloped to the valley below. Steep clefts descended and no habitation was visible. But Shah Riza, looking out with eyes narrowed with excitement over his own land, said that down in the main valley was a mill, where we could spend the night, and reach his people (and the region of the treasure) next day.

The tribes come every spring to pasture along this great ridge of Kebir Kuh. It is then deep in grass; the *arjiné* bushes and stunted thorn and *keikum* trees give fuel; and there is water a short way down the slope. They pitch their tents and spend a month or two in the mountain air; and it is a mistake to think that they do not know the beauty of their landscapes and the delight of high places, for the mere mention of the Great Mountain to any coolie in Baghdad will light his eyes with pleasure.

Alidad was not of the mountain people, and when I suggested lunch at the highest point, his feelings were outraged. A Persian guide does not look on his employer as a human being: he, like any other registered packet, is an object to be delivered safe at the other end: when and how, the guide considers his own affair. Alidad was a quarrelsome man with strong views on the proper place for women in the general scheme of things. Had he not treated me with a respect almost excessive; he asked. Had he not humbled himself so far as to allow me to put my foot upon his shoulder in mounting on my mule: what word of complaint could I find?

'No complaint,' said I, mildly but firm. 'What I want is lunch with a view over both sides of the landscape.'

Alidad had no language to meet this. But he opened both hands and breathed hard at the listening hills and looked at Shah Riza. The Philosopher, however, evidently knew a determined woman when he saw one, and he himself liked the look of his mountains. With my moral supremacy, as I hoped, firmly established, I sat down in rather a cold wind and pulled out my compass, and proceeded to disentangle, with the help of the three tribesmen, the names of the unknown hills.

Night in Garau

We made our way for hours down the northern slopes of the Great Mountain before we reached the mills of Garau in the valley.

The track was steep and bad, and little used at this time of the year; it followed a spur divided by a deep cleft from the precipices which buttress the eastern side of Walantar. Then it descended, and dipped into the oak woods as into a petrified sea. No wind stirred there, no undergrowth grew in the shade, no small creatures scurried among the trunks and branches. The leaves of these oaks look dark, as if some black had got into the colour by mistake; a tone I remember being distressed over in childish water-colours when the foliage was started before the sepia that had been used for the trunk had got well out of the paint-brush.

We came to a neck; the path mounted a little to push through a cleft so narrow that the saddle-bags could not go through together and had to be unloaded; and as I stood waiting there, eight ibex, four young ones and four does, leaped below our feet across the torrent boulders, and raced up into the sunlight along a slanting ledge of strata that shot peach-coloured into the sky. There was no water in the stream, except a pool or two by some willows where we rested, which dried up again lower down. The descent grew gentler; the trees spaced more openly; reddish stubble land appeared, ploughed by the little tribe of Ali Shirwan who own the Garau stream: their tents, not more than three or four, were hidden in a tributary valley out of sight. The Garau also was dry, but a little clear watercourse, led down from Walantar between damp earthy banks, fed the mill and the maize and bean-fields below it.

I ruscelletti che dai verdi colli
Di Casentino scendon giuso in Arno,
Facendo i lor canali e freddi e molli.

It was amusing, in this severe land, to think of the tilled and
tended Tuscan fields, and it was pleasant, in the mellow light, to
come upon signs of humanity, hemmed in by solitude, for the
mills of Garau and their tents have no neighbours but woods and
mountains for many hours on every side. Only one mill can be
seen: a small half-pyramid of stones put together without mortar,
and not large enough for me to sleep in. The miller, with a curly
beard, was digging in his field. He had no flour for our supper, but
he mounted an old mare and galloped off to get some from the
tents whose smoke rose from behind the hill. We made our camp
under an oak tree in the open. The cockerel was sacrificed and
neatly arranged with all his limbs outspread on a peeled stick,
sprinkled with salt, roasted, and eaten in the name of Allah. The
flour, kneaded with water, hardened slowly under the ashes; while
the miller at his pipe sat contemplative, and explained how he was
the father of seven sons. They were all useful, scattered within
sight beside bonfires of their own that twinkled here and there.
They were watching to keep wild pig from rootling in the crops.

The people of Pusht-i-Kuh have now been disarmed, and have
no means of defence; and all night long, from this side or that, the
boys would cry: 'Ware pig! *Wei khek, wei khek!*': the call would be
taken up by each of the little outposts; and it increased the feeling
of remoteness, of surrounding wildness in the valley hemmed in
by cliff-sides, where even the voice of water was silent under the
travelling stars.

We had no way at all to go next morning, said Shah Riza, who
felt himself at home. But as it turned out, there was a good four

hours' ride downstream to reach his tribe. The Garau runs eastward, and follows more or less a line parallel to that of the Great Mountain's ridge which connects the two highest peaks of Walantar and Warzarine. The latter, as we approached it, revealed itself more and more as a beautiful mountain, clothed in majestic slopes, and rising gently above its precipices to peaks not needle-sharp, but pointed as a wave is pointed where it breaks. These the sunlight struck, facing us as we rode, until we entered the defile of Gavan and threaded our way among light shadows and white boulders.

Here the most unfortunate contretemps occurred. As we rode eastward, we met five men and four guns riding west, full and inevitable on our path. They came from the tents of Saidmarreh lower down, and were at the beginning of the second day of a three days' ride to the capital, where, said Alidad, after a heart-to-heart talk with an inferior servant who marched on foot, they were going to fetch a bride and all her trousseau for one of their chiefs. They were unattractive men, and wore the *Pahlevi* hat with a European coat, and rode on embroidered saddles with silver pommels. The chief among them had murdered his father and was, Alidad explained, 'not a good man', even in a country where the standard is not very high. He looked at me in a glowering way, twisting himself round on his saddle to do so after he had passed, and calling to Alidad to explain me: and as we rode on I felt uncomfortably that my days of freedom would be numbered as soon as these ill-omened ones reached the capital with their story. Shah Riza, too, looked flustered, his grey hair sticking out in wild rebellion under the respectable superstructure of the national headgear as he told me the unedifying details of the great one's past. It took us half an hour's riding or so down the easy, tree-filled defile before we could capture again the morning's sense of peace.

A little narrow valley, coming down from north-west, opened up into ours at the end of the defile, and showed at its head behind us a bit of the cliff table-top of Barazard, to which we had looked across all day yesterday as we came down from our pass. This meeting and meeting again, from different points and in other lights, of the same landmarks, is the charm of hilly travel. The mountain shape, first seen as a dream in the distance, alarming as you approach, lost perhaps altogether as you become involved in its outworks and ramifying valleys, appears again suddenly, unexpected as some swift light upon a face beloved to which custom has blunted our eyes. Like a human being, the mountain is a composite creature, only to be known after many a view from many a different point, and repaying this loving study, if it is anything of a mountain at all, by a gradual revelation of personality, an increase of significance; until, having wandered up in its most secret places, you will know it ever after from the plains, though from there it is but one small blue flame among the sister ranges that press their delicate teeth into the evening sky.

After the easy threading of the Gavan gorge, our dry river lost its name of Garau, turned itself into the (equally non-existent) River Khirr, and became of so intractable and difficult a temper in the cleft of a gorge called Suratai that our path very sensibly left it and climbed on to a wide grassy shelf that runs, as it were, within the outer cliff rim of the valley along the greater part of its length. Here for some time we felt uplifted, looking across on an equal level to the similar and opposite shelf across the valley, where the treasure of Nushirvan and a summer house of his are reported under the summits of Warzarine at a place called Ganjeh, above another steep and inky gorge.

Our shelf was still cultivated here and there by the Ali Shirwan, though we saw none of them about. Most of it, however, was withered grass of summer, on ground gently undulating, with oak trees here and there. Warzarine filled the sky behind them. After a while our shelf developed a small rim of hill between us and the valley: the view was hidden: the heat increased: Shah Riza, when interrupted in his meditations, said we had reached the lands of his tribe, but seemed vague as to how many hours were still required before an actual tribesman might be hoped for: the day unrolled itself into the drowsy light of noon.

We passed a sort of obelisk, a pointed affair on a pedestal, built of stone and mortar and plastered over, which the Lurish tribesmen put up either as landmarks or memorials.

And then we came to red hills on our left, and lower red hills on our right; we wound round a corner into a pocket, and there in the bottom saw variegated green, apricot and pomegranate trees, a few sheep and goats lying about, and half a dozen tents or so belonging to the Philosopher's tribe.

The Tribe at Home

It is unlucky to reach a nomad's tent in the master's absence.

The laws of hospitality are based on the axiom that a stranger is an enemy until he has entered the sanctuary of somebody's tent: after that, his host is responsible, not only for his safety, but for his general acceptability with the tribe. He is treated at first with suspicion, and gradually with friendliness as he explains himself – very much as if he were trying to enter a county neighbourhood in England, for the undeveloped mind is much the same in Lincolnshire or Luristan. From the very first, however, once he is a guest, he is safe, in every district I have ever been in except the wilder regions of Lakistan. This is the only arrangement which makes travel possible in a tribal country: but it makes the adoption of a guest a responsibility, and the master of the house or some influential representative is alone willing to undertake it.

My young accomplice, Hasan, had given me two letters, one to an uncle and one to a cousin: but both were out for the day, and we were received by a cavalier and jaunty young man with shining slanting eyes and thin lips, and a wavy moustache he was proud of, dressed in a white coat quilted in patterns, with a tobacco bag hanging at his sash, and a coloured silk turban off the back of his head.

He was, I discovered later, the daughter's fiancé, and took the leadership of affairs upon himself. He went swaggering ahead to lead us to the chief tent with an air of: 'We'll think what to do with you later,' which distressed my Philosopher, unprepared for so cool a welcome from his own people. 'The young generation have no manners,' I almost thought he was going to say; he was, however, wiser, and said nothing at all, but squatted under the tent awning and concentrated his mind on pouring loose tobacco into the little paper tubes he smoked all day long.

A funeral had taken away our hosts, and no one of any importance was left of the little tribe. A few retainers and cattle-men gathered around, while the women came out from the seclusion of their screens and joined in the general curiosity. Shah Riza, still looking down at his tobacco, and treating the topic with the detached manner of diplomacy, explained that I travelled for pleasure and learning, and that I was one of the great ones of Baghdad. I had a passport, he added, and the police had allowed it to pass too, apparently an unusual distinction. I had letters to carry me anywhere. I wished to find old cities, and cross the river to Lakistan.

The lady of the tent, still young but with a middle-aged, disillusioned manner, sat smoking a short clay pipe, and looked sceptically at the ground. She had a nose tilted prettily under her turban, and a smile that gave a charming gaiety to her sulky little face. She presently undid a corner of her headdress and produced tea, tied up there in a knot: she handed it to the household with one hand while she held her pipe in the other and began a Kurdish oration, telling Shah Riza, as far as I could gather, that we were only on sufferance till the master returned.

This female eloquence appeared to produce a certain uneasiness among the men, inclined to be more tolerant. Her daughter, a shy and beautiful creature of fourteen, looked at me with timid friendly smiles. The young man, in his off-hand manner, made our tea: the ladies retired: the humbler visitors grew talkative and friendly. There would be no difficulty for Lakistan, they said: men with relatives on the other side could take us, and knew how to find out the day before where the bandits might be, and how to avoid them. It was constantly being done. All the routes are used by smugglers. Did Shah Riza think I could be induced to smuggle across some opium when I returned to Iraq? I could not do that, said I decidedly: Shah Riza had already made use of my saddle-bag to get through twelve boxes of matches and innumerable packets of cigarette paper without my knowing it. I had no wish to find opium there; I hoped to have plenty of crimes of my own to organize by that time. Opium, I observed, was an immoral thing to sell or buy. The tribesmen, who are not given to this vice, agreed with me, and grew more friendly still. But I was tired by this time: I took my *abba,* wrapped myself in it from head to foot, and went to sleep with my head on the saddle-bag.

The capacity for sleeping in public is one of the most useful things one can acquire, and takes a certain amount of practice: an *abba* is a help: in the midst of a crowded tent it will secure you privacy; and after a time, the murmur of voices, discussing you over the fire, becomes no more disturbing than the sound of running water to dwellers by a stream.

When I woke in the late afternoon, a big man, dressed in short loose black trousers and a striped black coat, was sitting by the fire with three friends opposite in a row. He had a stoop, from being so tall, and a big bony face with a fine brow spoilt by a scar: it was handsome but for a look of uncontrolled violence about it, and the fact that one eye was sightless. He was listening to Shah Riza expounding, and Hasan's letter of introduction lay open on the ground. This was my host, Mahmud.

He welcomed me without effusion but politely when I woke up, and continued to discuss with the Philosopher. He saw no difficulty, it appeared, in my travelling anywhere, so long as the police did not interfere. The police, in Pusht-i-Kuh, play the role of ogre in the fairy tale: every disaster is considered to follow in their wake. They have stopped all the traffic that used to travel over the mountain passes, and made all trade illicit, and all that the tribesmen have gained in exchange for the general stagnation is security along roads where nothing worth securing is allowed to be carried.

In spite of the correctness of my passport, Mahmud and all the tribe took it for granted that I was at one with them in the desire to see as few policemen as possible. Perhaps Shah Riza and his account of our diplomacy at Bedrah may have had something to do with that. It was at any rate a friendly bond.

In the late afternoon I wandered down with my host to where a few bits of walls show the site of an old village; a place of graves whence all I could glean was a Sassanian coin found, they told me, in one of the round jars used for the burial of the dead. But the actual ruins I saw were much more recent, and probably belong to a time some few centuries ago when this region must have been full of settled villages along the courses of the streams.

We discussed these matters, skirting the garden hollow along a slope of red hill cropped of all herbage by the goats and sheep. We were passing the cousin's tent, he of the second letter. As we reached its neighbourhood, Mahmud left me, with a chilly nuance that made me suspect a want of harmony in the family, and the two brothers, who welcomed me with almost excessive cordiality, confirmed the suspicion. They had not expected to be visited at all; it was only my insistence which brought it about. They were more gentle in looks than my host. The brother had spent some years in Baghdad in the government Survey Department as a porter; he knew a word or two of English, and had a pleasant frank expression one could trust. All they could do for me would be done, said they. They were unmarried, and lived in a small tent composed of two apartments only, one closed in by the usual palisade of reeds woven together with wool, the other open like a verandah where guests could squat for tea.

I had not been sitting very long under the awning when a gentle old man with a grey beard and nothing on beyond a very ragged shirt and short black trousers came up and murmured timidly to the least and most distant members of the circle that surrounded us, glancing at me with a hopeful air which one learns to recognize as that of someone who is asking for medicines. The poorer sort among such petitioners are apt to be snubbed away before ever they get near enough to explain their troubles unless one notices them and makes enquiries.

This man turned out to have a small son of about ten or so, who had been bitten by a snake two months before. He was a stranger, belonging to a tribe four miles away, and without relatives or natural allies among my hosts; and he lived in the extremity of poverty on the opposite slope of the valley. I climbed up there with him to a group of tents and found the sick child on the ground in a noisy circle, bearing up with the vitality of his age against what would long before have killed an ordinary European man. The snake bite, they told me, had been on one finger, as he pushed his hand under a rock. The poison had spread upwards, and first his hand, and then his forearm, had dropped off, the latter leaving the bone still sticking out. The poison had now corrupted his upper arm to the shoulder, leaving it a swollen mass of raw flesh which the tribespeople covered with a mess of oak leaves and a muddy bit of old shirt. The boy's pulse was racing at 120 beats to the minute, and the poison had evidently spread over his system and was coming out in small sores on his back and sides.

In spite of it all, and when he had got over his first fear of being touched by me, the lad took a certain pathetic pride in being so the centre of attention. In the high monotonous voice of his fever he explained how it had all happened, while the tribespeople, pressing round, called on the name of Allah. I gave him not more than a day or two to live, but did what I could by washing the arm in strong permanganate, clearing away every trace of the oak leaf poultice.

By the time this was done, very little was left of my supply of gauze and bandages, and I had to part with my face towel as well, as the surface to be medicated was so large. The child's mother escorted me on my way home, weeping and kissing my hand, but also improving the occasion by asking for more clothing and anything I could spare from about me. In such poverty small wonder that when anything comes to them they grasp it with both hands and try to get more, but it is a discouraging experience, and I came away feeling sick at heart over the general misery of mankind.

But now there was friendly welcome in the porch of Mahmud's tent. My old Philosopher had evidently not wasted his time, and, left to himself, had been exerting eloquence on my behalf, explaining the mysteries of archaeology at second-hand. From inside the tent, where bread was being baked, the ladies called to me in a cordial way. The young Kaltuma, the daughter of the house, with beautiful downcast eyes, very shyly brought water in a long-beaked ewer to pour over my hands before the meal. There was another cousin now, a handsome fair-skinned young man who might have been English, but that he wore a long black velvet coat tied in with a white sash round his waist and a curved dagger to finish it off in front. In his hand he played with a stout stick, the knob sheathed with fluted iron at one end, a substantial weapon fashionable in the Pusht-i-Kuh. Tassels from a black, green, and purple turban dangled round his head. Behind him was a gun, for he alone among the tribe had a permit, and he promised partridges for supper next day: it was a harmless little weapon not fit for bigger game.

'Why do you not get a permit, too, Mahmud?' said I.

'It has its disadvantages,' said my host, with one of the rare and charming smiles that lit up his heavy dark face. 'If a malefactor comes along, and I have a gun, I am supposed to do something and questions are asked: and if I do something, I get into trouble and feuds with his tribe, who take his part. But if I am unarmed, the police cannot expect me to help them, and anyone who is in trouble can come through my territory without being arrested, and we all remain on friendly terms after the police have come and gone. All we need guns for are the wild pig.'

'Do the police come often?'

'About once a month, or once in two months. Not often unless they hear of any trouble.'

'And what about Lakistan across the river; do they ever go there?'

'Hardly ever. It is a bad country. But we can get you across. My wife's mother's sister is settled there.'

Apart from the treasure, and the lands across the river, I wished also to visit the idolaters' country on the south, and the lands of Shirwan on the north of me. I thought I would make two preliminary expeditions in these directions so as to pass the time unsuspected while waiting for my accomplice from Baghdad.

We discussed the plan after supper, over glasses of tea in the semi-darkness, while the tribesmen came in by ones and twos after seeing to their animals for the night. The lady of the house, her clay pipe in her hand after the labours of the day, sat in the doorway, joining now and then in the conversation, but still sufficiently secluded for propriety. The men knew all the paths, which are more used since smuggling has become so common.

I decided to let them take me south-east to the lands of the Larti and Hindimini, and to return to the tribe after a three days' tour, by which time Hasan, if he were coming at all, should have arrived.

The funeral, however, which was the subject of interest at the moment, was to go on all next day, and the Philosopher asked me to postpone my journey for so long while he went to visit the tents of the dead. I agreed to this, and retired to sleep under the porch. On one side it was open to darkness and to the dim forms of the mares and kine and their herdsmen. On the other, behind the screen of reeds, eyes of whispering unseen women watched my undressing. The roof was of dry and dusty oak leaves, and cows came lumbering up in the night to eat at it over my head. On the outskirts of the camp, the dogs kept up a racket, chasing wolves and pigs. There is never silence in these small oases. And early in the morning, before it was light, so that I might move undisturbed and not outrage the herdsmen by the sight of satin pyjamas, I woke and dressed and lay down to sleep again and meditate till the sunlight should come and the fires be lit for tea.

This was a lazy, pleasant day. The Philosopher left with Mahmud, and I sat reclined on quilts under the tent awning, watching while the swaggering young fiancé broke in a mule. He and the mule seemed to me very much alike, and looked each other in the eye with the same expression of untrustworthy and inflammable wildness. He would approach softly along the taut halter, murmuring soothing Lurish noises to which the mule listened with an obvious lack of conviction, till he got quite near, and already his arm was nerved to throw over the animal's back its first burden, a gaudy piece of green and orange weaving. But the mule saw with the corner of one eye: reared, turned, and snorted, and put the whole length of the halter between them again. And the morning slipped by.

In the afternoon I had a bath. The women of the tribe boiled a cauldron, and screened off a place in the middle of the tent where they sat twisting black goat wool into ropes. They put a copper tray for me to stand on, and a bowl beside it with which to pour the hot water over me, and retired only to return and gaze over the top of my screen when I was defenceless, and murmur with praises to Allah how white and soft I was, while they pulled up the sleeves of their gowns to show me the contrast of their own darker skins.

In the tent we drank tea with the pleasant sense of leisure that envelops harems when their masters are absent. My hostess threw aside her turban, disclosing a fragile little head plastered over with flattened curls, with an ugly gash across the forehead. She had tried to separate Mahmud and a cousin when they were quarrelling, and Mahmud had inflicted this wound by mistake. He was rather ashamed of it, and his wife was quite ready to make the most of it, and often put her hand up to her head and groaned; whereupon Mahmud would appear to be interested in some distant part of the landscape.

He and the Philosopher came back late and sat discussing politics in the night. A stooping, hale old man joined them, with eyes surrounded by wrinkles, and a paternal air of authority, who turned out to be the tribal *kadkhuda,* or headman. Between them they arranged that I should have Mahmud's white mare next morning; it had green leather reins and a silver pommel to the saddle, and leather flaps embroidered in mauve and green. The Philosopher on the other mare was to carry what little luggage we needed, and Sa'id Ja'far, the cousin, would guide us.

But the morning brought very little sign of movement. Imperturbable and meditative, the Philosopher, after many prayers and glasses of tea, continued to fill his little cigarette eases. The mares were still unsaddled. The family sat chatting leisurely. A guide from the Dusan tribe, through whose lands we were going, was ready to join us. The young man with the velvet coat said he was coming too, because he had a gun; but no one showed any sign of actually moving. I left them and went over the hill to look at the boy with the snake bite: his pulse was still racing, but the poisoned flesh looked healthier. After what seemed a long time, the washing and bandaging being accomplished, I returned to Sa'id Ja'far's hut only to find things just as I had left them. We called and shouted. Sa'id Ja'far was ready himself: he therefore said that my impatience was only too justifiable. The Philosopher, however, appearing at last with a grey lock bunched over either ear and a bulging saddle-bag under either knee, screwed up his eyes in cheerful and amused surprise and asked where was the hurry.

'There are tents everywhere,' said he. 'We will not need to sleep in the desert even if we do not start till the afternoon.' A point of view unpromisingly non-progressive for someone about to travel.

At this moment, however, the tables were turned, for it was discovered that I was taking no passport.

'A passport is *always* good,' said Shah Riza with conviction, and began slowly to make the movements which precede the actual preparations for dismounting; but I was not going to let him go back to our tents: he was wound up, it would be simply disastrous to let him unwind again.

'Go on,' said I, 'I will overtake you.'

I set off to run back without remembering the dogs, who seeing a swiftly moving object, flung themselves on me in a body, and had my skirt in shreds in no time. The tribe hurled clods of earth and curses, while I stood still among their unpleasant fangs, and the men drew near, beating their breasts, with horrified faces.

'That this should have happened in our tents,' they repeated again and again. The dogs turned snarling away.

More annoyed than ever at this conspicuousness, I reached the tent in a grim silence, applied iodine to a slight scratch on my leg, and took advantage of the general horror, which kept even the women silent and petrified around me, to get away as quickly as I could. To keep the dogs off their visitors is one of the chief preoccupations of the tribal host. I was always absent-minded, and not inclined to be afraid of dogs, and gave constant uneasiness; and I would find that on my most private walks a woman would silently rise and follow me to keep the dogs away. Now I had actually been bitten. It was my fault entirely, but that seemed to make no difference to the feeling that it was a blot on their hospitality. Only my Philosopher took that side of the question into consideration when I returned and found him and Sa'id Ja'far waiting side by side, ready at last.

'Why do you run?' said he, 'and get bitten by dogs, so that I am made anxious?'

The Defile of the Unbelievers

We now rode, in pleasant and restored tranquillity, by the pomegranate and apricot trees of the hollow, until we left the garden of the tribe and came again to rough pasture between red sides of hills.

The lesser ridge that shut out the main valley of the Khirr (our Garau River of the days before) soon sank into nothingness upon our right, and we came out into the openness of the main valley, and saw again in the hot blues of the middle morning the noble barricade of Kebir Kuh. On our left an uncompromising red wall with splashes of white limestone rose steep and near and treeless. Here was the road to the treasure. I saw it, winding up through the crumbly powder of the lime and asked the direction, which corroborated exactly with what was written on my map.

Now, however, we were not attending to this part of the adventure, and rode straight on until we left the Musi lands and came into the boundaries of a small tribe of Arab origin, who take the name and guard the shrine of one of the saints from Medina, a certain Jaber, buried in this valley under a white plastered obelisk. Indistinct remains of old buildings and Muslim gravestones surrounded the obelisk in its lonely place.

For some reason unknown it made me think of what I imagine to be a Tibetan landscape: the round and ugly hills behind, and the small tower rising in polygonal tiers about a foot high, with dingy discoloured plaster above the half-subterranean building of the tomb. There was no name and no date, but the place is probably old; it has an air of secrets about it, a life now long under the ground. The Dusan guide and the young man in the velvet stooped down the steps into the tomb to make their vows while Shah Riza gave himself the airs of an archaeologist, wandering about and picking up shards of pottery as he had seen me do.

After leaving this place of ancient piety our track went down into the river bed, flat as a table between the long ridge of the limestone hill on our left and the first rise of Siah Pir on our right, a hill which, as a far blue smear on the skyline, we had seen on our ride down from Garau. Our non-existent river was now the Ruá, having taken on the name of a westerly stream which we could see descending by steep black places and step-like defiles from the Maimah pass of Kebir Kuh. It watered rice-fields, a little behind us and some way off as we emerged into open ground: they shone in the sun beside the black tents of their cultivators, the Dusan tribe.

The wide river space was now all tamarisk and sand, but in spring the water comes raging down in spate, and for a few weeks carries all before it. In the middle of its alluvial waste lies a strange round crater hole, with water called Zem-Zem in its bottom, about three hundred feet wide, dirty but holy. Saint Jaber once, walking along here, with a goatskin of water as they use to-day, met Shaddad the son of Nushirvan, whose castle was downstream in the defile.

'Have you any water in your goatskin?' asked the son of the king.

'Ah,' said the pious old man, anxious not to lie, but also anxious not to give drink to an unbeliever.

'Is it cold?' asked the king's son.

'Not cold, not warm,' answered the saint.

'Is it sweet?' asked Shaddad.

'Not sweet, not bitter,' was the reply.

The son of Nushirvan asked to drink, but the old man, as he pushed a slip of reed into the goatskin for him to put his mouth to, also placed there the obstruction of a pomegranate seed, so that no water came to the heathen lips. Shaddad in disgust threw the goatskin to the ground, and the water, spreading around, made the pool of Zem-Zem in Luristan, on whose banks ever since the tall reeds have been growing, and also a pomegranate tree, though I cannot say that I saw it. And the water is neither sweet nor bitter, nor cold nor warm, and all the year the same. But it did not look very attractive.

A half-witted retainer of the Musi chieftain had added himself to our party to look after the horses, and was supposed to lead my animal by a halter over the rough ground. The real necessity for such assistance lay in the fact that I did not understand the Lurish manner of talking to horses. To make the creature go, one was supposed to give it a violent jerk in the mouth, and to flick its back perpetually with a long, plaited thong which formed the prolongation of the rein. Three or four energetic pulls were supposed to make it break into a canter: my efforts in this direction – being possibly rather half-hearted – merely induced the tired grey mare to stop altogether. An unwilling horse and a dragging child and a woman who insists on explaining her motives are the three most wearying objects in creation. I soon saw the advantage of someone in front who would automatically give the jerk as he walked along whenever my steed became meditative, while I could write things about the landscape in my notebook. The half-wit was asked to do so. He smiled with gentle foolishness, slouching along in the dislocated manner of his kind.

Such people are treated with tenderness by the tribesmen, and life must be pleasanter for them than it is for many an asylum inmate. This specimen had just had a wife found for him, the young men told me with a delighted amusement which might have made the founder of the Eugenic League turn in his grave. With the halter held loosely in one hand, and my sunshade, open and incongruous in the other, and crooning his little songs, the half-wit went mooning on, 'through brake, through brier', regardless of the obstacles presented to the surprised and outraged horse behind him. We went more slowly than ever, considering each bush as we came to it. Shah Riza, who was behind, and liked to go slowly because it allowed him to fill his cigarette papers with tobacco between one jog and the other, looked at me in surprise when I said something about it.

'There is no hurry,' said he. 'We can sleep anywhere in this country. There is no danger.'

It was only the fact that the Dusan tribesman wished to reach his home this night, which made us improve our speed at last, for that active lithe young man came striding back impatiently, saying: 'Shah Riza is like the accompaniment to a funeral.' Seizing the halter in his own hand, he walked me and my charger at a rousing semi-trot across the flat lands of the Ruá to where the ruined city of Shaddad and a camp of the Dusan tents lay near the entrance to the Unbelievers' Defile.

A few sad rubble stones on the side of a naked hill was all that was left of the traditional city of the king. The black tents stood among them, showing their slovenly dinginess in the noonday light. Dogs came snarling to meet us. Donkeys and mules, resting among the tent ropes, rose with a sputter of hooves and the dust upon their coats. Under their lopsided houses which, scattered there, looked like so many black boulders in shallow water with a little foam of children, cooking-pots, kids and puppies breaking perpetually around each of them, the various tribesmen of the Dusan looked out at us as we rode to the chief tent.

I insisted on examining the defile and the castle of Shaddad immediately, leaving lunch to prepare for our return. The opening cleft, a steep black natural gateway, was only a couple of stones'-throw below us. At its entrance, out of a very white bed, the Ruá stream was reborn, rising from its underground journey in a deep pool which turned into a river, blue and brown down the defile. It was banked off to work a mill, the last small sign of human masonry, almost invisible among the high works of nature around it.

Like most of the Pusht-i-Kuh gorges, the place looked as if it might have been sliced through by a titanic knife. The uncovered strata on either side ran almost horizontal, with gentle curves, like galleries in a theatre; the corridor between, not more than fifty feet or so, was filled with reeds and oleanders and willows, and the half-hidden noise of the stream.

The way was bad, though not impossible for horses, but we went on foot, the Dusan guide wading with me on his back through long river stretches, a proceeding which I always dislike. In the very middle of the defile about fifteen minutes downstream, the way went up, they told me, to the castle of Shaddad on the height. A large boulder lying across the track still showed the hollows where his two knees rested when the Presence Ali beheaded him, whose sword dint was visible, bitten into the rock. Ali's sword marks are freely scattered over Persia, and it does not do to take them too seriously. What was more interesting was a remnant of masonry sticking here and there to the solid rock of the gorge; evidently once a built-up way where probably a *derbend* or gate closed the valley in this so obvious a position for defence.

Nobody, they said, had climbed up to the castle at the top except the brother of a young Dusani who accompanied us. The brother was employed in Baghdad in a drapery store, but still came to spend incongruous holidays in Luristan, and was the best climber of his tribe. Up there he had found, they told me, remains of rooms, a cooking hearth, a corridor and walls, all of which he had demolished as having belonged to the infidels. We climbed some way up, Shah Riza, like a nervous and very scraggy hen, imploring me to stop at every step. The old way followed one of the ledges and was very narrow; it finally melted altogether into the cliff-side, but not before it had reached a spot where a few graves had been opened, though nothing appeared to have been found inside them. I gathered there was nothing very much left to see of the Sassanian castle and relinquished the thought of the precipice, though with some regret.

The Dusani promised to dig during our two days' absence: and when we returned he had unearthed a cornelian bead and a bit of stucco work, a slender piece of column moulded in a pattern of overlaid leaves, and probably once intended to be covered with metal, for it was made of very fragile 'gatch'. Two broken daggers and three light spear-heads of bronze were produced as having been found some time ago close to the site at the bottom of the defile. These meagre results, such as they were, fortified the supposition of some Sassanian post in the valley, as the old legends implied.

We climbed down and followed the defile to where it opens on the banks of the Saidmarreh, where rusty flanks of hills lie one behind the other in the sun, like hippopotami after drinking, ponderous in their folds. Opposite to where we were sitting a little zig-zag showed the Sargatch Pass and the way to Tarhan. The river wound between, a green water, its sunken bed lined with tamarisk, *kurf,* and broom and oleander. This is a warm valley, and the half-hour's walk through the Unbelievers' Defile brings one from a summer to a winter climate: in another month the Dusanis from the west and the Tarhanis from the east would have their black tents pitched in little clumps for miles along these banks. But now, except for the half-obliterated track and the opened graves beside us, no sign of anything human was in all that land. This country has been hardly explored and never surveyed. The river banks are dangerous, open to raiders from the south and east, Sagwand and the other tribes of Lakistan. A little to our right across the Saidmarreh, black as ink in the sunlight, on the way from Sharwan to Tarhan, another defile came down to the water, Tang-i-Berinjan, which wise travellers avoided, since robbers had ensconced themselves in it for some time. These sleeping monstrous hills, this inhuman emptiness and silence were full of awe: a kingfisher down by the water, and the figures of my companions as they climbed about the rocks in their cotton shoes and medieval tunics, seemed strangely peaceful in the lawless land. And then we turned back again into the shadow of the defile, and reached the Dusani tents for lunch.

The City of the Larti

The Dusanis, when we left them, promised to hunt for antiques as busily as they could during our absence. We, on our side, engaged ourselves to return that way, and started in the afternoon heat, southward for the lands of the Beni Parwar. This is an agricultural tribe which inhabits the broad trough, something between a valley and a plain, north of the Kebir Kuh. The land was smiling and prosperous, a rolling stretch of plough, then brown in autumn, but with the pleasant homeliness of man's labour printed upon it. We dipped down to it gently, over a low col which finishes the range of Siah Pir. The river and its fierce and lonely banks were out of sight, flowing away from us south-eastward; all we saw were easy curves striped by fine lines of ploughing, rolling up to the forested black outworks of the Great Mountain, which continued against the skyline its long unbroken wall.

The outwork was a separate range, parallel but lower, so that in section the two would look like the descending graph of a fever chart. It was called Kuh Siah, the Black Mountain, and continued the formation we had already seen in the valley below Garau: here, as there, it was broken at intervals by black ravines. The Larti and Hindimini, the two tribes we meant to visit, lived each in one of these ravines, under the shadow of the mountain wall. Between us and them, across the open stretch of plain, were white and red small salty hills, untidily scattered in a straggling line. Our track, dotted through the afternoon by wayfaring labourers, made straight for them, passing in the open plain a little cemetery with domed tombs, and the obelisk memorials of which the Lurs are fond.

The Dusani guide was near his own home, but the darkness threatened us before he could hope to reach it, and no one is willingly out in this country in the dark. As the sun sank, we stopped to water our horses at the only spring in the neighbourhood, the Eye of Bitterness, which slips into a green hollow out of a cavern in the limestone hills. It is good plentiful water, and cold, with a slight salty taste, not unpleasing. After leaving it, we wound among the hillocks. The plough-land ceased; we came into a grassy downland; and on an eminence found a Dusani camp, just as the last women were shouldering their goatskins at a water-hole below in the dusk.

Here was no question of a doubtful welcome, for our Dusani was among his own people, and Sa'id Ja'far was also a man of consideration and well known, though of a different tribe. The place was high and windswept: from the tent door it looked out westward to Warzarine, and east to the open valley spaces beyond whose horizon the invisible Saidmarreh flowed. To the north we could see the day's travel, and the hill where the treasure was, and ridges in Lakistan beyond.

A thin mountain wind, imperceptible in the pure and luminous sky, moved the leaves of the roof as we sat on rugs in the porch of the tent. Oak branches, heaped on the fire, made a good warmth. Shah Riza, comfortable in my waterproof, set about the saying of his prayers, while I tried to solve as well as I could the various medical problems of the camp with the help of an army medicine box which had been given me as a most kind gift at my departure from Baghdad.

Our host was a middle-aged man with a round, sensible face marked by the smallpox. He was ill with some internal trouble. He had been to the hospital in Baghdad, where they had kept him four days, and had sent him off with some recommendation whose usefulness was destroyed by the fact that he knew no word of the language in which it was given. I wrote him a chit to take with him next time, and suggested an Arab interpreter as advisable if he went to hospital again. He was a man of the world with some property in sheep and lands, which gave him an easy courtesy of manner. He owned mattresses and bolsters, and had them spread out for me in a partitioned space not far from the fire. There I slept, more safely than in Chicago, a wanderer not only in space but in time also, living a life that most of the world has now forgotten.

We got up so early that we saw the first sun-shaft on the peak of Warzarine. But we turned our backs upon it and rode up and down the dry and treeless downs, till we came to Kebir Kuh itself, advancing with oak trees here and there, and to the place where the Larti torrent bed descended northward at the bottom of a steep and wooded valley. Here we turned and led our horses along its difficult side among boulders and roots of trees, till the ravine below us divided, embracing between two beds of tumbled rocks the ruined city of the Larti on a cliff.

An old barber at Bedrah first told us of the Larti and the Hindimini, their sister tribe in antiquity. They were, said he, the oldest tribes of Pusht-i-Kuh, the last descendants of idolaters to whom once it all belonged. They fled before the invaders, retreating ever higher into the fastnesses of their land, till these two ravines were all that was left them under the uncompromising wall of the Great Mountain. This towered 3,000 feet and more above us, black and unscalable to all but genuine climbers, though they told us that there was a way among its almost perpendicular slabs for men who went on foot. A thin thread of water dispersed itself in spray on the enormous flank, making it shine as if a strip were varnished. The steepness came down a little above us, where loose stones rolling made a gender slope covered with trees. Here on a cliff-encircled promontory the ruined city stood, with traces of stone walls and ruins of houses jagged as an old crone's teeth against the mountain background.

We had to dip down into the ravine and up again, to go either to the city or to the present metropolis of the Larti, a company of seven tents or so on an opposite promontory. The tribe had had misfortunes. What with feuds and wars their numbers dwindled, and most of what remained had fled and is settled in Kermenshah, while the Dusanis have taken over the lands left empty. Such as there were, however, the Larti were as friendly as could be. Their two small mills were down in the valley, fed by a runnel with soft muddy banks. Traces of older and once prosperous gardens were visible on what had been hillside terraces. And at the top, the Larti families were grouped each round an oak tree whose branches made a natural roof, whose boughs were used as wardrobe and larder, while a palisade of woven reeds made the walls. No more simple form of house can be thought out, and they were simple people who lived there, dressed in rags that fluttered round the children with that complete detachment one admires in the pictures of gods and goddesses, wondering how the things stick on.

Like the Golden Age too, as the poet describes it, these people fed on acorns. They expected to do so this winter because of their rainless cornfields; but they still had some bread left and a mess of pumpkin for our entertainment, and spread it on the ground before us.

We were not the only visitors. A civilized Lur was here on a holiday from Baghdad, where he lived in a shop and thought he knew what Englishwomen were like until he saw me. My contentment, so very ragged (after the encounter with the dogs), was too much for his politeness. He looked at me and slapped his knee at intervals, ejaculating 'Allah!'

'Is this as good as Baghdad?' said he.

'Better,' said I. 'There is cool air, and good water, and wood for a fire, and shade.'

The inhabitants of the seven oak trees agreed. The townsman, defeated, sank into silent bewilderment.

After our meal, we climbed down and up again into the Larti city. As we crossed the valley head, we dipped into a dark delightful shade, made by fruit trees and vines over a stream cold as ice and black as velvet, that sprang here from among stones out of the mountain, and probably first caused this site to be chosen by prehistoric man.

An old peasant, who had lived all his life in the region, came with us, saying that he knew the places of graves. He had a short white beard and the kind of blue eyes that grow light with excitement. He shouldered a concave tray on which the bread is baked (*saj*), and a pickaxe for the digging; and he walked along before us flapping his old shirt and cotton trousers, a small felt cap on his head round which his grey locks curled. He hoped that I would use the magic glasses that everyone knew I carried to look through the earth of the ruined city and see its buried treasures. His was the arm, he considered, mine the guiding brain – an embarrassing attitude seeing that I had only one afternoon and no real knowledge for the making of discoveries.

Where the promontory of the city is joined to the mountainside, an upper road leads east and west from Ganjeh and Kulm and the Puneh and Maimah passes along the flank of Kebir Kuh to the Saidmarreh. These upper roads, all the world over, nearly always follow the traces of very ancient sites: either because they were usually safer for the inhabitants than the lower, being less accessible, or because their very existence in difficult mountainous country can only be caused by a demand spread over a very long area of time.

Anyway I have often noticed that it is the older and upper track which leads by the important places of antiquity. Here it dipped down over a shoulder towards us, where sure enough, the old man said, skeletons had been found in jars. We, however, were taken on to the promontory itself, and found there a Muslim cemetery of upright carvings round a white-washed altar of stone and mortar, beneath which is a tomb whose present holiness was shown by a collection of large pebbles and a few of the black fossils of the country, which they call Peri stones, laid there as votive offerings.

We had no use for the Muslim cemetery, and left it piously alone, descending by what was once a street among the ruins of houses. I suppose the city is three or four acres in extent. Its upper part is dotted with small squares where Muslim tomb-stones lie half embedded, carved with a florid script which show them to be not very old. A very few shards of pottery picked up among the houses dated the place as thirteenth or fourteenth century, or thereabouts. The line of the streets was marked by boulders, which must once have formed the first layer in the buildings. Wan and poplar trees as well as oak grew over and among them, giving their green fugitive beauty to the sense of the passage of time. Here and there I saw round holes, about eight inches in diameter, in flat stone surfaces on the ground, and came to the conclusion that they served possibly to hold the doorpost, as they still do in the stone doorways of the Jebel Druse in Syria.

All round the northern side of the city, where it overhangs its cliff, the walls are still plainly visible, and we followed them to where the gate and gatehouse in the north-west lie open to a stony track, that winds from under the cliff and the valley. Our old man's grave was below, in a dry place, sheltered by the preci-pice as by the side of a ship. It was marked by a stone at head and feet, and had been opened once and carefully covered over again. The old man said the 'Things' were inside it. He worked with his pick, and then used his shirt and the bread-tray to shovel out the earth. All he produced were bits of bones, a shard of rough crockery, and a triangular stone cut like a flint. His hopes, to tell the truth, were not in the objects themselves but in what I might find in them – a belief which I did nothing to strengthen, for I was disappointed.

As we sat there in the clouds of dust watching the work, a noiseless figure suddenly appeared by the side of the grave. It was a young man in an old green coat tight at the waist, tied with a sash, and his dagger inside it. His brown naked feet in cotton shoes made no sound. His light hair and beard were almost she same colour as the little felt pointed cap on his head, bleached and tawny like the woods and rocks. He seemed the genius of the place and smiled in a friendly way, looking down into the shaft of the grave, which now showed narrow sides of dry built masonry made just to contain the outstretched figure of a man. We bent eagerly down to look, but found only a small stone and two shards of reddish earthenware at the head: and when we stood up again, our silent visitor had vanished among the sunlit trees of the ravine.

'Is it true,' said our digger as he shouldered his implement to try for better luck with another grave he knew of, 'is it true that the skeleton of a man has been found with horns growing out of his forehead?'

Shah Riza, who loved fairy tales, and was delighted with the discovery of archaeology, at which he gave himself expert airs, pricked up his ears and joined us. He was in disgrace, and had been loitering behind. He had taken my pointed stone, the only find of the afternoon, and lightly chipped off the tip of it, saying airily: 'This is nothing.' The storm of just indignation which had broken round his ears surprised but did not disconcert him; women being in his eyes so inferior that they could say what they liked without its mattering to anybody. He merely continued to murmur at intervals: 'It is nothing', keeping, however, prudently out of my way.

'You had better ask Shah Riza,' said I, replying to the matter of the horns. 'He seems to know more about everything than anybody else.'

The Philosopher smiled in a disarming manner, not however denying the imputation of knowledge nor refraining, as we pulled small bits of bone and pottery out of our next grave, from giving his opinion in a decided manner as to their value. We were no luckier. The grave was of the same kind, also built under the lee of the cliff and city wall, and formed of a narrow shaft where the skeleton lay on its back with head turned to the right and feet pointing east-north-east. Under its elbow was a sharpened stone, a piece of pottery at its head, and that was all. It was already after four o'clock, and some way lay before us to the valley of the Hindimini eastward. I gave the blue-eyed old man sixpence, and told him to prepare more digging for our return next day, and we joined Sa'id Ja'far and the horses and our impatient Dusan guide at the top of the ravine.

From here we rode across country eastward over an easy but very stony shelf of Kebir Kuh, dipping into small combes and out again, but keeping more or less to the level of the Larti city, at about 4,500 feet. The great wall stretched out of sight before and behind us, as near and overwhelming as a wave about to break on the head of an insect swimming below.

Across the open lands beneath us on our left, we could see in its full outline the small tree-dotted range of Siah Pir, divided by clefts into separate hills. Blue enticing distances of Lakistan lay before us. Sa'id Ja'far, one of the pleasantest of companions, chatted about that country and its ways.

'The women there are more cruel than our men,' said he. 'Last year, while they were at war with the government, one of them had a baby. When her husband asked to see it, she said: 'This is no time for children,' and took it by the feet and dashed it against the rocks. Many of them use a gun and ride like warriors with their tribes.'

Sa'id Ja'far told me about Saidmarreh, which is the name of a camp and tribe as well as of the river. It is well watered and lies surrounded by rice-fields in a wide plain. It is more or less a centre of government and an outpost against Lakistan, though there are no houses other than the black nomad tents.

I asked him about the idolatrous worship of the two tribes we were visiting, but this is a matter on which the people feel, as Mrs. Langtry did about history in general, that bygones had better be bygones; and probably very little is known about it except among some of the very oldest men.

The sun sank and we were still high up on the mountain. The Dusani guide, striding ahead, again observed that Shah Riza, on horseback, was synonymous with a funeral, and implored me to trot, which I did, rising in my silver inlaid stirrups as on a platform with a flutter of tassels around me. These stirrups, like most things invented for the country in which they are used, are very sensible in their own place. Their sharp corners, sticking well out beyond the rider's footwear, save him from innumerable knocks against the rocky sides of narrow mountain paths.

In the dusk we descended to the Hindimini ravine. Surrounded by a chaos of enormous boulders, tumbling down to a small amphitheatre, a clear spring of water is made to run in wooden troughs where half a flock could drink at a time. We took off our horses' bridles and let them enjoy themselves. Two other travellers, a brown black-bearded fellow and his companion, were also on their way down. The Dusan guide, who had observed one of my feet sticking out from the dilapidated remains of my cotton *giva* shoe, remarked that this was the man to make me a new pair before to-morrow morning. The Hindimini, he said, are a famous tribe for the making of *givas* and for the beauty of their girls. The bargain was on the point of being concluded when the Philosopher, scenting danger from a distance, came trotting up, flapping his elbows in his anxiety to inspire his horse with speed.

'You will never get them,' he shouted when barely within earshot. 'Why buy what we can make ourselves? Do I not know how to sew *givas* from the time of my childhood? By the Hand of God, why do you believe people when they speak to you?'

The Dusan guide was a man of insight. He knew the impossible when he saw it. Leaving the black-bearded stranger without a word, he strode on down the steep hillside which formed the ravine's eastern border. I followed, also on foot. The light was fading off the path as we descended. Far down, the first of the Hindimini tents, some four or five, showed on a little spur. Their fires began to glow in the darkening air as we approached. Their sheep were home already from the pastures. As we entered through a circle of snarling dogs, the shepherds were attending to them. A hairy man with shining brass dagger in his sash looked up from among the woolly waves. He did not ask questions.

'Where is the tent?' said the Dusani. The man pointed and resumed his labours.

And we introduced ourselves to the Sheikh of the Hindimini.

The Valley of the Hindimini

The Hindimini had received a lot of visitors that day. They were all sitting out in the open, round three sides of a square formed with strips of carpet. In the post of honour a Dervish sat cross-legged. The Hand of Abbas cut out in brass at the end of a rod about four feet long was stuck into the ground behind him and appeared over his shoulder. His companion was an Indian, with fat and pleasant face, who had travelled with British and Americans in Iraq.

I chose a place as far as I could from the Dervish, so as not to inflict on him the unholiness of my sex at closer quarters than necessary, and saluted him with becoming respect. A dark, long-faced man sat next me, member of a family called Malak, which he considered as equivalent to a tide of nobility, and as showing some old tradition of supremacy in pre-Islamic days. He was travelling with a small son from the eastern lands, and took the lead in conversation. The Dervish had kind and wise eyes, used to the observation of things and men. I asked him why he travelled.

'To see,' said he.

'We all travel,' I remarked, 'even though we stay at home.'

This philosophical contribution was received with a murmur of approval, and I was accepted as someone with whom rational conversation was not impossible. There were holy places in the mountains, said the Dervish: he went from one to the other. He was not a common man. I wondered what had first so detached him from the roots of ordinary living. Not religion: he spoke of that almost with indifference, as might a Catholic in the worldly days of Rome: nor learning, for he did not appear to be a student. He rested there like a Buddha with voluminous draperies, the master of his company, 'seeing' the world with a quiet superiority and tolerant aloofness.

That night was even noisier than usual. The dogs rushed here and there, chasing wolves or pig with unearthly yells. Cocks crowed. In the darkness, the Dervish and his Indian set forth, after a baking of bread for their journey: and before dawn the women started with their goatskins down the hill for water. When I woke up after all this, the Philosopher's lanky figure, with my Burberry loose upon it, was already saying its prayers against the morning sky.

In this camp of the Hindimini I saw for the first time the loom which the tribespeople erect for the weaving of their carpets. It stood outside one of the tents, tall enough almost for a gallows and looking not unlike one in the half light. It was an upright square made roughly out of the branches of oak trees, at which on a high bench the young girls sat. They fled with assumed terror from my camera, but I think the Hindimini still have some touch of the old paganism in their hearts, and the women show it by a gayer ease of manner than is usual in strict Islam.

There were graves round about us under half-buried boulders on the little spur on which our camp was tilted, but the master of the tent thought them Muhammadan, and was obviously unhappy at the risk of sacrilege. The infidel town, said he, was down in the ravine.

The ravine narrowed below. It had a steep, wooded side on the left, but on the right, where we descended, was a precipice wall overhanging in horizontal strata above us, at the top of which pastures began, such as we had ridden over the day before. Under their eaves, as it were, the young men of the tribe led us, leaped ahead by an invisible path along flat ledges, and came to where houses had been built under a hollow rock, like cells of a wild beehive, plastered to the side of the ravine. They were very rough, of small stones thrown together with mortar, and looked as if they had not been either comfortable, beautiful, or strong. Nor were they very old: probably the last places to be inhabited when the city of the Hindimini was falling to decay. Tombstones lay about, carved with a running Persian script. The Larti valley, besides its tombstones, has an inscription carved on the face of a rock; so that anyone will easily decipher the dates of these two cities, which probably flourished and decayed together.

The Atabeks of Luristan are known to have done much building in this country, and probably these sites were inhabited in their day: but although I am no expert in script, it seemed to me that what I saw belonged to a later date. There is a sadness in coming on these once inhabited places, built by prosperous and settled communities, where now, for many days' ride on every side, the nomad in his black tent dwells alone.

Below the houses built into the rock, ruins of an older city go in terraces to the valley bottom. The remains of a good causeway, still used, led up to it from the plain of Dusan, and showed, better than the heaps of stones, that it had once been a place of some consideration. Below the slipshod late work, the remains of a more massive and primitive style appeared. As in the Larti, boulders as big as a man, or nearly so, had been used for the ground work of the houses, and showed, by their alignment, the old streets running horizontally above the valley bottom. Here, in a promising spot that a druid might have chosen for his burial place, under an oak tree with low branches, where three boulders, arranged like a tripod, marked the tomb, we started operations. We were embarrassed by too much help, having eleven young men besides various advisers and onlookers, and I hastened to look round for more tombs to distribute their energy. But even so we were disappointed.

After digging down two feet or so, we came upon the horizontal boulders that cover in a grave. We dug carefully until all was laid bare, then lifted the lid; with sticks and fingers, so that no treasure might escape nor its position be confused, we laid bare the skeleton, stretched out exactly like those of the Larti, with head on one side and feet south-east, but nothing further was there. A few shards of unglazed pottery; a fragment of mortar that can obviously not have belonged to prehistoric man; and nothing else between the carefully built sides of the narrow resting-place. No graves had ever been excavated, no bronzes had ever been found here. The bronzes, I was becoming more and more convinced, belonged to people who followed the rivers and ever clung to the neighbourhood of waterways. If these valleys were indeed the refuge of the country's first inhabitants, as is likely enough, they probably remained in their rough and primitive condition long after the river-lands were civilized.

The graves we discovered might have been early Muslim. Our men had fears about it, owing to their lying in an orthodox direction.

'Are you sure,' they asked me, 'that these are unbelievers' (*Gabri*) graves, and not graves of the children of Adam?'

They think of the pre-Islamic Zoroastrians as a race of giants, not human; for they people the world, as most simple folk have peopled it, with a primitive society of Titans destroyed by the advent of Jove. And Shah Riza, squatting in the dust of the labourers, and filling his paper cigarette tubes, peered down at intervals at the strange shapes of the tree roots among the bones to see if the horns which he expected were not really there on the foreheads of the *Gabri*.

It was ten-thirty before the end of our labour and the satisfactory disentanglement of those who had worked and must be paid and those who had not, but hoped to be paid likewise. We did not retrace our way, but climbed due westward up the slope of the ravine on to the pasture-land at a lower point than yesterday, and rode pleasantly with the world spread round us. The flat lands of Dusan and Beni Parwar were below us on our right, and Siah Pir beyond: and over its shoulder we could see more plainly than ever before the hills of Lakistan. Oak trees were dotted park-like about us, and the sky so blue over our heads made their leaves white against it, motionless as the wings of a kite in the sun.

The Dusani guide knew of a Hindimini camp on these uplands, conveniently near us at noon. We turned aside and found it scattered about a large enclosure fenced with boughs where its flocks were kept. Children, even more naked in their rags than usual, gathered in a shy crowd at a little distance, while the young master of the tent, which was so poor that the branches of its central oak tree had not even been roofed, came out to hold my stirrup as we dismounted.

Yet nothing, you might imagine, could have delighted him more than to have to lay out all he possessed in the way of food for our entertainment. He had a pleasant brown face with eyes well apart, and quick, neat manners. He had been for a good many years in Baghdad and Basra, and knew the ways of civilized life. When I had been accommodated on a carpet, and water was brought me to wash my hands, he knelt beside me, and out of his voluminous sash produced a small piece of soap. He offered it with an air of modest triumph. He evidently felt about it as an Englishman may feel when he dresses for dinner in some outpost of the jungle. It was the symbol of a different order of things, a little treasure kept among the difficulties of nomad life as a reminder of something better which might otherwise be forgotten. Even so, perhaps, in the decline of Rome, some relic of imperial opulence might be preserved amid the northern forests, embodying in its dim way ideas long since shipwrecked and submerged.

What a delicate plant is our civilization, I thought, as I sat in the shade with the circle of the tribesmen around me, in that short silence which is good manners in the East. You would imagine that these people, who know the life of cities and its comforts, would reproduce it in some measure when they return to their own hills. Far from it. They return and live just as they lived two thousand years ago or more. The force of primitive circumstance is too great for them. And these amenities are not, like freedom, or religion, authority or leisure, among the indispensable necessities of mankind.

The father of our host was an old patriarch very nearly blind and dressed in strips of rags so multitudinous that only a principle of mutual attraction could, you would imagine, induce them to remain all together on his person. He carried them with a serene dignity, having reached an age when the mere fact of being still alive at all entitles one to indulgence and respect. His son, who was obviously a charming and kind man, listened with great deference while the old sheikh apologized for the poverty of our meal and begged us to use all the tribe could afford as if it were our own. They brought a mess of pumpkins and a small chicken floating in a syrup of melted butter, a food which after a week or so of hard riding in the Luristan air becomes more appetizing than one would think. This winter, they said, there would be nothing but acorns to eat, as the harvest was poor for want of rain.

We hurried our leave-taking so as to have time for more digging among the Larti. I had promised the old man of yesterday to return and see what he had been able to find during my absence, and resisted all efforts of Shah Riza to miss the rendezvous and take the more direct route home. We accordingly hit the Larti ravine some little distance below the city, and made our way into

THE VALLEYS OF THE ASSASSINS

it by a path among trees and boulders. A foxy-faced old man came walking down behind me. He was the headman of Larti, the *kadkhuda*.

'You walk well in the hills,' said he after a greeting.

'But I am a hill woman,' I explained.

'You run as lightly as a partridge,' he said. 'Is not England a city?'

Sa'id Ja'far, who had left the horses and was also walking down, interposed.

'Perhaps you come from Scotland?' he said. 'When I was in Baghdad, soldiers came marching through: I saw at once that they were different from the others. I said to myself: "These people surely come from the hills. They walk better and they are dressed like us of the Pusht-i-Kuh. Perhaps they are our cousins." And when I asked, I was told that they were Scotchmen, of the mountains.'

The Graves of the Beni Parwar

The old Larti man lived in a little house of reeds and leaves down by the mill in the valley. It was a semi-detached residence in a row of three huts, each consisting of one room and an open porch; and the animals – fowls, goats, and donkeys – browsed about in open stubble-fields which filled the valley bottom.

The old man was not there. Not only had he done no digging, but he had been called away on business to the lands of the Beni Parwar. The keeping of appointments in Persia is a one-sided affair, and requires time, patience, and a philosophic placid nature. Shah Riza added to the annoyance of it by remarking that he knew all along that this would happen: but his innate love of virtuous platitudes made him in spite of all approve of my conscientiousness in the matter, which he used as a Moral Theme for many evenings after in the fireside circle.

Meanwhile we had to decide whether to wait or not for our old man. His plans were unknown, but his family, a buxom young bride about thirty years younger than himself, pressed us to stay. The afternoon was late already, we could not get far on our way home: we accepted the offer and settled outside his hut for the night.

Our Dusani guide now left us. He was surprised and a little chagrined to find that I considered my compass as a sufficient substitute for his presence, for he had hoped to hurry us back with him to his own tribe; but he gave in with a good grace, and took a friendly leave, looking upon me less as an English stranger than as a woman endowed with sense in the climbing of rocks, an altogether creditable distinction.

He had hardly gone when a pleasing jaunty figure came striding down towards the door of our hut over the brow of the hill. He wore a quilted jacket woven in a little Cashmere pattern, and had two knives in his sash. At the back of his bald forehead was a turban all on one side. He was clean shaven, with two bright dancing eyes very near together, and an enormous nose. His mouth was as ready to smile as his eyes. He moved with a keen decided air, and carried his luggage in a small handkerchief at the end of a stick. He called a greeting, took me in with one look, and came across the brook to join us. He was, they told me, a Malikshahi from the other side of Kebir Kuh. He would have made a very good picture for 'A Soldier of Fortune'.

Though the Bedrei, on the east of Kebir Kuh, always mention the Malikshahis on the west of it as lawless beings of an inferior kind, this wandering tribesman seemed to be on friendly terms with the Larti and with Sa'id Ja'far too. The country is so solitary that everyone in it is known who is anyone at all, and it is the most absurd fallacy to imagine that a lonely region is the one for inconspicuous secrecy. One could indeed travel for months in the Pusht-i-Kuh unknown to the authorities, but only by having all the tribesmen in the secret and in league.

The question of the moment, as we sat outside the hut on its poor carpets drinking tea, was the matter of my *givas*. I had bought an elegant pair in the Baghdad bazaar, but the hills had been too much for them, and my toes, innocent of stockings, which I had been wearing out at the rate of a pair a day, had nothing left between them and the stones. The Larti are not *giva* makers like the Hindimini, but the small boy of the neighbouring hut happened to be at work on a pair for himself. Unlike the city things, these were stout footwear, their uppers made with strong needle weaving of cord-like wool, and the soles of strips of leather hard as wood, arranged to be flexible on the same principle as the top of a roll-top desk, and sticking out about half an inch all round in proper mountaineering fashion. They were too big for me, but Shah Riza in his emphatic way asked if it was not his profession to fit clothes on to anyone at all, and pulled out of his tobacco box an enormous packing needle which had already served to mend my skirt when torn by the dogs. With his *Pahlevi* hat tilted at an incredibly rakish angle over one eye, he sat in the shadow of the porch of leaves, sewing round and round the opening of the *giva* until it consented to dangle more or less tenaciously round my ankle. It looked something like a snowshoe when finished, and later on amused the Governor of Pusht-i-Kuh when I called on him. Seven krans, or 1*s*. 2*d*., was the price of this pair of shoes.

We were still occupied over this business, and hearing from the Malikshahi about graves in the lands of the Beni Parwar, when the old man returned, hospitable and cheerful, and evidently with no idea that we might have expected to find him true to his appointment.

'You have been waiting?' said he. 'It does not matter. To-morrow we will go and dig.' And he was just sitting down to a few glasses of tea and conversation when I ruffled him by assuring him that we were going off to dig that very moment, before the darkness fell.

He gave in with a good enough grace, and after looking about among the tombstones of the old city, and coming to the conclusion that they were certainly Muslim, and not to be touched, we found another grave at the cliff's foot, on the side opposite to that of the day before. The old man dug hopefully. The results were identical. The same narrow shaft, built rectangularly of flat stones: the skeleton lying with head to the west: two sharp stones, not flint but pointed like flints, under the head and at the knees, and nothing else at all. The bones were intact, and I took the skull, and wrapped it up in my Burberry, to the chagrin of the Philosopher, who felt I was robbing him of his garment. And as the dusk was falling, we stumbled back among the obliterated terraced gardens of the city, to the hut by the mill.

This was a bad night, our host being so poor and his carpets full of bugs. The barley crop had failed this year, and he allowed me to give him two krans with which he wandered off to buy our horses' dinner from luckier neighbours who still had some in store. Otherwise he would accept nothing.

'What I have, I give you. What is not here, you cannot have,' he said with the unconscious dignity that comes of true courtesy. But I learnt the poverty of the little family from the wife, for she put my fourpence into a fold of her garment whence it dropped out and was lost, and I found her sobbing as she baked our bread as if her heart would break.

Poor as they were, these people had two guests poorer than themselves, a widow woman and her daughter from Lakistan across the river. 'The widow and the fatherless and the stranger.' Among the nomads one realizes the Bible sorrow of these words; the absolute want of protection, the bitter coldness of charity when obligations of kinship or hospitality have ceased to count. These two women worked about the fields for their small share of the household bread, until they must wander on, weak, helpless, and indifferent to their own fate as driftwood.

They were not a likeable type; they had the narrow, foxy faces and shifty eyes that I remembered in northern Luristan, unpleasing in a successful robber, but ten times more so when he has become a cringing victim of fate. Some war or raid had driven them from their home: they fingered my belongings with an eye to begging what they could, ready to steal if possible. What little I gave only made them ask for more. The young mistress of the hut, who, with her old husband behind her, could face poverty with a brave face, looked at them tolerantly, understanding and despising.

Next morning we were late again in starting. We had decided to dig among the graveyards of the Beni Parwar, since our Malikshahi friend had a brother staying here who knew of a site, and our host also told of places in the plain where graves with jars had been found, and beads and bronzes. At the last, however, there was great reluctance and an hour's delay before we could get off, and then the two men came with nothing but their hands to dig with, and had to go back for their ineffective tools. I started ahead down the valley, keeping to our path of two days before, and coming out again where the slope descended, free of trees to the plain.

A little stream, the Ab-i-Makulà, runs in spring through the lands of the Beni Parwar and Dusan and into the Saidmarreh out of sight, but it is nothing of a stream, and vanishes completely in summer. The crops of all this tilled ground depend on rain alone, and the far-spaced camps get their water from muddy holes in the ground.

Here, however, the people of the Bronze Age lived, and their camps or graves can be found everywhere on the slopes of the small gatch hills that ripple the surface of the plain. We tried two places and found chipped flints, evidently brought from a distance, splinters of bronze, rough red pottery and mortar, and a squared stone, probably used for dressing skins or as a loofah. There were no bones, and dim lines of dwellings appeared under the surface of the ground. But my party was discouraged by the size of the boulders to be dislodged. The morning was hot already in the open land; and the men's ridiculous pickaxe continued to separate itself from its handle and to require longer and longer interludes for its mending. Promise of pay had no charm for one who had already sixpence in his pocket from the Larti digging: in vain I talked of buried gold and silver to my old man, who merely spat upon his hands and smiled.

Another old man came presently riding on a donkey over the yellow plain. He had a long beard descending to his chest with a flattened silvery wave like that of a Sumerian carving: he had an aquiline profile, and a pleasant wise keenness of old age in his eyes. When, as a matter of course, he dismounted to hear all about us, I knew that the morning's digging might just as well be relinquished, for he and Shah Riza squatted side by side and began to smoke in that companionable silence which is the prelude to a long, long chat. The Malikshahi and our old host rested near-by with the pickaxe between them, ready to listen in. Our Odyssey was entered upon by the Philosopher with such slow and casual monosyllables as might belie any indecent sense of hurry. The old stranger, puffing at a home-made clay pipe, very like a small coffin in shape, gave me a glance now and then to see if my appearance corroborated the peculiar story he was hearing, and the sun climbed higher and higher in the sky. It was no use staying there, I thought. I made a note of the place as a fertile hunting-ground for future archæologists, and announced myself ready to start.

Shah Riza was ready too. He must have been hungry for his lunch, for he soon beat his mare into a trot and deviated from our path towards a little group in a bare hollow. Sa'id Ja'far and I meandered leisurely after. When we came up, our welcome was waiting. The master of the tents held my stirrup to descend: a carpeted space had been made for me under a woollen awning: and we had just settled down to the first friendly politenesses, when the sudden appearance of three mounted policemen on the skyline gave us all a shock.

Capture

The seriousness of the shock to all concerned was shown by our silence.

The policemen descended into the hollow, and the master of the tents hastened out to salute one who appeared to be the officer, a youngish man in a tidy khaki uniform. He had a rather heavy chin not recently shaved. His two followers belonged to the *nazmieh*, in blue, with guns, pistols, and cartridge-belts hanging all about them. They bent from their saddles to make enquiries. The master of the tents pointed to where I sat secluded. Shah Riza glanced at me uneasily. Quite imperceptibly our friendly circle of tribesmen had melted away: Cæsar's enemy has no friends in Persia when Cæsar is anywhere about.

I was feeling anxious myself, but determined not to show it.

'Do the police often come here?' I asked casually.

'Never,' said one of the tribesmen. '*You* must know why they have come.'

'They may have heard of me and come to see my passport,' said I.

'Have you got a passport?' said they, surprised and relieved. Those two tomans at Bedrah had been well spent.

As we spoke, another surprise came fluttering over the brow of the hollow. This was the old *kadkhuda* of the Musi, our friend, in a great state of agitation. He dismounted and walked straight to my tent.

'They made me follow you,' he burst out, scarce waiting to greet us. 'They thought you had escaped across the river, and they made me responsible for finding you. They refused to believe me when I said you would return.' He also looked at me with obviously great anxiety. I told him how much I regretted the long day's ride he had been made to undertake.

'That is nothing,' said he. Many worse things, he seemed to say, might happen in the immediate future.

Meanwhile the police had finished their enquiries. The lieutenant was striding up towards my tent with an official air, arranging his curved sword at a military angle as he came, prepared to exert in its full force the majesty of Law. It was a delicate moment. I greeted him with as ceremonious a composure as I knew how, and motioned him to a seat on the far corner of my carpet: the tent, I meant to imply, was mine for the time being, but he was a welcome guest: the lieutenant, though he had other ideas on the subject, could not very well express them. He bowed in a provisional manner and began to ask questions.

Having tracked us for three days across the solitudes of Pusht-i-Kuh from Husainabad, where, as I had feared at the time, the ill-omened wedding guests spread the report of our journey, the lieutenant of police felt certain that the very last thing we should have in our possession would be a passport. Else why were we here, unannounced and unknown? When, of my own free will, I asked him whether it would not interest him to see our papers, he began to be surprised.

He had obviously been pondering in his mind how to inform anyone as polite as I was that he had come to take me into custody. He accepted my passport with a beginning of doubt in his manner. It was in perfect order, and had been signed at the frontier by Persian officials. Shah Riza's document, rather more surprisingly, was in perfect order too. Shah Riza, it is true, showed a deplorable nervousness over it, but that might easily be attributed to the merely general effect in Persia of anyone who is an official on anyone who is not. The lieutenant studied the document from every angle: said it was very peculiar: wondered that we had been allowed to cross at so lonely and unusual a part of the frontier, and finally fell back on the method of direct questioning. I was hunting for buried treasure, he decided. He gave a glance towards my saddle-bag. Would he like to see what I had found; I asked. We had been digging in three places, but all I had carried away of any interest at all was a skull. The lieutenant, more intrigued than ever, watched with a long face while the object was extricated from my Burberry. I presented it to him. I was taking it, I explained, to the Iraq museum where people understood about such things.

The lieutenant was for the moment docile in my hands. Having seen that his premises were wrong, he had none to put in their place except such as I chose to suggest. And no motives could be too eccentric for someone who travelled about with a skull. He listened while I explained to him the interesting problems of his

country's history, and asked what were my plans. To travel round
the cemeteries of Shirwan and Tarhan, said I. I had been delighted,
I added, to see that there appeared to be no danger on the roads of
the Pusht-i-Kuh: it was a safer country than Iraq. This pleased the
police lieutenant. The whole of Persia, he said, was safe from end
to end. It had been the only point, I remarked, which had made
me a little doubtful about journeying into Luristan: now that he
reassured me, I felt there was nothing to prevent my going on. The
lieutenant told me, untruthfully, that I was free as air to go
anywhere.

It is a matter of regret that I did not take him at his word and
start right away to cross the Saidmarreh. I knew at the time that I
was risking the whole journey by delay.

But I still expected my accomplice, and felt certain that no
chance would ever come again of visiting the valley of the treasure
if once I left its neighbourhood. To the lieutenant's obvious relief,
I told him that I was returning to the Musi tribe that night. He
and his party, he said, would follow (to see that I really did so).
They would rest a few hours and catch us up on their faster horses.

The master of the tents now appeared with a chicken ready
roasted on its wooden spit: the lieutenant dismembered it with
delicate fingers and deposited half of it before me. I sacrificed one
of my three remaining boxes of sardines, and shared them with
my captor, who soon rode off, as I afterwards discovered, to make
further enquiries into our doings among the tribes of the ravines.
As for me, I slept for an hour while the ponies finished their unap-
petizing meal of chopped straw, and then, with a sobered retinue,
and leaving a hush behind me, set out again on a track that led
towards the Unbelievers' Defile.

We rode now in the late afternoon, and descended on the valley
of the Ruá with level sun rays slanting from our left. We were

made welcome from far off by our friends of the Dusan camp, who evidently expected to see me brought along in shackles, having been strictly interrogated by the police that morning. Now that our captors were out of sight, it became obvious that to be in disgrace with the law was one way of being really popular among the tribesmen. A feeling of cordiality was noticeable everywhere. The women came up to pat my knees and admire the new *givas*, and begged me to stay the night. Our guide brought out the result of his digging, a piece of carved stucco column and a cornelian bead from the centre of the defile: three spear-heads found there some while before, were added to the booty. We refused to dismount, as it was late already, but turned our horses homeward up the valley, at a brisk pace among the tamarisks of the river bed.

We had hardly crossed to the northern side, when the policemen and the old *kadkhuda* appeared in the distance, and shouted to as to stop the night. I still did not realize that I was virtually a prisoner, and, considering this mere unnecessary politeness, waved light-heartedly and rode on, the mountains now blue in dusk in front of us under a sunset sky. Nightfall would see us home, said Shah Riza as he ambled leisurely. Sa'id Ja'far was uneasy, and begged us to hurry before the dark.

'This is desert,' said he; 'it is not safe like the city.'

But Shah Riza never hurried except for a meal, and I was enjoying the cool peace of the evening air; and presently another delay came to meet us in the shape of an old man with a donkey, who looked at my Philosopher intently, and then exclaimed by the Hand of God, that this must be Shah Riza. And having recognized each other after years of separation the two old men embraced and kissed many times, with a charming tenderness, and ambled on together more slowly than ever, talking of the past.

By the time we reached the shrine of Jaber, its thirteen pagoda tiers were invisible altogether in the night. We climbed along a cliff-edge, trusting to our ponies' sagacity not to walk over, for nothing could be seen. The donkey, with flapping ears just visible in the shadows, wandered here and there among our feet delaying us, while its master and the Philosopher still talked, and Sa'id Ja'far, anxious in the loneliness, rode on silently ahead. The uninhabited valley seemed endless. As we entered its narrowest part, a jingle and clatter behind announced the policemen and the *kadkhuda*. The lieutenant rode up bustling and annoyed.

'Why did you insist on coming on?' he asked. 'Did you not know the night was falling?'

'I like riding in the dark,' said I truthfully. 'The air is cool and pleasant.'

The *kadkhuda* too came up with reproaches. To be out at night was, it appeared, a monstrous impropriety. As fast as we could, we hastened over the roughness of the ground, and filled the little valley with the jingle of bits, and with sparks when the horses' hooves hit a stone. The policeman's gun in front of me, slung over his shoulder, just showed against the dark blue of the sky. The horses in the dark gave a pleasant sense of exhilaration and movement, which, however, I was careful not to mention, as I felt I was in disgrace.

When at last the fires of the Musi tents showed on the hillside, a general relaxation came over the party. The lieutenant saw me home, bowed, and retired with the *kadkhuda* and his policemen: and I was left to the sympathetic welcome of Mahmud and his family, who evidently felt about the coming of the Law much as I did.

A Mild Affair with Bandits

That night, while the cows came and nibbled at my roof in the darkness, I tried to make my plans.

Hasan had not turned up from Baghdad. He was in prison, put there by his enemy, the vizier, to prevent his leaving the country, but I could not guess this at the time. It was clear that I should have to do what I could without him.

The first thing was to go up into the treasure mountain and see if the map was correct. The second was to shake off the police, if possible, and get across the river to Lakistan. I decided that the first was the more important of these objectives and the second must, if necessary, be sacrificed to it, since it is an axiom that one cannot be sure of getting more than one thing at a time. The police would probably refuse to be shaken off: already they had spoken of accompanying me to Husainabad next day, and only the assurance that I was far too tired to start on a two days' journey had put an extinguisher on the lieutenant's plans.

By the morning my tactics were ready. When the *kadkhuda* came, sent by the enemy to question me, I made, as it were, a reconnaissance by saying that I had decided to cross the river, to spend ten days or so in Lakistan, and then return by way of Husainabad and call on the Governor on my way home. I waited to see what would happen. There was an ominous nodding of heads between the *kadkhuda* and the chiefs of the Musi over this statement. Mahmud, his face very serious, sat looking at the ground. A little later, when all had been duly reported, the lieutenant came to call, sat on the carpet, talked about religion in the most elevating way, and asked if it was true that I meant to cross the river.

'I had thought of it,' said I. 'My plans are quite vague. So long as I can visit interesting ruins in this country, I am content wherever I go. What do you recommend?'

The lieutenant shrugged his shoulders. 'Anything you please,' said he. 'I only desire to serve you. You can go where you like best.'

My heart rose. For a few hours I hoped that after all I might visit the treasure valley and cross the river too. I told Shah Riza to have the horses ready next morning. After a decent interval, Shah Riza came to tell me that there were no horses left among the tribe.

'No horses?' said I, outraged at my old Philosopher's sanctimonious duplicity. 'What has happened to those we were riding yesterday?'

'They had to be sent off early this morning.'

I was on the way back from a visit to my small patient, and caught up with Mahmud behind his tent.

'What is this about the horses?' I asked.

'What about the horses?' said he.

'I have been telling her that there are no horses left here,' said Shah Riza in obvious discomfort.

Mahmud looked down at me from his great height and stooping shoulders. He seemed to be making up his mind.

'You shall have as many horses as you like,' said he. 'They are my horses, after all. And we will take you to Tarhan to-morrow if you wish, whatever anyone may say.'

This truly courageous offer touched me very much. I thanked Mahmud.

'I knew Shah Riza was lying,' I said. The Philosopher looked unhappy.

'I did it for the good of my people,' he explained. 'The lieutenant tells you one thing, but he threatens us with punishment if we let you have a horse, or guide you where you want to go. Mahmud is reckless: he will do anything: but it is he who will have to pay, and you will be far away.'

This was true enough, and I gave up there and then any thought of crossing the river that time. I decided not to take risks that other people would have to pay for, and by giving way grace-fully to improve my chances of a day in the treasure valley. When next we sat at tea round the fire, I said that I had changed my mind: if the lieutenant would wait a day for me, I would take advantage of the fortunate chance of his company and guidance and go to Husainabad *first*, and thence if possible to Tarhan, after having visited the Governor. I only required one day more here, to look at some old ruins I had heard of in the neighbourhood, and then I would be ready to start. The lieutenant was charmed. No doubt he was pleasantly surprised to find that his desires and mine coincided so happily. The day's delay was nothing to him; he did not even take the trouble to insist on escorting me to my ruins.

But now another difficulty threatened.

I sent a message to Sa'id Ja'far to ask if he would guide us up next day, and Sa'id Ja'far, when he heard the direction in which I intended to go, declared that he would not risk it, not with five tribesmen behind him.

'There is a track,' he said, 'which runs along the level ground up there. It is hidden from sight between two hills, and there are no tents for miles on any side. And always there are brigands: they come up from the river and lie in ambush. You know that we are disarmed. If I had a weapon, I would not care.'

'Providence has attended to this matter,' said I. 'We will ask the lieutenant to lend us a policeman. Then we shall be safe against anything.'

I wrote a little note and sent it to the *kadkhuda's* tent. The reply came back in the hands of a young policeman who was himself to accompany us. I begged Shah Riza to make his prayers next morning short and early; and feeling that I had done all that circumstances allowed, I left the party and went to think out in my sleeping-sack the details of the adventure, of which the most difficult day lay before me.

Next morning I dressed as usual before it was light, and made a few alterations to my costume. I emptied the map case I carried round my waist, and substituted for its ordinary contents an electric torch, a candle and box of matches, and a strong knife, suitable for opening treasure chests if any such were found. I pinned a small pillow-case, which happened to be travelling with me, round my waist under my skirt. And I looked again at the pencilled map, memorizing it thoroughly. If fortune were kind and I managed to throw off both the police escort and the tribesmen, and then to find the cave, I would be ready to take away some specimens of the treasure undetected. They would be sufficient to interest any museum or connoisseur; and the next step might be taken in a more orthodox way, with the help of proper antiquarians. So, full of hope, and with the excitement of action upon me, I went out to see my party.

Shah Riza, I decided, must stay at home. His sense of responsibility was so great that I would never shake him off. His ardour for archæology had worn rather thinner during the last days, and I had no difficulty in making him see that a quiet rest was good for his health.

'The *Khanum*, she thinks of everything: better than I do for myself.' I let the undeserved praise pass, and waited to see with some anxiety who else was coming with me.

Sa'id Ja'far was there, with black cotton trousers reaching half-way down his legs and *givas* on his bare feet, ready for walking. He had the heavy metal-headed stick of the country in his hand as a weapon. Husein and Ali, two of Mahmud's retainers, one dressed in black cotton, the other in white felt, completed the party, together with the policeman, whom we sent for as soon as we were ready. All were on foot, for the road was said to be difficult. The grey mare was there for me alone, with a water-skin looped over the pommel to last us for the day.

I had prepared the tribesmen by saying that I expected to find on the hill the ruins of a fortification of the time of Nushirvan, so that even if I could not escape from them, they would, I thought, be looking for ruins while I was looking for the cave, and something might yet be accomplished. For the rest, I left my tactics to time and circumstance, and watched, as I went along, how the landscape fitted in with my map.

We went up the valley, retracing the steps of our coming until, after half an hour, we came, as Hasan had said, to a path which tilted itself up the slope of the mountain through patches of white limestone like salt. The pony found difficulties here; the white rock crumbled under its hooves like powder, and the path had no thoughts for gradients. Under ordinary circumstances I should have walked. But I was making a plan, which involved fatiguing my escort while I myself kept fresh, and so I remained seated, watching the men climbing with easy mountaineering strides ahead. It was full morning and the sun was hot: the white slope, dotted with broom bushes and small shrubs, glistened in the sun: we were being lifted up again into the joyful loneliness of hills. At the top of the mountain's long torpedo ridge runs an important track from an *Imamzadeh* on the Saidmarreh banks, along the level height, and down into the plain of Shirwan on the northwest. The track keeps a little north of the ridge up to a point where that dips and rises again to another ridge, parallel, higher, and equally long; so that for a lonely stretch the road lies, as it were, in a hammock elevated between the two hills, out of sight of everything except their solitary summits. This, Sa'id Ja'far said to me, was a place almost always infested by thieves. As we emerged on to it, a man leaped out from a small gully below us, and sped over the rocks. Our policeman swung his gun and shot at him.

This was the first time in my life that I saw, as I thought, a brigand, and I cannot say that I felt anything except a pleasant exhilaration. There was a little band of them down the road, and our policeman, Sa'id Ja'far, and Ali were bearing down upon them, fast but cautiously, as if they expected to be shot at. Beyond, making downhill as fast as their legs would carry them, were two men with some goats. It went through my mind in a flash that this was curious impedimenta for a robber band to be burdened with, but I was too much absorbed in our own party to trouble with inferences. I stopped my horse under a little thorn tree, and watched the operations, like the damsel in a medieval romance, hoping for a battle.

The brigands, after wavering a moment or two, decided not to wait for our advance, and turned downhill, leaping like gazelles. Sa'id Ja'far and the policeman shouted to me: I hurried up to them, dismounted, snatched the extra weight of the water-skin off the saddle, while the policeman leaped into it and pursued over the long grassy shoulder of the mountain. Husein went running after: the other two stood by me, watching them out of sight.

They were away for over forty minutes, and a beautiful peace, an unbroken solitude, lay around us again. I began to fear that our policeman had been killed. Sa'id Ja'far thought not. The fugitives, he considered, were amateurs. Professional bandits, he said, wore white, which made them inconspicuous in the rocks: but quite a number of honest tribesmen might turn to a bit of robbery on a track as lonely and as notorious as this, especially now when they would hardly ever meet an armed opponent. One need never fear a sudden attack in force, Sa'id Ja'far explained. What happens is, that as you ascend towards the pass one man will step out as this man did from some gully, and ask you to allow yourself to be looted. If you comply, you can go on, denuded but not molested. If you resist, the robber will turn and usually get away in the rough ground. You and your caravan will continue in apparent safety until you reach the pass: this is usually a narrow passage between rocks: and here an enfilading fire from either side will make an end of you and your obstinacy.

Sa'id Ja'far had just finished his exposition of the technique of the national pastime in Luristan, when two wayfarers appeared, coming towards us along the lonely level of the track. One was an oldish, the other a young, man, and both had the heavy-headed metal stave in their hand. Sa'id Ja'far and Ali went to meet them before they came too close to me. It was amusing to watch the approach, for each side evidently had the blackest suspicions of the other. From a safe distance they called a greeting; then gingerly drew near, sticks held ready. They asked each other the names of their tribes, and where they were travelling. As the explanations appeared satisfactory, the grip on the sticks relaxed, the distance became less carefully maintained, and I was allowed to draw into the radius of conversation.

The two travellers said that they had seen the men who caused all the commotion. They were not robbers at all. They were Hindimini tribesmen.

'Why did they leap out at us from the rocks?' said I.

The party seemed to think this quite natural.

'Either they thought *we* were robbers, and wanted to be in the best position to begin with,' said Sa'id Ja'far, 'or they may have hoped that we were unarmed, and then of course they might have robbed us whether they were robbers or no.'

'It just shows,' said I, 'that when one goes about with a police-man one can always find somebody to shoot. How lucky to have missed the man.'

'Well,' said Sa'id Ja'far, 'it was his fault. He ought to have stopped when he saw a policeman, and not made him gallop like this for miles. Here they come back.'

The policeman was trotting towards us, with Husein jogging at his stirrup leather, and the old mare tossing her mane as if she felt that it had been a holiday.

He was very cross with the Hindimini. They had made him gallop half-way over the hill before he rode them down, and then they had turned out to be most disappointingly respectable quiet people.

'And the *Naib* [lieutenant], will think that I wasted a cartridge for nothing,' he added.

'Never mind,' said I, 'it was an excellent *tamasha*.'

On this we were all agreed, and set off again in the best of spir-its on our delayed expedition.

The summit of the ridge, when we came to it, was a delightful place. Oak trees, well grown and round as cabbages, spaced singly here and there, threw shady patterns on the grass like splashes of Chinese embroidery on a tablecloth. The yellow lawns spread more or less on a level with gentle ups and downs. From the edge on the right one had only a monotonous ridge in sight across the dip we had skirted that morning: but the other edge jutted onto space. It went steeply down like a wave just gathering, and looked on the Saidmarreh River, green as paint in the valley below. Behind us the wave continued, descending in tree-dotted slopes to the plain of Shirwan, visible with cultivation: that part of the mountain backbone was Waraq Husil; we had seen its other face from the pass of Milawur. From north-west, along the plain, the river came winding in a ribbon of flat land where the wintering tribes sow their corn: there it had eaten itself a bed between low cliffs filled with thickets of tamarisk.

At present, but for a small cultivated patch of Rudbar Arabs on our right, the land was empty. One beyond another, long hills, cuirassed with flat slabs, lay behind the river like a fleet at anchor, motionless and stripped for battle. Facing us there, was a wall of a ridge called Barkus; not a blade of grass appeared to grow upon it: its rusty boiler-plates of rocks were cleft into shallow cracks for water, and its base was decorated with a series of very regular pinky-white triangles, where small streams, descending in parallel gullies, had laid bare in so amusingly symmetrical a fashion the lower strata of limestone in the soil. The foothills between Barkus and the flat river-land, were all salty, and nothing, Sa'id Ja'far said, would grow upon them: but they had here and there traces of low mud walls which serve to surround and protect the tents of the Lurs in winter, for the tribes live on that higher ground above their *riverain* fields. The track from Lakistan, along which they would be migrating in a month or so, ran over these foothills from the country of Tarhan. We saw how it kept to the higher ground, avoiding the dangerous recess of the Berinjan defile, into which we could look straight down. Another black cut in the landscape showed the Tang Siah beyond, the Black Narrows, which, they told me, must be negotiated before one can emerge into Tarhan, a far, romantic landscape lost in mists of sunlight.

We sat down where we could look at all this. I feared now that I should never cross the river, but it was something to gaze at its unknown course, and see the way upon its farther side. No doubt was left in my mind that somewhere along this water highroad the old civilizations must be looked for; a natural law links its fertile plains together in a chain which probably continues unbroken between Kermenshah on the north and Susa in the south.

I had brought lunch on my own account, foreseeing that a folded piece of bread stowed away in their waistbands was all that my escort would think of in the way of food. Sa'id Ja'far, however, had been additionally inspired by two pomegranates. Apart from everything else, I was anxious that my people should feel as happy and somnolent as possible for reasons of my own. I fed them with sheep's-tongue in a tin, jam, bread, and tea, to which the goatskin water gave rather a depressing taste. I had asked whether the sheep's-tongue was safe for Muslims when I bought it, and having satisfied their religious doubts, I watched them take to it with enthusiasm. After we had eaten, and drunk our tea, I handed over a packet of cigarettes and remarked that, as they had walked while I had ridden, I might perhaps wander by myself and look for ruins while they rested: they could follow when they felt so inclined.

All went well. No one showed any inclination to move. Husein offered to come if I felt any alarm, but was obviously relieved when I remarked that, as the landscape would be clear of brigands for a week after the morning's doings, I would go alone. I strolled away slowly till I was out of sight: then I started to hurry as fast as I could, north-west to the *wadi* of the treasure.

For twenty minutes the ridge continued its broad and park-like symmetry, in a solitude so great that six ibex, standing on their hind legs to reach the lower branches of an oak tree, were frightened away by my approach. It was two-thirty when I left my party: two hours was the utmost I could allow myself before our return, and the men might begin to search for me sooner: and yet no *wadi* was in sight.

I was beginning to doubt the map after all, when a cleft appeared descending on the northern side of the hill to the river, and therefore invisible from the south as we came up. Here, by rights, should be the treasure. A black rock should overhang on the left side as one climbed down; four wan trees and an oak should make a group before it; and between the rock and the trees I ought to find the entrance to the cave.

Partly with the haste of my walk, and partly with excitement, my heart was now beating, my knees and hands shaking. I began to descend in a great hurry, pausing at every group of rocks to see if the cave could be there. The ravine, from a shallow grassy basin, quickly turned into a sort of funnel with overhanging rocks, a series of small granite amphitheatres descending in tiers, and every one of them capable of containing half a dozen caves or more. And trees, wan and oak, grew everywhere. In five minutes I had descended what would take me four times as long to climb up again. And the ravine grew more and more difficult. Black rocks were all about it, mocking me with little openings of possible caves.

I remembered a fairy story of my childhood. The Prince's Beloved had been carried off by a witch to Lapland and turned into a plant of heather: she would be frozen by the winter night if the word to disenchant her were not recalled: the word was forgotten: alone on the moor in the dusk, with the deadly night coming, the Prince could not distinguish, among so many like her, the little plant he loved: he tried word after word: only at the very last the right one came, and the figure of his love rose up in the twilight.

But my word did not come. Whether I had not descended far enough, or whether I missed the right place in that chaos of rocks, I do not know. But the very last of my time was up, and I dared not seek further. Somehow or other I must scramble back up the ravine and try not to arouse suspicion. So much time had gone already, that even if I now found the cave, I should not be able to explore it. I turned to hurry again, faster than ever I had climbed before, up the steep sides of the ravine.

The two hours were up before I reached the grass of the higher hollow. I saw Husein pass along the skyline, looking for me, and squatted down a moment among the rocks while he went by. Then I continued to race up, my ears filled with the drumming of my heart and every step feeling like the last effort of which I was capable. A little swarm of flies which travelled with me, buzzing round my head, was almost more than I could bear: they settled on my lips and rushed down my throat whenever I opened my mouth in the effort to breathe: I was too incapable of extra effort to brush them away: I came to the conclusion that the want of moisture in the neighbourhood made them such a nuisance: my lips were the only moist objects thereabout, and they tried to settle on them in crowds.

When I reached the top of the ridge again, I devoted five more minutes to a last survey. I reached a high point whence I could see how the end of the mountain dipped down to the Saidmarreh on one side and the plain of Shirwan on the other. In the east was the northern wall of the Unbelievers' Defile where we had travelled: the upper edge of that precipice was just visible. I made a careful note of the landscape and position, and with a little breath again in my body, started to race back along the ridge as I had come. A hare leaped out and scuttered from under my feet. A jay screeched in the trees. I could not think, but went counting my steps mechanically to make myself keep on. And after hours as it seemed, I saw the policeman and Sa'id Ja'far, still placidly resting under the oak tree, and the grey mare browsing near-by.

That was the end of the treasure hunt. And what there may be in the cave of the mountain still remains a mystery.

Sa'id Ja'far and the policeman had been getting anxious. Husein soon returned and showed great joy and surprise at finding me: he could not think how he had missed me on the ridge. As quickly as we could, for we had no time to lose, we started homeward; and had descended, and reached again the track to Shirwan, when we saw Ali and another man, a policeman, coming to meet us, with the lieutenant's fine bay and a second water-skin, a thoughtful offering on his part.

The rest of the descent was a long affair, and the white limestone as bad downhill as up for the horse's feet. Between one skid and another, the day's adventure with the brigands was recounted. Our own policeman, a pleasant healthy peasant lad from Kermenshah, showed his cartridge-belt with the cartridge missing: he was pleased and relieved because the lieutenant had sent words of praise. I took little part in all this, for my heart still seemed to be pounding my ribs after that hectic race. But presently I was roused by the man who came with Ali, who asked if I had seen the cave.

'What cave?' said I. 'I am interested in caves.'

'Far on the other side, a big cave near the river.'

'Some day,' said I, 'I will come again, and you shall take me to see it. Have you been inside?'

'Yes, indeed,' said he. 'It is a big cave, but with nothing inside it.'

And that is the last I heard about the place of the treasure, until I returned to Baghdad.

Return to Garau

The family of Mahmud was particularly friendly that evening round the fire. My avowed dislike of travelling about with an escort had, I think, something to do with it: they hated the police with an intensity which no one could guess at from their obsequious manners in the lieutenant's presence.

The lieutenant himself seemed to be a bombastic, empty-headed, but not bad enough man to deserve such violent antagonism.

'He is all words,' said Mahmud, with a virulence of scorn refreshing in a country where the excess of words is not usually looked upon as remarkable. 'He says all those prayers, and they are worth nothing.' The lieutenant was, indeed, always punctilious to turn the peak of his cap round to the back of his head and prostrate himself on a rug which his police spread out for him. Shah Riza, usually more timid where authority was concerned, whether human or divine, agreed with his kinsman, in a deprecating way.

The matter of the horses hung heavy on his soul. I taxed him with it in the evening circle, to the delight of all the tribesmen, who were a little restive now and then under his uncompromising sanctimoniousness.

'He comes with me as a guide,' said I, 'to make things easy in a strange land, and on the very first occasion on which I really need him, when it is a choice between me and a perfectly strange police officer, he tells me lies so as to please the policeman.'

'Hear, hear,' said all the tribesmen, or words to that effect, laughing and cheering me on.

The Philosopher smiled too, but in a shamefaced way. He was really unhappy.

'*Khanum*,' said he, 'you must forgive me. It was to save my people. I know Mahmud. He does not care what he does to the police. He would have got into trouble, and they have no scruples: they would come and take all he has away from him.'

'That is what you should have told me,' I retorted. 'Then, as you see I have done now, I would have given up the thought of my journey. It is a dreadful thing to tell lies to your own master because a strange policeman asks you to do so.'

Shah Riza would have argued still, but the meeting was against him.

'Go for him,' said the lady of the house, with her clay pipe in her hand. 'It is good for him to hear.' And the men, as they passed out of the porch to attend to the flocks just coming home, clapped him on the back with glee, telling him that now he knew what the *Khanum* thought about him.

The day's treasure hunt had left me rather exhausted, and I thought I would have my supper before going over the hill to see my patient of the snake bite: but the Persian is too accustomed to human callousness not to make all provision he can against it. As I sat resting in the porch, a pathetic little procession came up: the old man, holding his son on the back of a donkey, and the mother walking behind. I was annoyed because they had moved the child instead of waiting.

'To save you the trouble of walking,' they said, as they laid him down on the ground.

Though his pulse still raced, the arm undoubtedly looked better; it had turned to a colour of healthy flesh, and the boy himself seemed no weaker. The lieutenant, who had first been indifferent, was impressed when he saw that I put off calling on *him*, so as to see the sick boy, and evidently took it that philanthropy was the order of the day. He said that a government doctor would cure him if he could be got to Husainabad.

'How can they get him there?' said the old *kadkhuda*. 'It means two days for the going alone, and they have not a penny in the world with which to hire a donkey or a horse.'

'Let that not stand in the way,' said the lieutenant. 'If they find an animal for transport, I will pay for it and give them a letter to the doctor.'

I thought this a generous offer, and expected to see the animal appear. But nothing happened. When the evening came, I asked whether anything was being done about it.

'You don't imagine that that man meant what he said?' the tribesmen asked me. 'If we found a horse, he would not pay for it: and if the boy reached Husainabad, the doctor would not cure him for nothing. He only speaks to make himself great in your eyes.'

I am still reluctant to think so evilly of the policeman. But evidently nothing was going to be done.

'If the lieutenant does not pay, I will,' said I. 'I will give two tomans as soon as I see the boy actually setting out: that will take him to Husainabad and leave something over for food. And I myself will see that he gets the doctor there.'

'Your heart is full of compassion,' they said. 'If God wills, a horse may be found.'

But when they brought the boy that evening, nothing had yet been done about it. Since I was leaving the next morning, I gave the two tomans, knowing well that they would never be spent in the manner intended: but no doubt they would buy food, and the boy seemed to stand a chance of recovering with no doctor at all. After having the wound dressed, the little family sat watching me at my dinner with humble envy. The old man kept his quiet and admirable dignity, looking without affectation, but only with a natural sadness into space: the woman followed every mouthful I ate with her eyes, until I could bear it no longer. My hosts gave her some dinner at last: it was not for herself that she had broken the tacit Eastern code of courteous aloofness. She watched the boy feed with a sort of savage love, an animal ferocity, choosing out for him the more succulent pieces of meat from among the bits of bread in the bowl before him. It was by no means an invalid's diet: but I reflected that he was not to be killed by such trifles, or he would long ago have been dead, and probably a good meal was what he needed more than anything else. He ate and ate. And finally licked the last taste off his fingers with a sigh. I had handed him a little toy watch, which gave him great happiness. He began to talk in a high feverish voice, with a strange mixture of boyish-ness and hard stoicism of the poor. He had two brothers, porters in Baghdad, said he. He too would be a porter, if he did not die.

'I do not mind dying,' said he. 'But I do not like to think that my body rots and smells before I am dead.'

'It will not do that,' we said. 'Do you not see how your arm looks better since you have been washing it with the red water?'

He looked at the poor stump with distaste. 'God knows,' said he. 'But I shall never be able to shoot with a gun or cut with a knife.'

It was late and dark already. The old man held the donkey, and two tribesmen lifted the boy up. I said no more about milk or eggs or such impossibilities, or even about the journey to a doctor: but left it, vanquished, to Allah, in the manner of the East.

Next morning by seven-thirty the lieutenant was ready, and I parted from my friends. Mahmud had put all the best trappings on the grey mare, and was sending Husein with me to the capital in the hope that, having visited the Governor, I might yet be able to return by Shirwan and carry out the original plan of my journey. They would all wait and be ready to guide me wherever I might wish to go. They all came up for cordial leave-takings; not very welcome, I thought, to the lieutenant, who stood by with only the *kadkhuda* in a dutiful attitude beside him while these affectionate ceremonies were taking place.

'It is all lies,' he said to me as soon as we had got away. 'Mahmud is a bad man. He is only pleasant to you because of the presents you give him.'

We rode back by the way of our coming: the mills of Garau. I was not sorry to be going to Husainabad, for this way is not marked in the map, and the upper Garau valley was all new country to me, as it is to most other Europeans, though it is probably by this route that the Russian cavalry came from Kermenshah to Amara during the British advance on Kut.

I rode with a leisureliness exasperating to the policemen, whose horses were much better than mine. The lieutenant offered to change my mount at intervals: but I was anxious to take some bearings later on, and had no objection to going slowly, and soon to make him tired enough to leave me, either to rest behind me or to trot on ahead.

The valley was as hot and waterless as before, but less uninhabited, for people were ploughing here and there. They gave drinks from their water-skins to our police, who never appeared to travel with so necessary an equipment as a water-bottle in this arid land. As we came out into Garau by the defile where we had first met the ill-omened wedding guests, an old man came down with his plough on his shoulder; it was made all of wood with a blunted wooden blade, shiny and smooth with use. He, smiling up with shrewd peasant eyes under his matted hair and felt skull cap, looked as ancient as the instrument he carried.

We met the first advance guards of the tribes moving to winter quarters: a trail of tired people, donkeys and small black oxen laden with cooking-pots, carpets, and tents, and a few chicken on the top of all. Women, their long gowns catching them at every step, walked half bent with small children on their backs. The daily stage for a tribe on the move must be a very slow one; and one can realize why, a year or two ago, when some Lurs, settled by force in eastern Persia, wanted to break their way home across the hostile land, they eliminated the worst of the impedimenta by massacring their own families before the march.

Shah Riza had of course forgotten the merely terrestrial matter of lunch, though he had been reminded in good time.

'How wicked,' said he, without a moment's hesitation when I asked him; 'how wicked is the wife of Mahmud to let a guest depart without food for the wilderness.'

'She forgot,' said I, 'but it is only once, and you forget every day. Now what are you going to do?'

'*Khanum*,' said he, with an appearance of gentle reasonableness, 'by the Majesty of God, can I produce food in an uninhabited land?'

I gave up the effort to cope with my Philosopher and turned to the police. They were taking me where I had never planned to come; the least they could do was to feed me. This, I must say, they were more than willing to do, though I suspect them of very rarely paying for what we consumed. When the matter of lunch was broached, the lieutenant sent a man on ahead to the upper mill of Garau, above our former camping-place, while we followed slowly.

The lieutenant was waiting for news from Husainabad. He had, I guessed, sent a messenger as soon as he came upon me, and was still waiting for instructions as to his next proceeding. Just as we turned off the main track into a little side valley, where the mill lay low under the spikes of Walantar by a clear diminutive stream, a party was sighted coming down the valley. The lieutenant rode to meet it, while I continued towards the mill, delighting in the little watercourse in the shade; a built-out pier made of dry walling carried it into a hollow where the mill stood, like a truncated pyramid, about fifteen feet high by ten square at the base, like all the mills of Luristan.

Here two policemen spread carpets in a shady place and the inhabitants of three poor tents gave us a timid, very doubtful welcome. And presently the rest of the party, arriving, filled the hollow with the noise of their cavalcade.

The head of the visiting party was a young customs officer from Husainabad, with blue eyes and a black and grey European suit and an intelligent expression. He spent his time in collecting taxes and catching smugglers, knew the country well, and gave me details of the castles and ruins in the district of Shirwan, which I told him I hoped to visit.

'There is a castle there called Shirawan,' said he, 'which stands on a rock, and its watercourses, brought up from far below, are still to be seen. And in the city of Nushirvan itself, which is Shirwan, you can see the water conduits running among the houses.'

He was now on his way to collect taxes, and was waiting for an additional bodyguard to join him for this unpopular sort of tour. He had five riflemen already, Delivand tribesmen from Saidmarreh, which is the headquarters of this corps. They are volunteers, and get a small amount of money and some land given to them in exchange for their services when required: they were fine-looking men, with bushy moustaches and good fighting faces, and they wore white woollen *abbas* tied back over their shoulders, turbans, sashes, two knives stuck in front of them, and their guns slung behind them. Their chief was a weedy little city specimen in a

Pahlevi hat, very young, whose father got a lump sum from government for providing a fixed number of these people.

The Army and the Civil Service had lunch by themselves beside another tent, discussing no doubt the matter of my capture, for they threw glances in my direction now and then. I slept, until roused by a message from the lieutenant who was suddenly attacked by fever and dysentery and looked very ill indeed. I sent him quinine and opium pills, and hoped he might not die on my hands in this particularly lonely stretch of our journey. When I woke again, the volunteers from Saidmarreh were setting off as an advance guard: they were going down by the way we had come up. They were as friendly as could be when the officers were not about, and rode away looking fine against the skyline and as unlike the average figure of a tax-collector as can well be imagined.

I thought I too might be moving: I was anxious to have some leisure at the Milleh Penjeh Pass at the valley head, so as to take bearings and link up my map. I had had more than enough of the lieutenant and the police in general; and Shah Riza had irritated me by declaring that his matches were packed among my clothes in the saddle-bag, where, as he said ingenuously, no one would look for contraband, and whence he was now extracting them to the great disorder of what was left of my wardrobe. I left him, therefore, surrounded by chaos and protesting, while I walked away. As she saw me go, the old woman of the tent also protested. The police, she said, had not paid for my chicken, nor would ever do so. I handed over fourpence, the regular price, feeling like a guest no longer, but an intruder.

The Forests of Aftab

I set off at two-thirty, and walked for an hour along a delightful path that kept by ups and downs through open fields and glades on the higher level of the valley, where the sharp spires of Walantar run down in foothills. The valley bottom, with the stream and the main path from the Milleh Penjeh, lay all in sight below. A yellow domed tomb and the ploughed stubble-land was all the sign of humanity about, for there are no tents between the mills of Garau and the first Aftab camps, about six hours away. The upper part of the valley gradually clothed itself in a thick garment of oak trees, fair-sized and dappled with sunlight, and the low pass rose under them to a gentle skyline ahead. The silence and solitude lay pleasantly around in a delightful peace.

Solitude, I reflected is the one deep necessity of the human spirit to which adequate recognition is never given in our codes. It is looked upon as a discipline or a penance, but hardly ever as the indispensable, pleasant ingredient it is to ordinary life, and from this want of recognition come half our domestic troubles. The fear of an unbroken *tête-à-tête* for the rest of his life should, you would think, prevent any man from getting married. (Women are not so much affected, since they can usually be alone in their houses for most of the day if they wish.) Modern education ignores the need for solitude: hence a decline in religion, in poetry, in all the deeper affections of the spirit: a disease to be *doing* something always, as if one could never sit quietly and let the puppet show unroll itself before one: an inability to lose oneself in mystery and wonder while, like a wave lifting us into new seas, the history of the world develops around us. I was thinking these thoughts when Husein, out of breath and beating the grey mare for all he was worth with the plaited rein, came up behind me, and asked how I could bear to go on alone for over an hour, with everyone anxious behind me.

Husein dismounted so that I might ride, and walked ahead with the muscles rippling under his brown calves and the ancient remains of a pair of *givas* sticking here and there to his feet. The two valley paths met, and went over a low neck of limestone which enjoys the significant name of Jelau Geringé, or the 'advanced point where one is captured': it used to be well known for robbers before the present days of peace. Here the Chu'bid, a small stream, meanders down a sunken gully from Walantar, now hanging high above us. It runs into Garau, which starts here as the Ab Bank and runs a hidden course among trees from its low watershed. The trees hid the landscape. Except for the absence of undergrowth, we might have been riding through English woods: but the clear spaces with only rocks to variegate them gave a rather poor and barren look, and accounted, I imagine, for the absence of animal life; only a jay here and there, or a wild pigeon flew from tree to tree.

Two parties met us, riding the other way: the first, another squad of riflemen, was going down to join the tax-gatherers, and was evidently already aware of the fact of my existence from gossip at Husainabad. The other were strangers, also riding from the capital into these outer fastnesses, with an air of fashion conferred by the *Pahlevi* hat: they looked at me, astonished, while Husein lingered behind to explain. When he caught up again, we were in the most solitary depth of wood: a late golden light was slanting through. Husein stopped my horse by seizing the bridle, and gazed up at me with a smile which I thought most disquieting, so apt is one to be demoralized by imagination.

'I am tired,' said Husein. 'I am "tinim"'.

Tinim must be a Lurish word. I had not the vaguest idea of what it meant. He evidently expected me to do something about it and came nearer, repeating it. He then seized my water-bottle and drank.

Much relieved, I offered to rest for half an hour, or suggested that he should wait behind and get a lift from Shah Riza.

'It is not necessary,' said he, quite restored. 'If I had new *givas*, I would walk for you over the whole earth.'

'You shall get new *givas* at Husainabad, and I will give them to you as a present,' said I, full of remorse over my unworthy suspicions. With this moral stimulus, Husein strode on again, and we reached the top of the pass in time to take all necessary bearings before the lieutenant and his police overtook us.

The Milleh Penjeh Pass divides the Bedrei from the Mishkhas, a large and rich tribe that owns the lands of Aftab, and usually goes by the latter name. It grows tobacco chiefly, and is famed for its ewes, whence, with their usual etymological fatuity, they say the name Mishkhas (mish-ewe) is derived! The cultivated lands do not begin for two or three hours beyond the pass, and we still rode through woodland, now flat and running in glades with dry beds of the Ab-i-Baliaqin to be crossed as they descended from our right, and ran along the foot of Kebir Kuh, westward to join the Aftab water, and finally make their way through defiles to Iraq under the name of Kunjan Cham. Where the woods cleared here and there we could look ahead and see how the long ridge of Kebir Kuh came to an end: beyond it were isolated, less tidy hills, spaced irregularly at varying distances: a little puddingy range called Sardab Kuh ran alongside on our right, hiding the long cliffs of Saiwan and Barazard behind them. It was sunset. The lieutenant cantered on ahead and dismounted to prostrate himself for the fourth prayer by the side of the path, while the policeman held his horse. He then rejoined me with a certain swagger, an air of virtue devoid of humility.

'Prayer is good,' he remarked. 'We Muslims are bound to pray.'

'All people of the Book are taught to pray,' I observed.

The lieutenant agreed as if he were making a concession. Would I mind, he asked, travelling all night so as to reach Husainabad next morning before it got hot? He felt so ill that he could not face another day.

We had been riding eight hours already, and the horses had only had a feed of chopped straw. I offered, however, to set out at 2 a.m. or so, if a proper feed of oats could be procured. Meanwhile, we were still far from any sign of human habitation.

We turned northward across the Baliaqin towards the little hills, and in the last glimmer of daylight passed a very sweet spring of water called Chashmeh Qal'a Malik, the Spring of the King's Castle, which ran between banks of green turf, where our horses drank. Husein remained behind to fill my water-bottle. We thought he had followed, but when darkness had fallen completely, and we were already involved in the short slopes and sudden corners of the Sardab range, Shah Riza from the rear suddenly asked where Husein might be. He was not in the party.

We waited and called. No answer came. The night was now like velvet round us, with only the Milky Way above and a dim streak of limestone trade below showing vaguely. The lieutenant was for going on. But this could not be, and on my protest he galloped back with an air of voluntary gallantry, and we heard his voice and that of Shah Riza shouting in the woods.

Husein, however, had vanished, and only recovered us in the morning. After a time the lieutenant returned: there was nothing for it but to go on and hope that Husein might find the way by himself. The night was so dark that we could hardly see even the shapes of the hills against the sky. We knew vaguely that we descended: a dampness of cultivated earth presently came to our nostrils pleasantly, and soon there was running water, a sweet sound in the night. Scattered at wide intervals in a great open basin filled with streams, the Aftab fires flickered here and there. We stumbled down to the first of them, and found that it belonged to travellers like ourselves, a caravan camping in the open, without a handful of food of any kind for horses.

The next tent was very small and poor: our party could not have entered it: two people crouching inside pointed us farther on into the hollow. We waded in water. My horse, thoroughly nervous with the sound of streams flowing on all sides, refused to cross a leat which we now came upon, running along the slope. Shah Riza implored me to dismount: he leaped off his own mare and fluttered before me like a hen, or the ghost of one in the dimness, agitating my animal and asking whether, by the Hand of God, my life was not under his care. I dug in the corners of my enormous stirrups and got across finally, leaping down the unseen darkness of the farther bank with a heave which nearly gave a heart attack to the Philosopher. I was never able to make him understand that it was my physical and not my spiritual needs which he was there to attend to.

After the agitation of this crossing we came to what looked like a more promising tent, and found an old long-bearded man in an *abba* surrounded by snarling dogs. The old man had no room, said he. His words were disregarded, and I was told to enter under the flap: a crone inside crouched beside a new-born calf over a smoky fire. It was poor enough, and the lieutenant, when he followed me in, pronounced the place impossible. Better tents, we knew, must be about somewhere in so large a settlement: we went out again into the night and told the old man to guide us. But this he refused to do. If he brought the police to anyone in the tribe, they would be his enemies for life, said he; and he could not make enemies of people in whose neighbourhood he was living for us who might never come again. The young policeman from Kermenshah, the same who had pursued the brigand, seized him by the collar of his *abba* and shook him like a wet paintbrush. The old man called on the names of all the prophets but still refused to guide.

'Come on,' said the policeman, dragging him beside his stirrup. 'Son of a burnt father, son of a dog, we will pay you for coming: will you leave us out in the open all night?'

The old man stood his ground. He followed, because he was being dragged, but his spirit was unconquered, and nothing would make him disclose which of the many fires twinkling about the landscape belonged to a tent suitable for the reception of guests. We made for the nearest, and found there only two women and a small boy. They too would have avoided us if they could.

'You cannot come here: we are women alone,' said they. The excuse was one that a decent Muslim could not disregard. But the little boy was at last induced to guide us: the old man, muttering and dishevelled, was dropped with curses, and we followed through many more dogs to a large tent on the slope.

Here another white-bearded old man came out, but with a different welcome.

'*Hosh ati, hosh ati*, fair is your coming,' said he, and covered first one eye and then the other with the fingers of his hand in greeting.

His tent was roomy, but bare and cold, with no saddle-bags or mattresses to furnish it. But his son bestirred himself to build a fire in a new hearth hastily made by scraping a hole in the middle of the floor: his old wife was smiling and friendly: felt mats were found to sit on, and a handsome daughter sat down with the flour-bag to bake the bread. The lieutenant left us for another tent a little way up the slope, and an immediate increase of cordiality followed the departure of the police. Although I never saw any act of actual oppression, I found this unpopularity so general over the Pusht-i-Kuh that it is impossible not to suspect some justification for it when there is no foreigner looking on.

We were so late that there was little talk in the *manzil*, and I soon got into my sleeping-sack to get warm. Sheep or goats were just outside, and the high lost cry of wolves came in the night, with fearful raging and rushing of dogs. No one called us, so I realized with some relief that the idea of night travel had been abandoned. Next morning, indeed, there was no sign of life from the tents above, and I decided to start on ahead. We sat over our tea, our host drinking the first cup as etiquette demands, and telling us at intervals how welcome we were. He was charming and disinterested, for he would take no money, but allowed me to give pocket-knives to his two smaller sons. His tribe, he told me, follow the Kunjan Cham in winter to the barren lands we had come through, east of Zurbatiyah. An Englishman came here to Aftab to make maps, said he, about ten years ago: he travelled with seven tents and a wife, and spent his days 'measuring the hills'. At that time, he told me, there was more water, and many of the streams marked on the map are now dry.

By this time our ponies had finished their breakfast of straw, and we started, only pausing a minute when two beautiful girls came running after us in long red gowns and velvet coats and great turbans, and asked if I would mind stopping a minute, to let them look at me.

To the Capital of Pusht-i-Kub

The big basin of the Aftab is almost entirely filled with tobacco plantations, and new hills, hitherto unseen, stood up around it. But we left it immediately, and entered an untidy country of glaring limestone, amid whose unimportant valleys and ridges we spent the morning, circling towards the north round the outworks of a table mountain called Shalam. These hills with cliff-like tops are a feature of the land, which looks as if it had once been flat to the height of their summits, and then gradually been eaten away into small untidy chaos by the action of water and the soft backboneless structure of the hills. Kebir Kuh, alone, made of different and harder rock, looks as if Nature had intended it for a mountain from the first.

On our left now as we turned gradually north, we had the hills of the Iraq border round Mandali, the same inhospitable belt as we had traversed lower down from Bedrah. In the distance they looked pointed and wavelike; but the country ahead of us ran in long snouts level as moraines. The path was white, and so were the rocks around it: the oak trees parched and stunted: the watercourses mere empty gullies made for the transitory floods of rains: and not a flower about except the autumn crocus, that pushed anæmic, leafless blossoms through the dust.

At eleven, we dismounted by a long-promised spring of water, a black trickle like spilt ink among the blazing rocks, with the dusty shadow of one oak tree thrown across it. But we had hardly begun to take the packs off, when the lieutenant and his two policemen came up and begged us to ride a little farther, to some tents on higher ground.

The lieutenant was so ill that he could hardly ride at all: he crouched on the saddle, holding my sunshade to protect him from the sun, and murmuring dolefully at intervals that he was dying, while his bodyguard rode solicitously before and behind him.

They led the way, up a small rise, on to the edge of the open plain of Husainabad, or Deh Bala as it is still more generally known. Then for the first time since leaving Iraq, we looked at a flat horizon to the north, where ran the plateaux west of Kermenshah: long table hills enclosed us right and left, though so far apart that the impression was that of openness, given by the level land between. Only a high massif to the north-west, the Manisht Kuh, still dominated the view. The plain was rich and filled with plough-land: well-grown oak trees grew there, widely spaced, so that each tree had sun and earth around it; a warm breeze came across the level space, driving clouds across a blue sky. As soon as we topped the rise, our policeman led us from the track towards the right, and we came to three tents near together, small and poor under the trees.

The lieutenant collapsed beside one of them, while I with my party settled down for lunch beside another; and while the chicken was caught and massacred in the name of Allah, two cheerful little orphan girls, dressed with all fineries of beads and bangles, came to chat and experiment, in momentary awe, with the zip fastener of my travelling dress. They had been adopted by the woman of the tent: she looked at them smilingly, as if they were her own – but sadly too, for it was a very poor family, and the brother had just gone off as a soldier the day before: we had met him on the track with the riflemen of Saidmarreh. I distributed safety-pins, for their gowns had no fastening at the neck, and this gift in itself would have been considered as an ample equivalent for our luncheon.

Before leaving, I crossed to the lieutenant's tent, and found him so ill that I suggested riding on to send a doctor from Husainabad;

but he refused, and only consented to change mounts with Shah Riza, so as to recline on the pack-saddle and baggage, while I took his horse and set out as the leader of the expedition, feeling sorry for my captor, but rather amused at riding thus into the enemy's stronghold. The policeman from Kermenshah came with me to show the way.

The capital of Pusht-i-Kuh was still a movable city of tents three years ago, with only a fortified building or two of the Vali's to give it dignity. In 1931 the government rebaptized it and started to build a town. When I arrived, four or five straight boulevards were already laid out, from the police barracks at one end, an old building with round corner towers, to the new Governor's palace at the other. There were about twenty shops, and a square at the bottom of the hill, where a tall, unfinished pedestal in the middle of an ornamental waterless moat was waiting for a statue of the Shah. The whole place lies on a very gentle slope, on the track that inserts itself between the masses of Manisht Kuh and Shalam close behind. The houses along the boulevard were one-storied and most of them unfinished; the streets were dumping grounds for masons. The original city of tents had not yet removed itself, but stood in dingy compact rows, like seaside bungalows, outside and around the newly erected splendours.

The old summer residence of the Vali is four or five miles away to the west, visible among trees and known for the goodness of its water. Husainabad itself is arid and shadeless, and the slopes behind it sparsely wooded. It had just been linked to the rest of Persia by a motor road whose smooth surface ended abruptly a few yards below the Place de la Concorde, not used more than twice a week or so by cars, which the small boys still pursued shouting.

We looked down on all this suddenly from a little neck on the edge of the plain, where the policemen and I waited for our demoralized lieutenant, guessing that he would not like his captive to ride into the town ahead of him. When he came, we all descended slowly down a stony path. Signs of civilization, in the pleasant form of donkeys laden with water-melons, met us on the way. We skirted the main boulevard, until we saw, through a screen of poplar leaves, the light-blue uniform of a police sentry at the gate of the fort. More police gathered in a small knot. A trim little man in khaki, with blue aiguillettes, walked up. Everyone saluted. He went to the lieutenant, faint surprise visible at the unexpected sight of him on a pack animal: a few words were exchanged: then he came up to me, greeted me very courteously, and remarked that the Governor was expecting to see me.

Nothing, said I, could be more agreeable than to call on the Governor. I had come all this way to do so. But I must wash first.

The Commandant of Police, or Ajuzan as they called him, giving a cursory look to my appearance, evidently saw that I was right. He agreed without more ado, and took me through a doorway in one of the new streets into the court of his own house. Three rooms in a row gave on to a portico and a dismal little yard with a dingy tank below. All was new, however, and just whitewashed. A room with niches round it was cleared of the Ajuzan's things, except his ceremonial curved sword which they left hanging on a nail. A camp bed was in one corner. In the fullness of time, a boy called Iskandar appeared with hot water, a tray, and a basin: I ensured a precarious privacy by draping cotton curtains over the doorless entrances; and for the first time since leaving Iraq, found myself in the comfortable isolation of four walls.

My saddle-bags disclosed in their depths a crumpled gown and a powder-puff, of which I made the best use I could, and finally emerged to meet my host more or less like a lady.

He was waiting under the portico with a friend, a soft flabby young Persian of the worst kind. The Ajuzan himself, however, was a man of the world, very much on his guard, but pleasant, and evidently determined to get my secrets out of me by kindness. To this I had no objection. We settled down to a general preliminary conversation, like two fencers feeling each other's blades.

There were four points which quite naturally caused the authorities of Husainabad to look on my expedition with suspicion and disfavour. I might be coming from Iraq as a spy, to add to the intrigues which visibly enough were creeping about in favour of the Vali of Pusht-i-Kuh; the fact of my being with Shah Riza, who had been brought up in the old potentate's household, caused a serious prejudice in this direction. Secondly, I might be, as I declared, a student of ancient histories, but possibly merely with the object of digging up and smuggling away the country's buried treasures. Thirdly, I might be an innocent traveller, who was learning far more about the general state of the country and the troubles in Lakistan than the Persians like to have known abroad. And fourthly, apart from all this, I might get into trouble or be killed in the Ajuzan's district, and cause international questions afterwards.

The Ajuzan's difficulty was, that, of all these excellent reasons, the first two could not be mentioned at all with politeness, and the last two excluded each other. He asked whether I was not afraid to travel so unprotected in the hills.

'You must have slept out at least two nights in the wilderness,' he said.

'Yes, indeed,' said I. 'One could not dream of doing it in Iraq: but here I was told, and I have found it true, that one can travel with complete safety *anywhere*.'

'Iraq,' said the Ajuzan, falling neatly, 'Iraq is a most uncivilized country, but here the Shah has done such wonders that robbery in our land is unknown.'

'So I was told,' said I. 'And it is delightful to come here and be able to travel so freely. People spread such alarming reports. The Iraqis talk of the Pusht-i-Kuh as if there were only bandits; but I could see by the way your police went round that you have the country in hand.'

'Absolutely,' said the Ajuzan. 'All the same,' he added rather lamely, noticing perhaps that he was not getting where he meant to, 'all the same it is risky for a lady, alone . . .'

'I have travelled in many countries,' I remarked truthfully enough, 'and never found it risky. The study of history necessarily leads one into lonely places.'

'Is it true,' he asked, 'that you have a skull in your saddle-bag as they told me?'

I admitted this peculiarity, and produced the object, which the Ajuzan examined with a puzzled interest. He had been told, I afterwards heard, that I found bones of pure gold in the graves, but he was an intelligent man, and was evidently discounting a number of legends about me as he turned the Luristan aborigine round and round in his hands. He began to ask me questions about archæology, interrogating with perfect courtesy, but in a manner calculated to discover any weak spot in the defence; and I must say that I have never been questioned with so much acumen, or with so expert a knowledge of how a witness is most likely to give himself away. The Persian, living amid untruth, naturally becomes versed in the sifting of information, and I have noticed even among quite simple people that it would not do to pretend to knowledge which one has not got.

The interrogatory, disguised as conversation, lasted for over two hours, and left me exhausted, but with the certain and unde-served reputation of an archæologist to carry me through the diffi-culties of the coming days. The Ajuzan and his friend went, and only returned in time for supper, which they most courteously provided for me, together with the unusual luxury of a camp table and chairs. Next morning they escorted me to the Governor.

The Government of Pusht-i-Kuh

The Governor lived in the new palace, on whose Corinthian façade, at the end of a narrow outer court, a portrait of the Shah was uplifted amid stucco ornaments. The court had two long tanks in the usual Persian fashion, with petunias, carnations, and small pomegranate trees which made it cheerful and pleasant: a little boudoir, raised some four feet above its level and looking out on to it, was our reception room. Here the Governor appeared.

He was a tall, thick-set, youngish man in khaki uniform, with grey-green eyes and black eyebrows in a round, rather highly coloured face. He had an expression of simplicity and good humour, and the refreshing air of being more a man of action than of words. We sat in a symmetrical circle of upholstered chairs, while biscuits were brought, and tea in glasses with silver holders, agreeably civilized to the sight of a wanderer.

The Governor was extremely amused. He tried not to show it, but his eyes were dancing as he, also, asked me how I had lived and lodged in the mountains.

'No wonder,' said he politely, 'that yours is a powerful nation. Your women do what our men are afraid to attempt.'

After a few moments he asked to see my guide. Shah Riza, looking more than ever like a scarecrow, extremely agitated, appeared at the window by which we sat, accompanied by a policeman.

'What is your trade?' asked the Governor in a brusque voice.

'A maker of quilts,' the Philosopher replied, flustered, but with dignity.

The Governor was almost overcome with laughter over this incongruous answer. He cast an appealing glance of merriment at his Ajuzan, who was, however, looking at the floor with a serious expression calculated to increase the anxious feelings of my guide.

'And what does a maker of quilts do in the wilderness of the Kebir Kuh?' asked the Governor again, trying hard to be official.

Shah Riza, with every appearance of guilt in his manner, had nevertheless a straightforward story to relate, and a passport whose lucky existence now saved him, no doubt, from much unpleasantness. It was handed in through the window and carefully examined: no flaw was found: the two authorities were puzzled. 'They are mad, at the frontier,' the Governor murmured, and asked us again to specify by what police post we had entered. As far as the past was concerned, our position, I could soon see, was secure: the future appeared more problematical.

I told the Governor that I wished to examine the old graveyards and cities of Tarhan across the Saidmarreh. If a permit were needed I would write at once to Teheran, where I was known by name, and whence I hoped for a reply by return. 'Write, by all means,' said they politely, but I saw that, whatever answer came, I was not going to get across to Lakistan. The fact is that the country there was so disordered at that time that the police themselves had no dealings with the eastern bank: they could not send an escort beyond the river, and without an escort, I soon saw, I was not to travel any more. They meant, however, to keep me in Husainabad till instructions came from Teheran, and encouraged me to write and wait, taking care that my letters were not posted, while I for my part took care that the letters themselves should say exactly what I wished to have known.

On this decently artificial basis I spent the next four days in Husainabad.

The Ajuzan was kindness itself: he provided me with a small house, newly built, and furnished with his table and two chairs. The owner of the house was a Lur, called Mirza Farhad, who had been vizier to the Vali, and now worked for the Governor. He had good memories of the British: his wife sent mattress, pillow and quilt, a lantern and such small oddments as were indispensable to housekeeping, and in the evening, when I was more or less installed, she came to call with her daughter, a beautiful olive-skinned creature with brilliant slanting eyes under an enormous ceremonial turban scattered with jewels.

These were charming people, fall of gay and genuine friendli-ness, and evidently pitying me as a captive in a foreign land. The mother, fat, plain, and fresh-complexioned, told me she came to me for love of the Lady Mary, 'a woman to be honoured', and begged me to see much of her and her daughters.

'If it were not that we are suspected of loving the British too much, we would do more for you: it is not our hearts that are unwilling,' said she, and invited me to the house near-by.

'I have not a good room there,' she apologized. 'Every time my husband marries a new wife, I am turned out into an inferior room, and he has now three wives besides myself. It is not very comfortable.'

It was only a year, she explained, since they had a house at all. They used to live in tents like everyone else, and go down to

Mansurabad on the edge of Iraq every winter: but now they were settled, 'and it is not so good a life,' she sighed. The city people find it hard to realize how much the winter and summer change of home make up for all the discomforts of the nomad's housekeeping.

Twice a day, the Ajuzan came to call, and spent the time chatting and smoking, while his servant followed with a small decanter of *eau-de-vie* flavoured with lemon rind, which he deposited on the table.

'You do not take this, I know,' he remarked, assuming in the usual masculine way the negative virtues of woman.

He had come to like it, said he, in Russia, where he had travelled twice, and had learned to know European ladies, and nearly married one who refused him at the last. Now he had a Persian wife, but he never saw her. 'She does not count,' he remarked, as if he were talking of a mortgage.

In the intervals of these social distractions, I explored the town, and found that it had little to recommend it, though anyone who came here to excavate would probably find it more exciting. The northern hillside looks, and indeed is said, to have many ancient tombs, and the whole place is filled with things found during the digging of foundations of new houses, but which the people are far too nervous to show. Two of them were in prison at the time for selling antiques, all of which are claimed by government. Though everyone told me of the numerous finds here, the Ajuzan continued to deny them, and was evidently anxious that I should hear of nothing of the kind.

I walked a little way into the pass that goes eastward behind the town between the massifs of Shalam and Manisht Kuh, and leads out by Hizil into the lands of Shirwan. In the town itself I came on an old dome said to be that of Mahdi b-Illah, a Muslim structure of no great interest.

I returned the call of Mirza Farhad's wife, and found her in a large and sunny house overlooking the plain from an open terrace. Some of her rival wives and various friends were with her and made me welcome. They showed me seals and beads found round about here, and hidden in the heavy folds of their garments: they begged me not to tell the Ajuzan that I had seen such things. Though little was said, a feeling of great animosity appeared to exist against the government and the 'Persians' in general, and if any reverse occurred elsewhere, I imagine it would go hard with the officials and the shopkeepers from Kermenshah. The town is an alien thing in this country: its people, mostly imported from outside, look with contempt on the surrounding tents, whose people in their turn despise them. Mirza Farhad apologized for living in a house.

'I have to do so, because I now belong to the government,' he explained. I have never seen that the genuine tribesman has that respect for civilization which the *effendi* takes for granted, except in the matter of education, which the nomad looks upon with great reverence. The Mirza's family had a particular grievance too, for the beautiful daughter was secretly married, but dared not let it be said and was unable to get permission to travel to her husband.

On the fourth day of my stay, instructions at last came from Teheran. I was to be treated with the greatest consideration, to be given an escort of four men, and to be accompanied the shortest way to the Iraq frontier. All I could do, and that with some difficulty, was to persuade the Ajuzan to let me take the new road along the Gangir River to Mandali instead of the slightly shorter one to Zurbatiyah. The morning was fixed for our departure.

The last arrangements were causing the usual delay, when the sergeant in charge of the escort turned up with his three men: he was smart and red-headed, with thin legs and gold teeth, and a reddish moustache brushed outwards from his upper lip. He saluted with great curves of his arm that seemed to include a whole horizon within their sweep. Behind him the three police-men stood with a little less soldier-like smartness, each holding his horse by the bridle. One of them was the lad from Kermenshah who had escorted us before. They were reviewed by the Ajuzan with some solemnity. He described in a few well-turned sentences the extreme consideration with which I was to be treated. To be treated with consideration is, in the case of female travellers, too often synonymous with being prevented from doing what one wants.

'*Must* I have four men?' I asked the Ajuzan. 'I would much rather have only one.'

'Three soldiers and a sergeant,' he replied, 'is the very least we can consider adequate to do you honour.'

We shook hands with friendly feelings, bearing no malice. I turned from the splendours of my escort to my own humble mule, fastened by a woollen halter to the hand of a thin-faced Lur mule-teer who had been commandeered by authority at a price which left him very dejected. Shah Riza, already enthroned on his pack-saddle, destroyed any military air our cortège might have hoped to present. The Ajuzan accompanied us to the outskirts of the town. There he mounted his own handsome charger and watched us depart, a pained amusement visible on his countenance.

The Way to Mandali

The new motor road to Kermenshah takes off from Husainabad with a great sweep to the left through the plain of Arkwazi (distinct from the Arkwaz of our coming). But we went by a short and hilly track near the centre of the circle of which Manisht Kuh is the pivot. It led up and down over shaly spurs of detritus, white and grey in colour, and so steep as to be impossible in wet weather. Oak trees were scattered thinly, hiding shepherd lads who cut the branches and threw them down to their waiting sheep below. As we negotiated one little spur after another, our horses on the descents almost slid down into the small valleys, using their hind legs as brakes.

By dint of constant epithets and the use of a stick from behind, my mule kept up with the escort, who rode one ahead and three behind me. But Shah Riza, unprepared for this rapid travel, dropped out of sight in no time. We did not see him again, till we had once more come upon the main road, now running along the bottom of a thickly wooded valley closed by Manisht Kuh, which spread out ridges, long and thin as the tentacles of an octopus. One of these, the Kuh Renu, runs to the north, hanging over the plain with a cliff face worn to a lace-edge: the road climbed up it and crossed it by a tunnel about 100 feet long. Gangs of men were still working there, widening and blasting the rock over all this hilly stretch, a rough lot of mountaineers, less uncivilized to look at than the European navvy. Drinking water was being carried to them in sheepskins, quivering on the bowed back of barefoot porters. A car full of soldiers came up from the other side. It could hardly force its way over the rough surface and through the gangs of men; and Shah Riza and his mule made a terrified and lively obstacle for some minutes: but it got by and moved along slowly, a visible symbol of the military efficacy of roads in a tribal land. The sergeant, as we jogged along, told me how the tunnel had terrified the country people, and how a chauffeur from Kermenshah had to be bribed to run his car through it for the first time.

The land of Aiwan, a broad and shallow valley with Manisht Kuh to close it at our back, lay in evening sunlight. We travelled above it along the slope, under Renu, with Bani Kuh, a rounded ridge, across the open valley; and in the distance our night's objective, the police post of Sarab Bazan. It stood, a small square box with a flag, on a gentle rise in the middle of the open valley where, even from so far away, grey *débris* of stones half buried showed that a city lay under the ground. As we drew near, the sun sank: the water that gives Sarab its name welled out of stones in three quiet streams where light lay reflected. Flocks in long procession were drawing towards it. Women were filling their goatskins. My four policemen in their light-blue uniforms made no discord in the picture as they stood to water their horses. The sentry from the square fort had seen them. The small flag fluttered at the top of the keep in a light breeze from the north. Always, from the earliest days of built houses, such a chain of towers, spaced at convenient day's journeys, has probably linked these valleys with government: it is the only way in which the country can be held: and probably the same sort of sentry has watched the flocks and the tribes from his evening doorstep in the valley of Aiwan for longer than one would imagine, looking at the treeless nomad cornland now.

The tents of the Aiwan were arranged in two or three rows in the stubble-fields, and the chief who owned the first and best of them came out to greet and welcome us with more cordiality than I had ever seen since travelling with an escort. I began to notice here a great difference in the tribes, and a far larger measure of subservience than among the Bedrei and Malikshahi: and the sergeant explained it next day by telling me that here they do not, as in the region of Kebir Kuh, own their own land, but the landlord is the Shah, who sends his overseers to take a third of their harvest every year. Something of the tribesman has gone, something of the peasant has crept into their manner. I regretted it, though no doubt it makes them easier to govern.

It is not the turbulence of the tribesman that one admires: but the virtues that go with his turbulence, so that the two are associated together. His treasure is the freedom of his spirit: when he loses that, he loses everything. And if civilization is that state in which the unshackled mind bows voluntarily to Law, freedom and discipline are the two wheels on which it runs. The tribesman does bow to a law of his own, but his apologists must admit that discipline is in him the less developed of the two fundamentals: his freedom is more lawless than it should be. It is, however, genuine; it emancipates his being; through it

Metus omne et inexorabile fatum
Subiecit pedibus, strepitumque Acherontis avari.

And the discipline which the semi-civilized invoke against him is not genuine at all, a production not constructive but merely of fear. The tribesman in his heart knows that freedom, his own virtue, comes first in the order of things: it can at a pinch stand alone, while the beauty of law is of a secondary order, dependent for its excellence on the existence of the other as a basis. Even the worst politician tacitly admits this, bolstering himself up with words. The tribesman feels the falsehood of the alien code, and of the two complementary virtues, rightly prefers his own.

In many cases he will refuse the greater comfort of the settled life because he definitely prefers his spiritual heritage to more material things. He is an aristocrat. In our complicated lives the advantage of aristocracy is that of being able voluntarily to undergo those disciplines which are forced without choice on men less fortunately circumstanced: to eat bread and water from necessity has a depressing effect; to do so from choice is, in a reasonable measure, good for the soul: and the civilized use of riches is to become voluntarily independent of them. The nomad does not go so far: but he does prefer his lean emancipation to the flesh-pots of settled behaviour; and this makes him an insufferable neighbour but a gallant man.

The Aiwan, however, have gone some way already in the selling of their souls. Their lands stretch over a great deal of country, along the Gangir stream from near the Iraq border, to its source here at Bazan, and up to the spring pastures of Manisht Kuh. And in the shallow valley they have been induced by government to build small houses, which, however, they never live in, but use to store their grain. An older fashion of keeping it, which is still most generally preferred, is to dig a hole in the ground, to line it solidly with chopped straw, fill it with corn, and cover it over with a layer first of straw, and then of earth. This is done after harvest, before the tribe moves downstream to its winter quarters, and the stored provision is found ready when they return in spring. The Lurs of Pusht-i-Kuh nearly all follow this fashion.

My escort, having enquired carefully for my comfort and given orders for a chicken for supper, left me and went to spend the night in their own police post, while I sat and fraternized with the tribe, and Shah Riza slowly regained his diminished prestige. I distributed medicines as usual, and learnt about antiquities in the valley, which has several large mounds and, they told me, many graves where bronzes had been found. On the top of Bani Kuh, they said, were the ruins of an old city, near to a place where a spring of water leaped out of the ground: and there were ruins also among the Asiman, who inhabit the next valley eastward, parallel with ours.

I saw two mounds as we followed the new road next morning: one was on our left, called Qal'a Nargisieh, and another at Sarneh, on the road itself, but farther on than where we went, for we turned off to the west about three hours after leaving Bazan, and lunched while a small dust-storm with squalls of rain flew high about us, and pattered on the dry oak leaves of a camp where we rested.

We now turned definitely west, and picked up the Gangir stream, which gets its name only here where already it is a good-sized river among reeds. Flocks of sheep and goats were browsing, with Manisht Kuh, a fine background, behind them.

The sergeant, as we went, told me about the Lurs of Lakistan, to whom he was related – a better race and better fighters than these, said he, and with most remarkable women among them. He told me the story of Qadam Kheir, a lady of the Kulivand of Tarhan, who fought against the government five years ago. She was a beautiful woman, and married to her cousin. They used to go out together to fight, and she could shoot from horseback like a man. She finally submitted to government, and settled in comfort amid her tribe.

There were three other heroines among the Lakistani ladies, of whom only one, Naz Khanum, who now lives in a castle near Harsin, has reached old age. Gazia of Alishtar, sister of the rebel chief Mir Ali Khan whose brother I once stayed with in the north, and who was kidnapped and hanged a few years ago, killed herself when her husband divorced her: she was brought up just like a boy and used to ride everywhere with her brother and the tribe, who adored her. And Kak-Ali of the Kuli-Alis, after a long war with government, was finally persuaded to submit, and was to have married the former Shah's son, but when she saw him she declared that 'nothing would induce her to put up with half a man', and she remained unmarried till she died.

'The women of the Kakavend,' my Wakkil-Bashi concluded, 'are not like these women here. Here they are terrified if a guest comes to their tent at night: but a Kakavend woman would welcome thirty riders and know how to receive them.'

The Wakkil-Bashi seemed to be uncertain about the way. We had reached, he thought, the last camp before a long stretch of desert. It was a good-sized place with one or two houses used as granaries: it was called Sar-i-Tang, because it stood almost at the entrance to a defile into which the Gangir plunges. And everyone in the camp was out of doors, measuring the harvest. The Shah's agent, together with the master of each crop, superintended the division: the government pile was put on one side; the peasant's share was carried back in sacks loaded on black oxen, to be buried in the ground. Holes were being dug at a little distance. Out of the peasant's two-thirds, the seed corn for next season had to be found.

We enquired what lay before us, and the people of Sar-i-Tang told us that we should reach Bani Chinar before night. So we rode on, with the defile called Shamiran on our left, over a small col where oak trees still grew, already stunted in the warmer soil.

There was a ruined castle, we heard, on Shamiran: and graves with bronzes are found along the valley. It must have been a high-way for traffic in every age, since nature here provides a natural cleft from the Saidmarreh River system to the plains of Iraq; and Muslim ruins are traceable here and there at intervals along the valley. As we came to the top of the shoulder through which the river cuts its way, seven ranges spread before us, the red and barren ranges of the waterless belt of the frontier. The smugglers know them and slip in and out of the thirsty gullies. They are caught, but not so very often.

'Do I not always turn my face the other way?' my lieutenant captor had asked the *kadkhuda,* when the latter complained of the difficulty of getting tea and sugar now in the Pusht-i-Kuh.

Somewhere farther south in those hills, an ambush was lying in wait for Shah Riza and me, if we had only known it. The buried treasure, acting according to precedent, had inspired the wicked vizier to send six men after us to 'prevent my return'. They expected this to take place by the same route of our going, so that the police interference, and consequent change of plans, had something to be said for it. Until I reached Baghdad, however, I was ignorant of all these excitements, and rode on feeling neither more nor less safe amid the four policemen, than I had felt with Shah Riza and the muleteer alone.

The Gangir Valley

We came to Bani Chinar in the last light of the day, and looked down into a bowl among the hills filled with maize- and rice-fields, and the damp exhalations of the evening. The river flowed there under tufted clumps of reeds taller than a man on horse-back, and the tents were above on bare ground opposite. We had to get across. An old peasant, pottering about with a spade, pointed vaguely towards a ford, but refused to guide us. 'Father of a dog,' they shouted to him, and all four policemen launched one argument in turn, growing more emphatic as the effect seemed to be less impressive. At last the old man moved. We crossed the stream. It flowed nearly up to the horses' bellies in a cool atmosphere of its own. Mint and Michaelmas daisies grew among the willows and white-plumed reeds, and a moorhen swam into the shadows of the branches, leaving circles on the water behind her.

From the five tents of the camp one looked across the bowl to the other rim of hills; the sky above was pale and clear with one pink cloud: the evening cool and gentle, swimming softly into moonlight. This was our last stage within reach of oak branches for a fire: the men piled them high and lit up their handsome 'chits', the reed screens woven in patterns with bright wools like Caucasian carpets. When the police were safely installed in a tent lower down, our host brought out a few odd bits of bronze. He promised to show me ruins next day, but they were not worth looking at, and the sergeant was unwilling to linger.

In the evening over the fire the men spoke as usual of the difficulties of life here without a gun. They told me of one man whose gun was taken from him, who spent three days and nights at the police post, eating no bread and lamenting, until out of very weariness it was given back to him.

Next morning the chief of the camp, who was no other than our old guide of the night before, now full of friendliness and apologies, led us on our way down the valley.

We had a very long day before us, and made it longer by trying to shoot fish. Tantalizingly near and fat, they swam about in the clear waters of the Gangir and the leats that took off from the main stream. The policemen enjoyed letting off their guns, and finally one big creature, about eighteen inches long, turned up his fat profiteer's tummy in the water and was gathered in for lunch. He had been interrupted at his own breakfast, and half a small fish was still sticking out of his mouth, a sight which made us all exclaim that God is great. We then set off in earnest downstream.

The whole of this day, through an indescribably desolate land, we followed the Gangir River. We crossed and recrossed it, losing it now and then in the chaos of red hills, and coming upon it again, a green caterpillar in a cocoon of reeds under which one could ride for short stretches in aisles of shadow.

Small flats of rice-plots far apart had huts beside them: at Sepa there was a wide fertile hollow: at Kainmaru (below which place the track goes by a prehistoric graveyard, partly looted) and at Gangir, were tiny patches riddled with malaria. The huts here were no longer roofed with branches, but roughly made of the reeds leaning towards each other to a point, such as earliest man might have inhabited.

Though no visible tributaries came in, the river widened. It was a blue stream, as vivid in that thirsty solitude as a platinum blonde in a monastery, but with no fertile lands around it. The hills drew gradually apart, leaving a wide flat bed. Here and there, by the side of the track, were bits of masonry, old aqueducts or bridges: above Sar-i-Gatch, an open space which looked as if there had once been a city. The flora changed: we came to tamarisk, caper, and oleander. At Sar-i-Gatch were tents again and ploughed land, the last camp of the Aiwan.

We reached this after sunset and meant to spend the night, and the Aiwan gave us a friendly welcome. But the Gangir waters, let loose among rice-fields just below, hummed under a cloud of mosquitoes, and Saumar, the last Persian tribe, was not more than two hours away. The Wakkil-Bashi suggested a ride after supper to avoid that hot expanse by day.

So we rested and set off again at eight-thirty, and rode over the uneven ground in the moonlight while a policeman and my muleteer, trotting on ahead to scout, sang Kurdish songs, sweet and plaintive in the night: after the day, the air was soft and cool.

The land grew flat: the hills withdrew on either side. The plain of Iraq here runs a wedge into Persia along the stream, intersected with small canals, invisible but evident from the crops on either hand. Large animals were rootling among the maize stalks on our left. 'Pig,' said the Kermenshah policeman, and galloped in nonchalantly, turning out five humped and clumsy silhouettes in procession at the other end of the field. At ten-thirty we came upon the tents of Saumar, dim in sleep. A man lying across the entrance was roused, while a chaos of dogs sprang round us, guarding the huddled flocks. The people there soon spread a bit of 'chit' to enclose a bedroom for me: mattress and pillow were brought: without seeing the faces of our hosts, we slept after ten and a half hours in the saddle.

I woke next morning in a windy dawn and saw that we were in the desert. The huts of the Saumar were all around, built and roofed with reeds, whose leafy fronds stuck up like battlements. Some of these were real houses, with three good rooms and a porch.

At a little distance, on a mound, was the police post: the customs house and a rest-house for officials were below. Here, too, was the Shah's garden, a place of whose magnificence I had been told in Iraq, which turned out to be about two acres of untidy ground, just planted with young palms, apricots and pomegranate trees, where I wandered while passports were being attended to.

Four more police came on horseback to watch me: they added themselves to the escort, and, more like a cavalry patrol than ever, we rode along the Gangir bed to where, on a low cliff, a round tower shows the last of Persian land. Here we said good-bye. My presents, carefully prepared, were rejected. We spoke of the splendour and charm of the kingdom of Persia and our regret in leaving it instead. I would have wished to do something more tangible for my friends, for they had treated me with great kindness, and, although their incorruptibility impressed me, I felt that perhaps it was my management that was at fault. And there has been no safe way of sending a present to them since: but I should like, contrary to most recent travellers, to put on record grateful and friendly remembrance of the Persian police – for, whether on the road or off it, I have personally found them obliging, pleasant and honest, and ready to stretch authority as far in my favour as they could.

So leaving them, Shah Riza and I and the muleteer continued onwards to Mandali. We were anxious, as ever, to show our passports, but we missed the Iraq frontier post: we wandered among palm gardens, oppressed by the lowland air, until we reached the house of the Naqib, and the region of motor-cars, and thence finally Baghdad.

Finish in Baghdad

I came to Baghdad, and the matter of the treasure, overlaid by later experiences, had already faded from the foreground of my mind. I spent a day in the delirious pleasure of decent clothes and baths after a month's starvation, and then rang up M. to announce my return and to ask, without any great curiosity, for what reason, if any, my accomplice Hasan the Lur had failed to turn up at the rendezvous.

To my surprise I heard a sort of gasp at the other end of the line. It was M.'s voice saying: 'Thank God you are safe,' and declaring that he was coming round immediately to tell me all about it. Of the absurd events which he related, of most of which we were never able to disentangle the truth or untruth, I will give a short summary as an epilogue.

Hasan the Lur had not been able to join me because he was in prison. Though I am privately convinced that he never meant to do so in any case, the matter was taken out of his hands by his enemy, the ex-vizier, who no sooner heard vague rumours of our quest that were floating about the bazaars, than he accused the lad of the theft of a jewel box and had him clapped into jail. The jewel box appears to have been stolen in fact: Hasan declared they were his things, the first product of the treasure cave, which had been given to the vizier for safe keeping, and which he refused to give up. The accusation of theft at any rate could not be substantiated, but was sufficient, combined with a good deal of influence to back it, to ensure Hasan's retention in Baghdad.

M. heard the news two days after my departure, instantly bestirred himself, and succeeded in getting bail for Hasan. Meanwhile, however, I was beyond reach of recall: Hasan could not leave the town: and all that could be done was to send a cousin of his after me with a letter, which I never received since the bearer was seized near the frontier by the Persian police and imprisoned as an agitator.

The next event was the arrival of Hasan one morning in M.'s study in a state of great agitation. The vizier, he said, had heard of my departure. Fearing that I might return with the treasure, he had sent six men from among the bazaar coolies, with orders to prevent it. Each coolie had been given (or promised) 400 rupees – a flattering though improbable price – with orders to spread themselves out over the paths between Arkwaz and Zurbatiyah, the shortest and most obvious way one would take for bringing back a valuable load. In that completely uninhabited bit of country, Hasan rightly thought that murder might be committed without any chance of the criminal ever being discovered. My fate seemed definitely settled unless I chose to come back by some other way.

In spite of this awful conviction, M. could do nothing about it. No news could now reach me in time, and the Iraq or British authorities were powerless in any case to interfere in Persian territory. The British to whom he mentioned the matter, far from being able to help, merely added to his gloom by saying that he might have foreseen some such dénouement from the beginning, and by remarking that the British army would be well advised to discourage rather than incite the female wanderer. 'You can never imagine,' said my harassed friend, 'what agonies of mind I have been in all these days.'

To add to his trouble, my return was delayed more than he had expected. If Hasan had gone as arranged, and we had found the treasure, we had indeed planned to return with it immediately, and ought to have been in Iraq within a fortnight or so of leaving. But as the treasure had not been found, I had no thought of hurrying in any case, and it was only the interference of the police lieutenant which prevented my crossing the river, and spending another fortnight or so on its eastern shores. Even as it was, M. had been thinking of me as murdered for the last ten days.

And his troubles were by no means over when once I was in Baghdad again. A rumour soon spread that I had come back with the treasure. The vizier thought Hasan had got his share: Hasan thought I was keeping it all: and even Shah Riza murmured that I had been seen staggering down a mountain with a sack that I could barely lift. The report that reached the Persian police, and thence gradually returned to the tribe with whom I stayed, was that I opened graves and found inside them skulls of unbelievers moulded in solid gold. The result of all this whispering excitement was that M. found himself one day sent for to a Baghdad police court to answer questions, and was very nearly involved in the inextricable tangle of Hasan's affairs.

Hasan meanwhile went completely to pieces. He drank arak, and tried to commit suicide in the Tigris. He attacked the vizier's sons as they walked down the High Street, and suggested that twenty witnesses be bought and a counter lawsuit started. I used to be told unkindly that my friends were all in prison or likely to go there soon. And when finally we heard that Hasan had been seized again and was safe between four government walls, we accepted the news with no little relief.

As for the treasure, whether it really exists or not is still uncertain. And the mountain and the cave are still to be explored.*

* The skull from the Larti grave reached Baghdad safely, was presented to the museum there, and is described as follows:

'The specimen found by Miss Stark, and presented by her to the Baghdad Museum, consists of a cranium and mandible. It was found in a grave underneath an overhanging cliff in the valley of the Larti, which lies in the eastern part of the Pusht-i-Kuh in Luristan. It is extremely brachycephalic, with an index of 88·6. The face is entirely missing, although the lower jaw is present, and the cranium is intact. The principal cranial measurements and indices are as follows:

Maximum head length	167 mm
,, ,, width	148 "
Basi-bregmatic height	137 "
Minim. frontal diam.	97 "
Basi-nasion length	102 "
Cephalic index (length width)	88·6 "
Length-height index	80·3 "

'This is an Armenoid type of head, with marked flattening of the occiput. The post-auricular length, from rough observation, is about one-third of the total length. There are wide parietal eminences, and several Wormian bones. The supraorbital ridges are well developed, and the bone structure is heavy, with thick, smooth orbital rims. Therefore this must be a male skull, that of a man probably in the prime of life, for only the sagittal suture is closed, and there is not much wear on the teeth. The face is broken off just at the nasion, and only the ends of the molars are present. The age of the skull must be told chiefly from archæological evidence regarding the manner and place of burial.'

The grave was one of many found under the cliff. It was long and narrow, lined with flat stones laid regularly, and covered over with flat boulders. The skeleton was on its back with the head turned to the right side. Under the elbow was a stone (limestone like the cliff above it) worked roughly into a point, and another triangular one lying above the head. In the grave were also a few fragments of rough red pottery, poorly baked, and with bits of straw in it. The long bones were in good condition. The feet were pointing roughly south-west. The other graves seemed to have been dug in the same general direction. Each was marked by boulders.

Part Two

Mazanderan

III

A Journey to the Valleys of the Assassins

The Assassins were a Persian sect. They were a branch of the Isma'ili, who were a branch of the Shi'a, who still constitute practically the whole of Persia and give particular veneration to Muhammad's son-in-law 'Ali and the Imams of his house. The Isma'ili broke away from them over the succession to the seventh Imam Ja'far. But it is not their theology which is interesting so much as their politics. They were exploited by an able and unscrupulous Persian family then settled in Palestine, who devoted themselves to the undermining and gradual destruction of every kind of faith by a system of initiation subtly graded for all stages of superstition and belief till, in its highest ranks, it seems to have culminated in absolute free thinking. They established the principle of obedience to one of their own family as the depositary of the Divine Wisdom, and having seated themselves, on the throne of Egypt, under the name of Fatimite caliphs, they increased in wealth and power, encouraged the love of learning for its own sake, and, alone among the nations of their day, practised religious toleration.

Egypt truly became for a short time the centre of civilization; and the Isma'ilian propagandist could be met with from Morocco to China. One such came into contact with a young Persian Shi'ite of Rei called Hasan-i-Sabbah, who joined the sect in the year A.D. 1071. He was to become the first Grand Master of the Assassins.

Such adventurers have ever been numerous in Persia. But the young Hasan did more than most of his kind for – apparently out of his own inventiveness – he brought a new idea into the political science of his day and treated murder as the suffragette the hunger strike, turning it into an avowed political weapon.

Even in his own lifetime it brought him power which spread from north Persia to the Mediterranean. The secret garden where he drugged and attached to himself his followers became known through the Crusaders' chronicles in Europe, giving us our word of Assassin, or Hashishin. He was the fear and execration of his neighbours. Unable to touch him, they reacted against the whole family of the Isma'ilians, who had further added to their crimes by developing a bloodthirsty branch of Carmathians in east Arabia. The perfunctory censure of the orthodox turned to denunciation as the movement became more dangerous. The parent sect in Egypt, together with the Fatimite caliphs who represented it, now a feeble crew, paid for the unpopularity of their offspring and for their own degeneracy by going down altogether before the Seljuks and the family of Saladin.

The Assassins themselves, however, continued to prosper. They had taken over some Isma'ilian and other strongholds in Syria, which they governed as semi-independent colonies from Persia, and they there came into contact with the crusading princes. It has never been made clear how much the organization of the great Christian fighting orders owed to this unchristian confraternity. It has been suggested that the Order of the Templars was based in some degree on that of their opponents: a comparison of the hierarchy and general administration of the two shows them to be curiously identical; and this may have lent a certain colour to rumours and accusations which brought about the Templars' downfall when, later on, their riches tempted the lawyers of Philippe le Bel. By then the Assassins had ceased to be an active power.

No longer independent, the Syrian Fedawis degenerated from martyrs into professional murderers. In the days of Ibn Batuta their crimes used to be paid for in advance: if they survived, they enjoyed their earnings, which otherwise went to support their families. They are now quiet country people, and talk freely of anything except their religion.

But in Persia the Mongol armies came from the east and in 1256 under Hulagu Khan took the Assassin fortresses one after the other. The central stronghold of Alamut might and should have held out. It stands in an impregnable valley south of the Caspian in the legendary mountain range of the earliest fabulous Persian kings. Hasan had come there when, nearing forty, a failure and an exile from both the Turkish and the Egyptian courts, he decided to carve his own way unaided, and had spread his propaganda for nine years through Persia and Khorasan: and the tale has it that after being the governor's guest and seeing the matchless strength of the position, he returned and obtained it in 1091, seemingly by friendly means; and never left it until his death thirty-four years later. He lived there with his secret garden and his devoted Fedawis around him, and combined assassination with the liberal arts in his efficient way. But after nearly two hundred years, madness and weakness came upon the sovereigns of Alamut. Rukneddin, a hostage among the Mongols, ordered his unwilling garrisons to surrender before Mangu the Great Khan caused him to be murdered as he travelled, a prisoner, through the passes of the hills; and his posterity, migrating southward to Qum and thence to Sindh, continued in the spiritual headship of the

Isma'ilians who still exist scattered from India to Persia and Zanzibar. H.H. the Agha Khan receives, as head of the sect, the tithe instituted by Hasan-i-Sabbah: his family's right to it was investigated and confirmed during a law-suit before the High Court in Bombay in 1866, wherein their lineal descent from the Old Man of the Mountains was proven: perhaps no one now living, and perhaps no one among the ruling families of the world, can boast so romantic and unusual an ancestry. But the Assassins' valley and the Rock of Alamut no longer know their ancient lords.

I had long wished to go there. But there were obstacles. One of them was that I could not find it on my map. There was Alamut district, but no Alamut village, nor indeed is there such a village, as I discovered when I reached the valley.

By dint of enquiries, I learned that Alamut has been visited eight or nine times at least by Europeans. One starts from Qazvin; one crosses the Talaghan range and reaches the Alamut River; and the castle is at a place called Qasir Khan on the left. That was as much as I knew: and with that I packed my bed and saddle-bags one May morning and started from Hamadan for Qazvin in a car with a Persian and two veiled ladies and a little girl, who were returning to Resht.

The day was fine; our party friendly. At noon we lunched by the roadside among young poplars, and bought eggs from an old man sitting in the dust. My fellow-travellers had been to a brother's funeral in Hamadan: they were now taking his small child home to marry their little boy later on: they would send her to school first, they said.

'In our country, if you marry them too young their children die,' said I, trying to do the best I could for the little bride. She was seven years old.

'We shall wait another five years,' said they.

The old lady, the brother's mother, dressed in the fashion of her youth, with enormous full black trousers gathered and sewn into black socks so that she was encased altogether, was on her first journey. So was Fatima, and as gay over it as a sparrow. She and I amused ourselves by feeding a family of hens in the speckled shade of the young trees: her uncle gave us glasses of pale tea. Along the dusty road cars sped by: two British officers in sun helmets: they would be shocked if they noticed me sitting here like a gipsy. Luckily I was beneath their notice: I was free of all that: the empty Persian plains were around me, and crested mountain ranges: the beautiful world, full of surprises, rushing through space we know not whither, was mine to do what I liked with for a while.

That evening from the Grand Hotel in Qazvin I sent my letters of introduction.

One of them produced the landlord himself, an old Parsee with a business eye and the most discriminating taste in Shiraz wine. The second produced Mr. Sookias, of the A.P.O.C., who introduced me to Armenian society at his wife's house and devoted himself most kindly to my enterprise. The third was from Bahai friends in Baghdad, and gave me my most charming acquaintance in Persia, Dr. As'ad el Hukuma, to whom the very hand of Fortune herself must have led me blindfold, for he and his brother are the present owners of the Rock of Alamut.

Apart from these, the city leaders who run the local politics and gesticulate over the daily papers in the dining-room of the Grand Hotel soon heard the news and gathered round to discuss history and advice. For once in a while, the explanations I could offer for my travels were sufficient and reasonable. They knew about Hasan-i-Sabbah: they thought it natural that one should journey from England to see his castle. The Persian's mind, like his illuminated manuscripts, does not deal in perspective: two thousand years, if he happens to know anything about them, are as exciting as the day before yesterday; and the country is full of obscure worshippers of leaders and prophets whom the rest of the world has long ago forgotten.

In the East, too, one may yet travel disinterestedly to acquire wisdom only, and I have entered a mosque where Christians are not encouraged by pleading that I came as a 'seeker after truth'. But it is a reason which is never worth offering to the police. The Commandant of Qazvin, when he came for his evening *apéritif* and heard about it all, looked dubiously upon me. If I had not been surrounded and supported by most of the Town Council, there would have been trouble.

Next morning, one of the enthusiasts sent me a servant. I did not know what to do about it, for I did not want him. He was small and cringing and cadaverous. Everything, even his skin, hung loose about him. He was so apologetic for existing at all that he seemed to be trying to shrink out of his own body into some even more insignificant nothingness. If one had wished to hang him up on a peg and forget him, which one would do very soon, there was nothing stiff enough to do it by except his high starched collar.

The Doctor saved me. He alone had actually been in the Alamut valley, and assured me – as I knew before – that a servant from the town could only cause vexation and trouble among the hillmen. He brought a man of his own, Kerbelai 'Aziz of Garmrud, a *charvardar* or muleteer who spends his life between the Caspian passes and was to answer for my comfort and safety: a bit of a man, with a straight nose and shrewd little eyes as good-humoured in expression as I afterwards found him to be. He would 'be like my mother,' he said, and twirled his ugly peaked cap in his hands while the Doctor, portly, urbane, and slow, wrote for me to his brother in Shutur Khan.

Next morning we started.

The caravan was larger than I had imagined. Not only had 'Aziz brought Ismail and The Refuge of Allah, two sub-*charvard-ars* from Alamut, to do the work while he himself rode like a gentleman: but his mother, an eagle-faced old woman under a white cotton *chadur*, and his small sick son, were also on their way back to Garmrud. It was not my affair. I paid two tomans (4s.) a day and was to be provided with all I required, including food, for as long as I wished; and I was pleased with the company of the old lady, who was cheerful and friendly, would leap a torrent when necessary as if she were seventeen instead of seventy, and after a day's riding over the hills, would turn her attention to *pilaus* full of almonds and raisins, of which, like Dr. Johnson with his lemons in the Hebrides, I carried a store at my saddle-bow.

Little Muhammad seemed to be in the last stages of illness, unfit for riding on mules, and for hard-boiled eggs and *chupattis*, and I feared that we might have to bury him by the way. I gave advice, which was agreed to sadly, and disregarded: he took my biscuits, and proceeded to eat them as well as all the rest: and strange to say, got better day by day. His grandmother held him on her swaying high perch above the corded baggage, and whenever I turned round I saw his little peaked face against the receding landscape of the Qazvin plain.

The city wall crumbles there amid vines and yellow roses. We went north-east, and left the road, and made by a rough track for Ashnistan in the foothills across the desert in flower. The mountains were on our left. A far peak that shone with melting snow just showed above the nearer range whose long unbroken ridge ran brown and level from west to east. We approached, it slowly, rising gently across the plain.

Far-spaced villages under trees, like islands, stood with corn-fields around them; and black oxen busy at the ploughing: the peasants' cries came to us as they turned at the furrow's end. Between the villages, the desert grass already withering into summer was thick with flowers of many kinds, so that it was a joy to walk over, and 'Aziz, perspiring beside me, for he was too polite to ride when I walked, begged me to mount in vain.

The track goes beyond Ashnistan to a place of pilgrimage: but we left it and stayed in the village land among the foothills to rest through the hot hours beside a leat of running water, where the village itself, with flat roofs and arched mud gateway on a rise, and vines and fruit trees and a grassy glade of old mulberry trees where the crows cawed like English rooks in a park, were all hidden from us by poplar trees and willows.

I sent Ismail for 'mast' or curds; the village headman came back with him, carrying them in a blue bowl, not too cordially: I was a Christian; he would not share my meal. But his two wives by and by adventured their less important souls with a little chicken, while the men smoked, and I lay in the grass and wished I knew the names of all the birds. The peasants were not unkind. My mountaineers despised them, and apologized.

'To-morrow,' they said, 'we shall be among our own people in the hills.'

I thought of the Qadi of Qazvin, who used to walk abroad in the days of the Assassins dressed in a coat of mail against the hill-men: no doubt the mutual opinions of highlander and lowlander are always much the same.

The rich land of Ashnistan ended with the suddenness peculiar to the East, and we spent the afternoon climbing easily through folds of small uncultivated valleys, very barren. The sun shone in a pleasant loneliness. We met no human beings save two men with sticks and loose cotton trousers, travellers from the hills. An eagle on a rock turned his flat head and yellow eyes upon us, but did not move till Ismail, creeping up, frightened it with a stone, and came leaping back amused at my reproaches.

I liked my escort. I was their first European. They treated me with easy charming courtesy, as one of themselves, and tried to please me with stories and slow melancholy ballads and flowers brought with both hands outstretched in the pretty Persian gesture, which must surely originally be the same as the feudal giving of hands in homage.

When we reached some little trickle of water oozing out of the hillside among kingcups, The Refuge of Allah filled his black felt cap like a round bowl and offered it as the ballad knight his helmet. Black hair fell about his ears and made a wild frame for his high shaven forehead and brilliant eyes and meeting eyebrows. The tight blue cotton jerkin, a dirty old sash wrapped over it round the waist, a leather wallet behind for a knife, and the quaint black caps like overgrown skull caps, made these men look as if they belonged to some fifteenth-century Italian picture.

They were wild and simple and peaceful. They had not yet reached the point of sophistication where the miraculous is separated from everyday life, and were ready to believe anything in the vast and strange world. So they must have been when the philosopher of Rei tried his tricks upon them and gave them the dream of Paradise in exchange for their lives. They were faithful and devoted too. They separated the universe into two parts of which one was the Alamut valley: and by the third day I think they looked upon me as having acquired its freedom, and took charge of my money and all that belonged to me far more carefully than I could have done for myself, and if we slept in a strange village of the plain, would group themselves round my camp bed on the ground, with their heads on the saddle-bags, to guard my sleep – rather to my discomfort, I must say.

'Aziz was superior to the other two, with a certain amount of knowledge picked up during his sojourns in Qazvin and Khurramabad on the coast – or Tanakabun as it is known locally. Between these two centres his life was spent like a weaver's shuttle to and fro. He kept a shop, and could read and write, and has made the pilgrimage to the four Holy Cities of Iraq, walking stage by stage for a month across the Persian plateaux and ranges and the dreary Mesopotamian plain. He it was who ventured on a sardine out of my box, under the anxious gaze of all the party and several villagers, and with some nervousness of his own: that one should be able to carry these fish into the mountains seemed to all something so miraculously verging on magic that I had covert apprehensive glances from some who were not as sure of my harmlessness as my own *charvardars*.

In the late afternoon we reached Dastgird, at the foot of our first range. The Qazvin plain reappeared on the south, below the rounded foothills. Our mules had only walked for five hours, an easy first day's stage, but the solitude and the slow dreamlike travelling in the sun already made it seem as if we were remote from the world's business in some little backwater of time.

The village was small and poor, with a scanty supply of water which made its vines and apricots look stunted: and the people were fanatical and begged 'Aziz in whispers not to drink out of my cup – a piece of advice I was by no means unwilling he should take.

The Imams of Kadhimain seem to have scattered their families over this region: Musa's son Jacob has a little mosque here, with a tattered green shroud round the tomb and the hand of Abbas cut out in tin, all very poor and dilapidated: but the graveyard is grass-grown, surrounded by a low wall with the blue distance beyond it and a sycamore above, and this gives it an atmosphere of peace unusual to the bleak and dingy Muslim tombs.

'Aziz took me back through the village, a placid hen destined for *pilau* nestling in his arm, while the Elders, sitting over their long pipes in the sun, looked at us glumly. They did not come to call: they left us to the inferior company of the women, who were stingy with the melted butter, said the mother of 'Aziz after what sounded like a fight.

'They are people of the plain,' she explained witheringly, the light of battle still in her eyes.

The highlands must have won again as usual, for when the *pilau* came she poured the butter over it in a rich stream amid a cowed but regretful silence. Sobs from a little girl whose parent had just saved her from my toffee added pathos to the scene. I was careful afterwards how I gave things to children, though I never met this sort of bigotry again.

Meanwhile it was depressing to sit in the midst of so much disapproval. It froze to horror when they saw me drinking tumblers of what 'Aziz told them was arak out of my water-bottle: and though my small gift next morning restored harmony, with embraces and protestations, I left Dastgird as prejudiced as any of the party against lowlands in general.

It was five-thirty, in the cool light before sunrise.

We climbed northward up a steep, open ravine or gully towards the Chala pass. The air grew more buoyant with the height, and fold upon fold of lower land gathered between us and the southern plain. On the shaly slopes there was little soil; hard thorny grass and flowers, larkspur and lavender, mignonette, lousewort, delicate frilled scabious, and a pink cruciform blossom, æthionema, which grew in tufts on the rocky ledges so thickly that it gave a faint colour to the snow- and sun-bleached valley. No plough land or human dwellings were here, except black nomad tents in a far corrie, where the wandering shepherd people take care of the village sheep through the summer.

'My flock is there,' said 'Aziz, pointing to a far hill. 'In the autumn they bring it back to me.' He panted behind me, for I was leaping on, delighted with the mountain steepness underfoot.

We began to meet the stream of traffic which carries the Caspian rice across these passes. The rice is mentioned in a Chinese report of the second century, and is still carried along its ancient ways. The men from Alamut came striding down with their laden mules behind them. Their white frieze coats, fastened on one side, were wrapped tightly against the cold; the straight-stemmed Kurdish pipe stuck in their sashes; their henna'd red beards were trimmed short in the Muslim way. They had squarer faces than the towns-folk, with open brows and longish nose, straight or slightly curved, but not aquiline. They greeted us with jovial friendly greetings; looked at me wonderingly; and welcomed me to their country.

The small bells tied at the mules' hindquarters tinkled pleas-andy through the still morning air as the long trains came down the zig-zag path. And after three and a half hours we came by the source of the stream; and after that to the long whale's back of the ridge; and looked on the Alamut country below.

This is a great moment, when you see, however distant, the goal of your wandering. The thing which has been living in your imagination suddenly becomes a part of the tangible world. It matters not how many ranges, rivers or parching dusty ways may lie between you: it is yours now for ever. So did those old Barbarians feel who first from the Alpine wall looked down upon the Lombard plain, and saw Verona and its towers and the white river bed below them: so did Xenophon and Cortez, and every adventurer and pilgrim, however humble, before them or after: and so did I as I looked over that wide country, intersected by red and black ranges, while the group of hillmen around me, delighted with my delight, pointed out the way to the Rock in a pale green cleft made small by distance far below.

There was the Assassins' valley, tilted north-eastward: before it, among lower ridges, the Shah Rud showed a gleaming bend. Beyond and higher than all, uplifted as an altar with black ridges rising to it through snowfields, Takht-i-Suleiman, Solomon's Throne, looked like a throne indeed in the great circle of its lesser peers. Its white drapery shone with the starched and flattened look of melting snow in the distance. The black rock arms of the chair were sharp against the sky.

Below it and nearer, but still above the snowline, were the passes: the Salambar where we hoped to travel, and the Syalan still blocked with snow. The Elburz summits were hidden by their own range on which we stood, but one could see the general trend of the land from the uninhabited region of the north-east, descending on either side of the Alamut valley, which it enclosed in steep slopes, until it sank north of us into the smooth untidy hillsides of Rudbar, beyond the Shah Rud below us, a region now green with transient grass, but waterless and barren, where many easy passes lead to the Caspian shore.

Hence descending, we left the Alpine air of the heights, and dropped through flocks of black goats grazing, by steep ploughed patches in hanging corries of the hills, and by more numerous streams, through a small sacred grove of junipers to Chala village, and decided to spend the night there, for the Alamut bridge below Badasht was reported washed away.

It was a steep hamlet hung over a ravine and small torrent that tumbled down to the Shah Rud and wore itself a rocky bed far below the tilted cornfields and walnut trees under whose shade I spent a lazy afternoon.

Towards sunset I wandered above the village, into the mud-built mosque where the children had finished school, and up among sweet brier and narrow terraces of corn and beans, till I could see the deceptive green landscape of Rudbar shining like Arcadia in the last light opposite, and a snowy peak behind.

Three boys came up and sat beside me while I asked them names of hills. They talked to me with the pleasant eagerness of youth.

'That,' they said, 'is Gavan Kuh behind Rudbar. The others we do not know.'

Gavan Kuh and Takht-i-Suleiman were the only two mountains marked on my map, which confined itself to a few villages near blue and red lines of rivers and paths, with shaded unnamed ranges in between.

Henceforth I made up my mind to collect my own names and fill them in as I went along, and began gradually to discover the joys and difficulties of a geographer, and the general inaccuracy of human beings which, I believe I have read in the *History of European Morals,* is the cause of half the troubles of mankind. I came to endorse this. Six people would each give me a different name for the selfsame hill: when in doubt they invented or borrowed one from somewhere else to please me. There was an economy to begin with: people had not sat down like Adam and Eve, who had nothing else to do, to look at objects and say: 'What shall we call it?' They gave a name to a whole region, and then made it do for whatever village, river, mountain, or pass belonging to it they happened to wish to define. This explained the difficulty of locating Alamut, which is neither village nor castle but the main valley only, and by courtesy the river whose proper name is Alamut Rud.

By sifting and collating, by telling Ismail that he was a liar and getting 'Aziz to ask every likely man we met, I gradually got the landmarks of my line of march; and also acquired such a reputation for geographical curiosity that strangers would come up and bring me names unasked.

In the villages in the evenings I would show my map to the men squatting round the *samovar*, and explain how it is gradually made by the report of travellers who give what they can for the benefit of others after them, so that to offer a wrong name is like wilfully misleading a stranger when he asks the way. This they understood and became careful to tell me what I wanted, and even Ismail, whom I accused of being the father of every mistake printed between Alamut and the Caspian, occasionally managed to say something one could believe.

I returned to Chala to find him erecting my bed and mosquito net on our host's roof while all the young inhabitants sat in rows on the roofs opposite, like the audience in an amphitheatre. Europeans were seemingly not frequent here, but 'Aziz had been right, and the good mountain hospitality did not fail us, though the people were so poor that even the bride's clothes hung in rags about her, and her ornaments and jewels were but lead and glass.

Graves of Achaemenian or Sassanian kings, which provide beads and talismans for ladies as far east as Hamadan, are here unknown. The mud houses too were poor: an outer room; an inner *anderun* where the women slept among the year's sacks of grain; an inmost little storeroom, and a porch roofed with boughs and hardened mud where the rugs were spread for tea, was the extent of our house and one of the best in the village. Its furnishings were a few rugs locally woven, a few copper, tinned or wooden vessels, some quilts, a jug or two of the lovely Qazvin shape, and the *samovar* and little glasses for tea.

We sat over these while the *pilau* was cooking, and watched the oil wicks go out one by one in the Chala houses while our host and his sons in their dark-blue rags and old frieze coats talked to us with the grave good breeding of the hills and, between long pauses, while the pipes glowed in the dusk, told us of the snow-bound winter life, when wolves in packs fight the village dogs; of bears and foxes and hunting; and of the mountain streams that swell in spring and wash away the small precipitous fields.

Next day we climbed down by the torrent, and by a steep descending crest came to the Shah Rud and the road which Hasan-i-Sabbah must have followed to reach his home. The ruins of an old brick bridge still show the way. Here, where the Alamut stream swirls out of a dark and narrow canyon, and the Talaghan comes to meet it from the southeast, a great ridge and headland of rock stands between the two and closes the valley of the Assassins as with a wall. It is, I believe, one of the 'mountains' which Marco Polo mentions in his reference to the Assassins' home.

The entrance to the valley is so well hidden that Dr. Eccles and his party who came before me, did not notice it and had to wade upstream. But 'Aziz knew the ancient way, and we climbed from boulder to boulder over the face of the cliff up a path evidently used and neglected by many generations, the sort of path that in the Alps makes short cuts above and below the new road that has superseded it, and still retains a sort of dilapidated solidity from earlier days.

After an hour's climb it brought us out across the ridge into the sunlight.

Far below, flat and arid at our feet, gleaming with interlaced streams, was the Alamut valley, and Badasht its first oasis far ahead. Somewhere to the right a castle held the entrance: but 'Aziz, whose education was only beginning, said nothing about it, and took me past its dead sentinels unchallenged, downwards among steep slabs of granite where roses and jasmine and fragrant shrubs of many kinds gave us the same pleasure as to those earlier travellers who reported to Marco Polo seven centuries ago.

There is no cultivation in this first part of the valley, and the waterless gullies of Rudbar come down on the left nearly to the water's edge. Whatever ancient road there may have been is long since washed away, and indeed the valley road must always be carried down by floods here and there. Even in its broader stony bed above the canyon, the Alamut water lapped dangerously at the bridge below Badasht in muddy waves and washed away the earth from the flimsy poles which sagged in the middle.

The men got one mule over, but thought it safer to wade with the other two, and Ismail managed skilfully, taking the current slantwise, up to his thighs in water, while the old lady and I took the bridge as far as it went and paddled through the rest of the stream.

It was stifling enough now: the round white stones of the river bed and the red earth walls of Rudbar radiated heat upon us. We were glad to reach the willows and meadows of Badasht, where the water was channelled in smooth streams, and the grey-leafed sanjid tree in flower gave us delicate scent as we passed. Badasht – Bagh Dasht – is Garden of the Desert, an attractive name for the historical detective. But it is not nearly so much of a garden as Shahrak farther along, where there are vines and corn and walnuts, and a green valley opens northward to villages and poplar-fringed meadows. We had our lunch here by a spring; the wayside travellers joined our circle, and white and black magpies walked up and down before us.

In a barren country roads cannot alter much, for they are ruled by the wells of water. This one was light and clear, and no doubt Hasan himself and many travellers before and after sat here in the shade: merchants from China and India; messengers from Egypt or Syria; governors of scattered strongholds from Isfahan to the Kurdish hills. Not a memory of it all remained. The legends of the valley belong to Muslim Shi'a or to the old native myths of Persia; for this is the beginning of the Elburz country, which borders on the demon province of Mazanderan, where Rustum on his horse rode and fought and the early Persian kings waged superhuman wars. The memories of Hasan and his followers seemed to be non-existent except in the villages nearest the Rock, where foreigners probably have brought them back.

We left Shahrak and went again through burning reaches of red, hardened earth to Shutur Khan, where the Doctor's brother lives in summer and the Rock of the Assassins stands out like a ship, broadside on, from a concave mountainside that guards it on the north. It was two hours' walk away up its own tributary, but it shone clearly distinct in the evening light, an impressive sight to the pilgrim. I contemplated it with the feelings due to an object that still has the power to make one travel so far, and then followed the mules to the low house of the laird beside a little terraced orchard and waterfall a few yards above the level of the path.

The laird was elderly, wrinkled and rosy-cheeked, with mild manners a little rusted over by the country, dressed in a long frock-coat and the new peaked hat. His newest wife from the city also came to me in the guest room, a blue satin bow in her hair; and presently the young policeman who lives at Mahmudabad across the river also arrived to look at me.

He was anxious to see my maps.

'So these are the pictures you take in your black box and show to no one?' said he, when he had examined them with attention.

My feeble attempt to explain the difference between a map and a snapshot was not believed for a moment. But he was politeness itself, and glad of novelty, for in all the district of Alamut and Rudbar, which is under his sole control, he has no distractions except the conversation of my host and the quarrels of the inhabitants, who keep him riding from village to village throughout the year. He knew no language except Persian, but he was intelligent, and must have had some character to stand the lonely life so contrary to his city tastes.

'Do you have a permit from my colleague in Qazvin?' he asked.

I remembered the scowl of the Commandant in the Grand Hotel, and lied boldly.

'It was not needed; he told me that you yourself would be able and kind enough to do all that may be necessary for my assistance here,' said I rather unpardonably: but Persia is bad for one's morals.

Anyway, the speech had a soothing effect. The policeman, deciding to postpone suspicion till he had searched through my luggage in private, devoted himself to pleasant conversation for many hours, till the lamp and the *pilau* were brought out to us and we ate supper under the stars. When, after that, I went to give some last order to 'Aziz and Ismail, their obvious surprise at seeing me still able to make plans of my own showed me that I had done rather well with the 'government' of Shutur Khan.

The sun was shining next morning, for I slept late. The waterfall made a pleasant noise outside my window, and the poplar trees glittered in a blue sky. I woke up with the delightful feeling of a pleasant day ahead, so near the journey's goal, and after tea and bread and honey on the terrace, set off with our own mules but with Ibrahim the major-domo to guide us, and Mahmud, the Arbab's twelve-year-old boy as company, across the sunken bed of the Qasir Rud to flowering wild meadows above, and northward towards the castle.

There the sentinel on the Rock might look down and watch who came and went along the slope till the path turned down into the ravine beyond a small white shrine, where I stooped to leave a coin on the tomb while 'Aziz kissed its stones. As I had been to three of the four holy cities, he and indeed all of the mountain people looked upon me as a sort of *hajji* regardless of the fact of my being a Christian. We were in the country of heresies.

I walked with the sun at my back through this open pasture, and thought of what strange destinies had climbed the path before.

Hasan himself must have glanced up at the mass of the castle and the cliffs behind it with an appraising eye while the Fates and his own fearless spirit were weaving his future. The disciple strode down here unquestioning to murder his chieftain's son. Rashid-ed-Din came penniless and on foot from Basra, stayed to spend his youth in study with his young lords, and finally left to end as the equal of kings in Syria.

That was in the days of the third Grand Master Muhammad, when Hasan, the young heir, thought to throw away the last vestige of Muslim tradition and to claim divinity for himself as so many like him had done before. Many a time the two friends must have walked along these hillsides talking over their revolutionary plans and spreading them in the houses of the villagers, till the anger of the old chief put a stop to it all for a time and the reformers had to wait for his death. That was in 1162. Hasan then allowed wine to be drunk in the valley, and abolished the formal prayers, and renounced even the nominal allegiance to Egypt. The old books which he studied, written by his namesake and kept with many others in the library on the Rock, would throw much light on the ideas which governed the valley at this time, what Manichean or Magian heresy, with possibly some pagan survival of philosophy lingering as among the Sabæans of Harran.

Then the Mongols came, and their slant-eyed armies must have camped in these meadows through the winter months till the Rock capitulated and the devastating horde went by, and the heretical library was burnt and lost for ever. The castle fell to ruin till other obscure lords somewhere about the eighteenth century settled there again; of whom nothing but a few shards of broken pottery remain to tell the story.

Meanwhile we had descended into the deep bed of the stream, and climbing out upon the western side, came into the lanes of Qasir Khan and to its village green under four great sycamores.

The village turned out with greetings for the young laird and Ibrahim.

People often came to see the castle, they said: someone came every year. They would call the man who always guided the strangers. This sounded rather like a tourist resort, but our expert examination soon reduced the crowd of visitors to two parties within the last two years and an 'English Ambassador' and his wife from Teheran some years ago. The rules for the sightseeing were well established, however.

A red-bearded old Assassin appeared with a *samovar* under his arm, and another, grey-bearded and less important, with a pickaxe and shovel to make steps up the slope. The women, grouped together under the trees, unveiled and barelegged with short kilts, and white kerchiefs over their heads, shouted good wishes: and our mules started off again along the shaly hillside, across the Qasir Rud, now a small brook, to the steep ascent of the Rock.

The particular name of the Rock is not Alamut, as travellers ancient and modern seem to take for granted. It is they and not the inhabitants of the valley who call it so, and they have done it so effectually that now the people of Qasir Khan also begin to talk of it as Alamut to strangers, and only after questioning admit that this is not its proper name. It is the 'castle' of Qasir Khan, on the Qasir Rud: and Alamut is the whole main valley with the Alamut Rud flowing through it: and as the matter might have some bearing on the old descriptions of the Assassins' stronghold, it is worth mentioning before the natural Persian amiability makes the people of the Qasir Rud valley rechristen their fortress to please the yearly visitor. Except for these, who had learnt it from foreigners, I met no one in the whole region who would know where to direct one if one asked for Alamut. 'You are in Alamut now,' they would say, and sweep their arm over the long reach of the valley in its mountain cradle.

Whatever its name, the great Rock looks a grim place. Mount Haudegan behind it rises in shaly slopes with granite precipices above. A green patch high up shows a small spring whence, said the guide, with obliging inventiveness, the castle's water supply was drawn in conduits. East and west of the rock, far below, run the two streams that form the Qasir Rud; they eat their way through scored and naked beds. There is no green of grass until, beyond a neck that joins the castle to this desolate background, one climbs under its eastern lee, reaches the level by old obliterated steps, and from the southern end looks down nearly a thousand feet of stone to the fields and trees of Qasir Khan, the sunny shallow slopes of the northern bank, and beyond the Alamut River, to the glaciers of Elburz in the south-east and the heights of Chala beyond Shirkuh in the west.

Here from some buttress in the castle wall, Hasan-i-Sabbah could watch for the return of his Fedawis. Here, no doubt, he would look out for his messengers when the benefactor and enemy of his youth, Nizam-ul-Mulk, the great minister, sent his army against him; and from here perhaps saw the emissary striding up by the Qasir Rud to say that the Assassins' work was done. Here as an old man he might stroll in the last sunlight and look on his lands already in shadow, peaceful below him with their crops. The place was now covered with wild tulips, yellow and red, among the stones and mortar. Patches of wall clung here and there to the lip of the rock and showed the extent of the enclosure: but nearly everything is ruined beyond the power of imagination to reconstruct, and the lower part of the castle, where rooms and a tank of water are dug out, were inaccessible without climbing-shoes which I had not brought with me.

Down there, so they say at Shutur Khan, seven black dogs guard the treasure and breathe fire, but fly – rather inadequately – as one approaches. The vine of Hasan spreads over the face of the Rock – perhaps of that second Hasan who released the valley from teetotalism; and the roses of Hasan grow on a narrow ledge whence my host had brought slips for his garden and gave me an Assassins' bouquet before I left.

We lit the *samovar* and sat round it in our coats, for a cool wind was blowing. I had chocolate with me, and persuaded the rather nervous party to share. Mahmud was the boldest, a proper descendant of the valley, and a true boy: our picnic was a joyful event to him. He had often climbed up the southern face of the Rock, he said, and had picked grapes from Hasan's vine.

When, after hunting for shards of pottery which lay all over the ground below, we returned to the village and went into our guide's house for tea, it was pleasant to see the people with their master's son, and his friendly young air of authority among them. It was very much like the squire's son in some old-fashioned English village. The men of Qasir Khan came one by one to sit in our circle, while the women stood beyond, and the children scrambled about on the wall; and they told us their stories of Hasan, but I thought they sounded like echoes of other travellers; the genuine note was only heard when they came to speak of Kaiumars, their legendary king, who first built the Rock, said they. No doubt in a winter's evening one might collect many an old tale, but I think that the lords of the castle would scarcely figure in them.

Meanwhile the sunlight came to us from the west. Through its level shafts we descended across the meadows, and talked of hunting-eagles with Mahmud, while Ismail, ahead of us with the mules, sang the melancholy ballads of the *charvardars*. They seemed to be hendecasyllables, three rhymes like the quatrains of FitzGerald, a long sad story of Miriam of Tanakabun. Here as among the Arabs song still springs naturally out of men's daily life; the incidents of the market, the gossip of the valley, are woven into ballads as they come: ever retouched and readapted to their modern background, they keep their original substance perhaps through centuries, like the ballad of Rosmunda the Gothic princess, which, in modern garb, is still sung by Italian peasants in the hills of Piedmont.

I had promised the policeman a visit, so that after a talk to the ladies of the house, and another futile effort for the baby's welfare, I went with the two boys across the river-lands to the police house in Mahmudabad. My luggage had been thoroughly gone through in my absence, and had disclosed nothing more criminal than a Persian grammar, so that I found both the police and the *Arbab* as cordial as possible. The little office contained a table and chair, but we sat independently of them on the floor, and were presently joined by an elderly unshaven man who proved to be not only interested but also intelligent in old castles, and told me so much of the one above Shirkuh and its reservoirs and the ruins of ancient water channels that I made tentative suggestions about a journey to investigate and was only dissuaded by noticing the consternation of the young policeman, whose suspicions were evidently returning in full force.

I had by this time decided to come back to Alamut some time or other, and left it at that.

The policeman's wife was not there; she could not bear the country life; but he brought in his two little girls, veiled in pink cotton *chadurs*. They were eight and nine years old, with pretty demure manners, very solemn. In spite of so much decorum, however, one of them had managed to fall off a ladder and scrape her knee; I took them home with me to dress the wound, and found that they turned into natural little human girls as they trotted with their hands in mine through the starlit valley now filled with damp night smells of earth after the ploughing.

The unshaven man joined us on the way and we discussed cuckoos, whose voices I had heard in Alamut for the first time that day.

'It is a useless wicked bird,' I said, and told him how it grows in a strange nest.

'Is that so?' said he. 'If your eye is diseased, and you smear ointment made from the cuckoos' eyes upon it, it will heal. Allah makes all things useful. This is written in a book called *The Peculiarities of Beasts*. It is true. You can buy it in the bazaar.'

We were polite about it; but we neither of us believed the other. Next morning we left Shutur Khan. We were to follow the valley to its upper end, to 'Aziz's village of Garmrud, over the pass northward, and through the Caspian jungle to the sea.

It was another fine day. I found the Arbab dispensing judgments at his door: he squatted on the carpet and wrote on his knee in purple ink, while his villagers waited with a look of confidence on their wrinkled peasant faces. It was a rare and pleasant sight in Persia.

Something weighed on 'Aziz's mind. When we had left Shutur Khan a few hundred yards behind us he came up to me and asked whether I had given a present to the Arbab's servant.

'Yes, indeed,' said I. 'I gave him half a toman.'

'That was more than sufficient,' said 'Aziz. 'But how was it that we did not see it given?'

'It is our custom,' said I, 'to give these gifts as quietly as possible, lest the master of the house should feel ashamed.'

'Indeed,' said 'Aziz, 'that is a good custom, but not for our country, for Ibrahim will not tell his master of your noble generosity, and your face will be blackened. I will make it all right.'

He hailed a passing hillman and spent a few moments murmuring earnestly.

'It will be well,' said he as he rejoined me. 'This man will tell the Arbab, and you will be fairly spoken of among them all.'

We were now hailed by a woman at the side of the path who had evidently been waiting for us.

'My mother is ill near-by,' said she. 'Out of your mercy come to see her. There is no doctor here.'

Which is true, for the nearest doctor or chemist is three stages by mule from the Alamut valley, and there is no track fit for a cart. Though I said I could do nothing, I dismounted and followed to a small group of houses off the road where a white-haired woman lay with a broken thigh.

'Welcome,' she said, with little hope. Beyond a rough splint to ease the pain, there was nothing to be done. I came away sorrowful and helpless to my party under the trees.

Our caravan was small now, for the Refuge of Allah had gone home and 'Aziz's mother with the boy had gone on to Garmrud the day before.

We rode for some time along the stony bed of the stream, admiring the caper in flower which spreads there from boulder to boulder along the ground, and which they call the Unbelievers' Flower, *Kafir-gul*. They use it in *pilau*.

'Is it true,' I said to 'Aziz, 'that the slope of Elburz is so rich in minerals that the sheep browsing there grow golden teeth when they happen to eat a certain herb?'

'I have not heard of it,' said 'Aziz. 'But Ismail belongs to that country: I will ask him.'

Ismail, whose mule had strayed off the path, was busy with a short but vivid sketch of its family history; he paused with stick uplifted when 'Aziz questioned him, and thought the matter over.

'There are hot springs with healing waters up there,' said he; 'and also in the region of Takht-i-Suleiman. But I have never heard of the golden teeth. It may be true, but I think not.'

'I heard it from the Arbab's daughter,' said I. 'Perhaps she exaggerated.'

'It does not do always to believe,' said 'Aziz.

'There is a true story about the Shah Nevisar here in the valley,' he added after a while. 'You can see its truth for yourself, for the landmarks all remain and his castle above Garmrud is still known as the castle of Nevisar Shah. He was an unbeliever, and our lord 'Ali blockaded him in his castle. Now you will see if we go there to-morrow that it is very steep, and there was only one gateway to pass in or out by. Our lord 'Ali placed a sentry before it and told him that no one was to be allowed to leave the castle, for he meant to capture the Shah Nevisar. But the Shah's mother was a witch, and she changed him and his son into a ram and a black dog, and they trotted out through the gate unsuspected by the sentry and fled. Down there across the river is a great rock cleft in two: they call it Kafir Kuh, and that is where our lord 'Ali overtook them and cut them down.'

We had now left the bank, and, turning a corner, saw a rich green basin before us where the villages lay among rice-fields, overshadowed by the most beautiful walnut trees I have ever seen. All here was fertile and fragrant: roses, vines, and hawthorn grew in the tall hedges, and where the rice-fields ended, the corn began. Water ran everywhere in little channels which flooded the shallow plantations: and the shadows were full of birds' voices.

But the people in these villages are sick with malaria, a poor crowd compared with Qasir Khan or Garmrud which stand too high for the rice to grow and are free of mosquitoes. Quinine seemed to be unknown. Indeed, except for sugar and tea and paraffin, and rice, of which the home supply is inadequate, and which comes with the tea from the Caspian, the Alamut valley seems to be sufficient to itself.

In the next oasis, on which we descended from a narrow and dangerous path of sloping shale above the river, we came through the chief village of Zavarak, where there is a little booth filled with European odds and ends, which are gradually beginning to find their way among the home-made things.

The valley was narrower now. A rocky wall, 3,000 feet or more, ran along it on our left. On one of the pinnacles, invisible to the naked eye, 'Aziz pointed out the castle of Nevisar in front of us. On our right were narrow wooded glens with the snows of Elburz at their head. The lane we rode along was almost over-arched by mulberries and walnuts. Well might the old travellers speak of this as a garden, when they came upon it from the bleak ranges on either side.

About half an hour's ride beyond Zavarak we found a meadow under trees, and had just spread the felt mule cloths, with my cotton quilt as a pillow, when a woman came to beg me to see her child and lured me back to Zavarak in the sun with the promise that her house was round the corner. By the time I had seen the invalid, uselessly as usual, and then seen about a dozen more, and given all the quinine and castor oil I could spare, and refused their poor offers of payment and left among blessings that I felt I had not earned, I made my way back to the resting-place, hot and exhausted, and promptly discouraged 'Aziz who was just ready to start off for his home.

Here we sat at lunch, and the folk of the house near-by joined us, together with a wayfarer or two as the custom is, for your food is free to all who come; and this in itself is an argument for not carrying more than is absolutely necessary, for if you share them with all the country-side your tins of biscuits last a very few days.

As we were sitting there in a circle, a stranger came up, a Bakhtiari with a peaked modern cap, the only one I saw worn in the valley except by 'Aziz and the Arbab. This was against the man to begin with, but he made matters worse by beginning to talk of Europe and its politics and asked me whether the British still consider Berlin as their capital, as they have done, said he, since the war.

'We have given that up some time ago,' said I, but wished he would go and cease from troubling our less intellectual peace.

Might he have a pencil, he asked, to remember me by?

I gave him the pencil, and he went: we were all polite to him: but two days after, when 'Aziz happened to mention the people whom his religion commands him to curse, he added after the names of Abu Bekr, Omar, and Yezid: 'And the man to whom you gave the pencil, him I curse also.' I then realized his feelings in the matter.

'He was a stranger in the valley,' said 'Aziz. 'He had no business to ask you for anything.'

We came to Garmrud in the sunset. An immense precipice which closes it in at the back and through which the Alamut River finds a narrow cleft to enter, was shining like a torch in the last sunlight. The flat houses on the slope at its feet were also made rosy in the glow. No more stupendous exit could be imagined for the Assassins' home. Here was the second mountain of which the travellers spoke to Marco Polo: and there above it, 'that none without his licence might find their way into this delicious valley', at the top of 3,000 feet of sheer rock, stood the castle of Nevisar Shah to which no Frank, so they told me, had ever climbed.

Anyone who wishes for scientific information about these matters is referred to the classics on the subject of the Assassins, Von Hammer Purgstall, Guyard, etc.; to Mr. L. Lockhart's article in Vol. XIV of the *Bulletin of the School of Oriental Studies;* to Mr. Ivanow's paper, and to my own itinerary in *The Royal Geographical Society's Journal,* of January, 1931. What I write here is for pleasure, for other people's, I hope, but, in any case for my own, for it is always agreeable to go over the wandering days. History and geography, arguments and statistics are left out: I mention the things I like to remember as they come into my head.

My stay in Garmrud was among the best of them, for the whole village received me as a friend and made me as happy as they could. Not only was I their first European visitor for years, but I belonged, as it were, particularly to 'Aziz, and therefore to his village. His mother was on the house-roof to welcome us: his pretty wife stood behind her with the last baby tied into the shawl on her back as is the Alamut fashion; his sisters and cousins and aunts came greeting us one by one.

The house was at the lower end of the village with the Alamut torrent in front of it and the cliff at the back. It was a prosperous clean little place, with a tiny walled garden full of lettuce and beans, two good rooms and a few dark places below for stabling and stores. And the inner room was well furnished with rugs woven by the young wife, and bedding, and the baby's cradle, and various treasures pushed into niches in the white-washed wall. Here Ismail set up my bed while the women squatted on the roof (in Garmrud every front door gives on to somebody's roof) and picked over the rice for the *pilau,* and gave the news, and 'Aziz showed his friends, who soon came dropping in in twos and threes, what he had brought from Qazvin in his saddle-bags for his shop across the stream. The chief treasure was a print of the Shah, and an oleograph of a Victorian lady in a bustle, which the young wife looked at with interest, bending over it in her black trousers and frilled kilt and bright waistcoat, her twisted red kerchief tied at a rakish angle at the very top of her head.

She was furious with 'Aziz for staying away so long. She had to spend all her time in the shop. It was not fitting, she said – and should be his business. And what was he doing all this time in Qazvin? It was not a woman's place to sit in the shop. It was not that she cared particularly whether he were here or no. She knew that whenever a friend said 'Stay' he stayed, and forgot about his wife. He could never say 'No' to anyone. It was a poor affair to be a married woman, anyway. Perhaps if I did not mind I would let her sleep in my room that night. This harangue, delivered in a series of short attacks whenever the *pilau* in the next room could be left for a moment, and addressed in general to the circle on the floor, caused much amusement. The final threat and climax was addressed to me with a mischievous and engaging twinkle. 'Aziz continued to smile unperturbed.

We spent the evening discussing geography. When the guest room was empty Ismail, now well trained to the routine, gave instructions for hot water: the children were tucked to sleep under a quilt on the floor; and the rest of the family settled in the outer room.

'Aziz had never been to the castle of Nevisar Shah, nor had Ismail. It is, indeed, unvisited except by shepherds or hunters of ibex, and of these there are not many.

The only weapon I saw in Alamut was a muzzle-loading gun immensely long, which appeared next morning slung at the back of a tall long-faced man dressed in blue cotton who was to take us up. He was the village dyer and his hands were stained dark blue, but he was also a hunter, and took the rocks on our path with the slow easy stride of the hills while 'Aziz and Ismail panted behind him and the mules seemed to be standing on their hind legs. The path wound up to a green col where the old people of the fort were buried; their graves lay open, robbed long ago. There we left Ismail with the mules and the *samovar* and the water-jar, and climbed over shale and grass and slabs of granite, round corners where hands and feet were both required, where one could look down over the cliff of Garmrud into country even wilder and more desolate beyond, or eastward over spurs and pinnacles to the sunlit valley and Marco Polo's mountain of Skirkuh in the distance.

As I climbed, I saw a gleam of blue glaze among the stones, and picked up a shard of the selfsame pottery we had found at the Rock of Alamut two days before.

Thirteenth-century pottery in this deserted place, 3,000 feet above the nearest habitation! I seized on it as a proof required; for here without doubt must be Marco Polo's castle, at the entrance of the valley as he describes it. We hunted among the stones, and found more and more broken bits all corresponding to the early samples of Qasir Khan, and blessed the destructiveness of Assassin housemaids long ago.

There is nothing left of the buildings except a bit of wall here and there; a piece of the keep still upright with a loophole on the highest point; and masses of *débris* of masonry over all the top of the crest, which is a good-sized place and must have contained a little hamlet as well as the castle itself. On every side the natural walls fall away in precipices; and from the highest point, 10,000 feet at least, for my aneroid could rise no further, one can see the great half-circle of the eastern mountains covered with snow, nameless on my map.

People who know nothing about these things will tell you that there is no addition of pleasure in having a landscape to yourself. But this is not true. It is a pleasure exclusive, unreasoning, and real: it has some of the quality and some of the intensity of love: it is a secret shared: a communion which an intruder desecrates: and to go to the lonely and majestic places of the world for poor motives, to turn them to cheap advertisement or flashy journalism, jars like a spiritual form of prostitution on your true lover of the hills. The solitary rapture must be disinterested. And often it is stumbled upon unthinkingly by men whose business takes them along remoter ways: who suddenly find enchantment on their path and carry it afterwards through their lives with a secret sense of exile.

I did not think of this, however, nor of anything nor anybody: the loveliness of the world being enough in itself. I sat in the sun and rested my eyes in the sight of the hills. How hillmen love them everywhere. 'Aziz and the guide, lazily contented, stretched among the wind-flattened juniper, pointed to the mountains by their names.

'There is pasture,' said 'Aziz; or 'Here is water'. 'There you will find ibex in winter', or 'There is the pass to Talaghan'.

The long saddles and sharp ridges, the black gorges and far vaporous snows began to group themselves in friendly lines.

We returned in the afternoon to Garmrud and rested, and were treated like heroes by the village, who do not often climb to Nevisar Shah.

Towards sunset I wandered out along the bank of the stream, and looked back at the cliff and the climbing houses against it, and wondered how the Mongols got into the valley, which is north of and off the usual route from Bokhara and Khorasan – the great route which saw the flight and death of Darius and the march of Alexander's men. Until the sixteenth century, when Shah Abbas built the causeway along the Caspian shore, the region between the sea and the great road must have been almost impossible for any army. Only a native and popular leader, wishing to cross north Persia unperceived, might use it and – like Bahram Gur with the White Huns – fall like a thunderbolt on the enemy from behind the screen of the Elburz.

This valley with its great walls should have been impregnable: north of it, over the passes, the country was so indeed. There, among forests and lagoons, the fleeing remnants of Persia found refuge from the Tatar hordes. When Hulagu's armies came from the east, they may have taken the Tundurkhan pass from Talaghan and forced their way through the ravine or over the shoulder of Salambar. It was not the first Mongol effort against Alamut, and there must have been those there who knew the ways.

While I loitered, considering these matters, an old man greeted me, who was cutting hay in his meadow by the stream. He strolled up with his sickle in his hand, to talk about the crops and the view. Then who should appear, as it were out of the ground to disturb the evening quiet, but the Bakhtiari of the pencil; insinuating as ever, with his air of superior information, he began to tell me of the castle in the hills, 'up there, impossible to reach'; he waved a vague arm.

In the old man's eyes, surrounded by innumerable folds and wrinkles, there passed a little twinkle of a smile; it never reached his lips; it was like a far flicker of faint summer lightning scarcely seen; but it was extraordinarily friendly.

'She has been to the castle this morning,' he said gravely. The interfering stranger was put in his place; and feeling it in some subtle way, took his departure and left us to stroll home through the shadows and the twilight peace.

In the evening we sat once more over glasses of tea and discussed the names and the passes of the hills. It was my last night in the valley of Alamut. Next day, beneath its high overhanging walls, we climbed out of the Assassins' country, over the pass, into the legendary forests of Mazanderan and down to the Caspian shore.

IV

The Assassins' Castle of Lamiasar

When Hulagu the Tartar devastated the Middle East in A.D. 1256 he took and destroyed among others fifty or more castles of the Assassins. Of all these strongholds, which one hears of over the north of Persia from the borders of Khorasan to those of Arabian Iraq, only two are mentioned as having put up any long resistance. These are Girdkuh and Lamiasar, of which the sites have hitherto been unknown. They held out for six months, long after the last Lord of Alamut had been taken away a captive and murdered in the hills by his enemies, and long after the Rock of Alamut itself had, against its will, been forced by its own master to surrender. Lamiasar and Girdkuh held out, and the story goes that, as far as Girdkuh is concerned, it could have resisted even longer, but was forced to capitulate owing to a shortage not of food or water, but of clothes.

The Mongols were not a mere horde without engines of war. They carried out their sieges in a scientific manner, with Chinese engineers, and every appliance, and with special auxiliary troops familiar with countries unknown to themselves. The places that could stand so long against them must have been particularly formidable. There are not many clues to their whereabouts, except that Girdkuh is mentioned by both Yaqut and Mustawfi as being visible and about a day's journey from Damghan. Lamiasar is only

known before its final siege and fall as having been captured for
the Assassins in the year A.H. 495 (A.D. 1083) by Kiya Buzurg
Umid, the vizier and successor of the first Old Man of the
Mountains. He was a native of Rudbar, the mountain region
north of and including the Shah Rud valley from its junction with
the Qizil Uzun at Manjil to the beginning of the Alamut and
Talaghan valleys on the east. When I was in Qazvin, and a Persian
friend, knowing my interest in castles, told me of an old ruin
called Lamiasar, in the district of Rudbar, I was therefore very
much interested, and though I had nothing but the name to go by
in a country of about 10,000 inhabitants, and though it is very
malarious there in summer, I decided to cross the ridge from
Qazvin and to explore.

I went north to Rashtegan and had lunch there in the heat of
the morning under plane trees and willows by a shrivelled summer
stream. It was the beginning of August. The only flowers left were
mint and willowherb, michaelmas daisies, and a small pink stock
growing round the water. The corn was out on numerous threshing-floors terraced up at one end of the village: its yellow heaps
stood against the mountain background, fine in a barren way,
where the northern passes climb across the ridge. In the foreground in the sun old men and boys drove black oxen slowly
round in a circle, dragging clumsy rollers with wooden spikes to
tread out the corn; while in another place the young men were
busy with the winnowing; the chopped straw, as they tossed it up
on forks, hung like dust in the air.

The party consisted of Ismail, myself, and two mules. My own
man, 'Aziz, was kept in his village in the Alamut valley by the
illness of his small son, and when at last my message penetrated to
him, after I had been chafing in Qazvin for a week, he hastened to
send for his mules, who were enjoying their yearly holiday of

pasture somewhere a day's journey into the hills, and dispatched them to me together with his servant Ismail. Ismail looked like a convict: he had one of those heads flattened at the back, and his limbs, as they slouched along, seemed to keep together by pure accident. His clothes had the same sort of casual dilapidation; the sleeves of his tunic began half-way down his arm and ended long before his wrist; his loose blue cotton trousers were suspended by some inadequate method which demanded constant hitching up; and he was hung round with about six different straps and bags in which his amulet, his money, his knife, packman's needle, and other objects were all separately housed. He wore a battered cap with a peak. My field-glasses, slung across him jauntily, gave a last incongruous tourist touch. He was terribly stupid. His daily food, which consisted of an ancient cheese in a furry bit of goatskin round his neck, made him very trying at close quarters.

'Into the hands of God may you be entrusted,' said the waiter of the Grand Hotel, as we left Qazvin; and as I started out for the hills with Ismail as my sole companion, I felt that some such pious wish was required.

At Rashtegan we had difficulties because the patch of grass under the trees where I sat was the only village patch, and too precious for mules to eat it up. Ismail was made to tether them some way off, while a shrill woman, who had argued the point, suddenly collapsed into friendliness and, squatting down with her *samovar*, prepared to feed me with tea and eggs. She had a quick, lively face, with dancing eyes and a gaiety apparently accounted for by the non-existence of her husband.

'This,' I find noted in my diary, 'often appears to be the cause of cheerfulness among the Persian ladies.' With her was a girl of thirteen or so, a bride of one year, who told me that she spent the summer up here in a little hut of boughs to enjoy the open air away from the village. It is a charming trait in Persia that anyone you meet understands the pleasures of a picnic and will make the best of all the trees and brooks and grassy places that they have.

We rested here till the worst of the heat was over, and then climbed upward among fields where the corn was cut, stacked in round heaps with the heads towards the centre, and covered with leaves and stones against the birds. The peasants were about, gathering it in to the threshing-floors, and ready to pause and greet us as we passed. The little stream, hidden in its sunken bed by a tunnel of trees, kept on our right side, until we reached the level of Razigird, and forded it, and began to climb in a bare dull landscape streaked with strata of light-green rock and outcrops of white limestone here and there. The stream, which they had called Pile Rudkhaneh, the Big River, in the plain below, now appeared on our other side, coming out of a steep uninhabited valley with clumps of willow trees and planes but no cultivation. Here it changes its name and becomes Pas Duzd, the Track of Thieves.

A little parallel range of foothills with grassy lands behind them runs between the main range and the Qazvin plain. We looked down on these, and on the gardens of Qazvin and its minarets beyond, nearly invisible in the distance. The track to the Simiar Pass was on our right, hidden from us by the round and shapeless contours of our range. Round us were many flowers as we rose higher, dianthus and thistles of various kinds, thyme, borage, a tiny forget-me-not on a long stalk, and many others I did not know. And we met company all the way – men from the Shah Rud valley bringing loads of melons to the Qazvin market – for this is one of the lesser passes for local traffic only, and the strong mules of the more eastern tracks are here replaced by donkeys, who do the journey in a day. Laleh Chak, the name of the pass, is not marked on the map, though its height is given.

We were three hours climbing up from Rashtegan, and were disappointed at the top, for there was no forward view, but only the one behind us to which we had become accustomed over the plain. But after walking twenty minutes along the grassy level of the ridge, with its points rising in low outcrops of rock from the rounded knolls, the Shah Rud valley suddenly opens below. Its saw-edge of pinnacles runs in a long eastward line to Alamut and the high massif of Takht-i-Suleiman beyond, like lines of a fortress rising to the keep. There was no snow, for we were looking at the southern face, but a bitter wind blew down this great funnel of the hills. Opposite, rising to a gentle blue peak on the other side, lay the straight valley of Javanak, open like a map. The slopes below us were squared in cornfields; their green village patches and ravines of unseen rivers were already melting into the dimness of evening. The most noticeable thing in the landscape was its silence: immense and grey, without a voice of any kind, it lay under the falling night.

I told Ismail to make for a small wooden shanty far below which we had been told of as an inn, and to order *pilau* while I stayed to take some bearings. This took longer than I expected, and when at last I started down in the dusk I felt singularly lonely at the top of so wide a solitude. Soon I came to the first cornfields, high up and still un-harvested. Ismail and his mules had long been invisible, and my feeling of solitude was made rather more acute than before by the sight of three men with reaping-hooks leaping down the hillside to intercept me. A reaping-hook looks unpleasant in the hands of someone whose intentions one is not sure of, and the three were waiting for me in silence as I came along the path. But a Druse guide long ago taught me two things: that one should be careful to keep behind people one is doubtful of, and that one should call out one's greetings from as great a distance as possible.

'Peace be upon you,' said I. 'Is the hotel a long way off – or words to that effect.

'Upon you be peace,' they replied in chorus, and came forward in the most friendly way. The hotel, they said, only gave tea by day to the donkey men, and by night its owner went to sleep in a village much lower down. But they would take me to their own village.

'Where is that?' I asked.

'Just here,' said they, and pointed almost perpendicularly downwards to where, on a spur of our mountain, a little patch of houses and trees in a fringe of threshing-floors pushed out between two ravines. This was Mirg.

'Very well,' said I, 'but you must call Ismail.'

Ismail was now visible, a small figure far away on the curve of the next hill. The tallest of the three men put his hands to his mouth and shouted down into the dusky spaces: 'Ya Ismail, ya Ismail, heh!'

A faint voice answered.

'Take the path to the left, the left, heh.'

We waited, and a faint voice came back.

'Above the stream, the stream, heh.'

Again a reply.

'To the village, village, village, heh.'

Ismail turned his mules round.

My new friends were Kurds. The Shah of that time had settled them here about a century ago, and they had lived in Mirg ever since, still keeping their own language, though they all seemed to speak Persian, as well. Englishmen who had mapped this country years ago had stayed in their village.

'And what are *you* looking for?' they then asked, having answered my questions.

'I am looking for a ruin called Lamiasar,' said I.

'Lamiasar?' said an old man, who had just come ambling on a donkey behind us with a load of grass under one arm. 'Lamiasar is there,' and with the sickle in his other hand he pointed far away across the Shah Rud to a fold in the hills. 'You can get to it from here in one day.'

So kind is fortune if you trust her.

Rustum Khan, the owner of Mirg, was a long-faced Kurd with pleasant manners. He sat in a whitewashed room furnished with carpets and quilts and three or four chests covered with painted tin and gilt and nails studded in patterns. In the niches in the walls were lamps with glass globes, two pink and two green. Little brass trays to hand glasses of tea hung on the walls between the niches, two by two. The brass *samovar* was in a central position. All these furnishings belonged to the young wife, blonde and fresh and plump as a German, who spoke a quite incomprehensible dialect from Muhammadabad in the valley below.

It was a friendly village. There were only twenty houses. The school, for such as wished to go, was several hours away down by the river. The village itself, however, owned a bath. In winter, they told me, it is so cold that even wolves do not venture out much. Rustum Khan sits under his *kursi* burning charcoal from the Caspian Jungle, which takes four days to reach him. He was an educated man, who had spent a year in Teheran, and had been a friend of the Emir Sipahsalar at Tunakabun, the great man of these parts whose financial difficulties with the Persian government caused him to commit suicide at the age of eighty. Rustum spoke of him with affection. He also spoke pleasantly of the British who had been his guests, and told me how one of them had brought a Persian lady; but while staying at Mirg, he received a cheque from his father together with a demand for his prompt return without her, and seems to have left her in Qazvin – a proceeding which the Kurds thought amusing but very comprehensible.

They were under the impression that Arabic is the British language, and surprised when I told them that we have a language of our own.

About eleven I was able to go to bed – on the roof. All the village laid itself to rest on the roofs around, so that we lay, as it were, in one flat dormitory under the stars. Over the hills of Rudbar, Cassiopeia and the Milky Way hung below me as it seemed. I was troubled through the night by incessant snuffling and grunting close by, and thought indignantly, as I lay half awake, that there must be pigs, and that my hosts must have thought that, as a Christian, I would not mind sleeping beside them. Then I sat up to trace one very loud grunt which seemed to come from just under my head, and discovered its origin in the sleeping form of either my host or hostess, who had arranged their mattress close to my bed on the roof. The pigs in daylight turned out to be nothing but a flock of sheep penned in among the houses.

Next morning a Scotch mist hid everything. It hung in drops on the cobwebs and the brambles, and the cornstacks in the fields. It often covers the Shah Rud valley for days like a ceiling, coming up from the Caspian; one can see it from below, breaking like waves over the northern ridge. It made the earth smell deliciously as we left Mirg. With Rustum Khan as our guide, we followed a track tilted on the hillside like a sailing vessel under canvas, so that it was hard not to slip off it now and then. Rustum Khan was taking us to see the castle of Qustinlar, which is on his land. It holds a commanding position, and must have been built to guard or prevent communication with the Qazvin plain over the passes; but there is nothing left except the rudiments of an outer wall badly built of rough stones embedded in mortar, and enclosing a space about 800 by 50 feet. Having seen this, we left Rustum Khan, and came down by the cornstacks and threshing-floors of Qustin, and thence after four hours reached the rice-fields in the lowlands of the Shall Rud at Siahdasht.

The bridge of Siahdasht and that of Shireh Kuh higher up were said to be the only ones not yet washed away, and the river was too full to ford so low down. The bridge was therefore important. Rustum Khan, however, had been giving us statistics of mules and muleteers drowned with the bridges they happened to be crossing. The new one is never built till the old one is swept away, which usually happens under the weight of the last muleteer, so that the crossing of bridges towards the end is rather like musical chairs when the music may stop at any moment. When Ismail saw what he had to get over, he was nervous, for the loose poles were shaking even under my weight alone; the mules were led after, separately and very reluctant; and Ismail wiped his forehead and thanked several Imams when the strain was over.

We were now in the region of mosquitoes. They buzzed about even by day, and it was impossible to escape. One could only take quinine and hope for the best. We found a garden, a little above the rice-fields and stagnant pools, and rested there in the company of a wandering tortoise, some village women, and an inquisitive, suspicious man. The garden was dark with fruit trees and deep grass; from its shade one looked down the glittering sunlit windings of the river whose enfolding mountains, high but far apart, sank into lower and bluer distances in the west.

It is a beautiful valley, rich and open and remote, the ancient kingdom of the Daylamites, who held Rudbar as a fortress and hence descended on the townsmen of Qazvin. It now grows cotton and rice, castor oil, tobacco, and much fruit and vegetables. There is no road worth speaking of. As we rode on again in the afternoon I had to dismount for long stretches where the track, clinging to red cliffs steep to the river, and nearly washed away, was almost too narrow for the mules' feet. Then we would climb down to the water level, cross the estuary of some tributary from the north, and go for a long stretch through rice-fields or flat stony waste ground flooded in spring.

Far ahead of us we saw Shahristan Bala, the capital of the district, though only a large village in groves of walnut trees. It seemed to get no nearer as the hours passed, and I began to have difficulties with Ismail, who was tired and furious at being made to come into this hot unhealthy country. Near seven o'clock, in the sunset, we reached the *Imamzadeh* to Muhammad, one of the sons of Musa of Kadhimain. It stood on a river cliff with cornfields and half a dozen houses round it; and we decided to stay for the night, and take such hospitality as we could find.

The little *Imamzadeh* was whitewashed, and held a wide view from its flat headland. It had seats all round it made out of carved tombstones a century or two old, laid on mud ledges. As I sat there taking bearings a black scorpion came crawling from under one of them and walked off with malevolent dignity.

Through my glasses I could examine the ruins of Lamiasar, now clearly visible on a truncated hill to the north and at about one and a half hours' distance. The people knew the way up, for the big sloping space within the walls is used to feed flocks of sheep. It and the villages around belong, the peasants told me, to a Sardar who lives in Qazvin, but comes in summer to look after his cattle. Next morning we passed by his house above Shahristan, a smart country place on the way up to the castle, with wooden colonnaded portico round its yard and a decent track and avenue of poplars leading up to it.

Meanwhile we sat among the peasants in a circle round their fire, hoping to keep mosquitoes away, and distributing quinine.

A fine old man, an old Aryan with the long face and short beard of the Persepolis friezes, volunteered to lead us next morning. We left our baggage in the care of the peasants, and, taking only lunch and a *samovar* for tea, started off across red stubbly hills and little dry valleys.

The castle of Lambesar, or Lamiasar, is about two miles north of Shahristan, on the banks of the same stream, which is called the Naina Rud. The easy way is to keep up on the side of the western hill and to reach it by a neck which joins it on the north to its mountain background. We, however, were misled, and after getting involved in rice-fields of the Shahristan villages, which spread a long way northwards from the estuary of the Naina Rud, we struggled up towards the castle from a precipitous ravine, until the smooth, steep ledges became too much even for our unburdened mules, and leaving them, with the battlements looming above us, we scrambled up a slope of blackish rock where pomegranate bushes grew, to the western gate of the fortress. The walls are no longer intact on the summit of their mountain of rock; but their ruins, and the fierce and gloomy valley, are impressive as ever. Some such places Dürer etched, with no softness of vegetation anywhere around them, but high buttresses and precipices alone. The battlements of Lamiasar have crumbled, but they still dominate the landscape at a little distance as they follow in and out the contours of the truncated cone of hill and enclose a sloping surface about 1,500 feet long by 600 feet wide, where the remains of buildings are scattered.

There is not much masonry on the long western side; the natural precipice must always have been a sufficient defence in itself, and a series of small towers stood here on every out-jutting point, a bowshot one from the other. On the south and east the ramparts still exist, built of rough stones taken from the hillside, apparently at different dates, for some parts are made of much smaller stones than others. They go in and out, following the natural line of the hill with the effect of a Vauban fortification long before its time, and the attacking forces must have had their flank exposed almost at every point. On the north alone the approach is possible, for here is the neck which joins the castle to the mountain-side behind it, and here the water conduit once came down from the upper village of Viar, visible through a narrow defile of the Naina Rud. This must have been the most delicate part of the defence, though I could see no trace of any ditch or outer fortification to protect the northern gate; but the gate itself and all this part is very much obliterated, and some strong defence there must have been, since, once this height were captured, the whole of the castle enclosure sloping away from it downhill would lie at the attackers' mercy.

The southern gate, which is 500 feet lower than the other, is much better preserved. Its outer entrance faces west, then turns, with the ruins of a guardhouse on its left, north-west into the enclosure. There is a difference of about twenty feet in the level of the inner and outer gates, and their actual doorways are built of big squared stones. In the enclosure itself are the ruins of a good many buildings, some quite modern and probably left by shepherds in later times. It does not look as if the castle had ever been used again after its capture by Hulagu. There are shards of pottery by the thousand lying about on the ground, all of an early kind such as are found at Alamut also; but of the eighteenth-century ware which witnesses to the later existence of the Rock of Alamut, Lamiasar showed not a trace.

The chief building seems to have been right at the top, below the north gate. It covered a space about 100 feet by 85 feet, and there are twelve long narrow rooms facing to the east, with a tower in the south-eastern corner. The southern part of this building is the best preserved, and still has its doors with pointed arches leading from either end into a passage, and doors opening on each side into rooms 6 yards long by 2 yards wide, vaulted, with very rough windows, and with places for bolts visible in the stone. The thickness of these walls is 3 feet 10 inches. It is all very clumsy work, and part of it composed of enormous stones or, rather, boulders.

Along the outer ramparts no buildings are left standing except part of two small towers on the western side, built of much smaller stones than the keep above, and with two rounded niches and small pointed windows still left intact. The windows have no keystone, but a tongue of mortar instead, and looked to me more recent than the great blocks higher up. The general level of the ground does not seem to have altered much, for the drainage holes visible on the outer face of the rampart are still in their proper places according to the present level.

Besides the more modern buildings, there are vaulted rooms here and there half buried in the middle of the enclosure, and doubtless a very little digging would restore the original plan of the fortress. The most interesting part of it at present is its arrangements for water, which can still be clearly traced. The leat from Viar came down to the castle along the northern neck and was received into rectangular cisterns, about 6 by 2 by 2 yards deep, dug into the solid rock. I counted three of these just outside the castle walls on the north and east. In times of siege numerous other cisterns of the same kind, some finished inside with mortar and vaulted over with masonry, some merely cut into the stone, stored the water within the walls. They are scattered everywhere, and probably each dwelling had a tank of its own, like the Assassin castle of Sahyun, in Syria. In the lower part of the enclosure a stone belt which runs across from west to east contains a row of these cisterns close together, the largest one being over forty feet long. Here the rock still shows traces of a small conduit cut to run water from one cistern to the other, so that the leat, entering through the higher north wall of the castle, filled all the reservoirs as it flowed down.

This was not the only water supply. From the eastern rampart, about half-way down its length and close to where two of the outer cisterns are scooped out of flat slabs of rock beneath the wall, a covered way dropped about 900 feet down to the river. Part of it still exists: it is 3 feet wide, covered in with arched masonry, very rough, about a foot thick, and ends at the water's edge in a tower ten feet square. Both tower and passage are now filled in with earth, but no doubt they were built in rough steps, as the gradient of the hill is much too steep for a path. The people of Shahristan have a curious tradition, and call this passage the Gurg-u-Mish, or Wolf-and-Ram. The rams, they told me, were put into the tunnel with skins of water tied under their bellies; the wolves were let in behind. Terrified by the pursuing wolves, and with no escape from the narrow way, the flock rushed up the slope and provided the castle with water. But it would need the imagination of a folk-lore expert to find the origin of this remarkable tale.

A man from Shahristan, who had given us figs on the way up, came and joined us as we sat over our *samovar* in one of the half-buried, vaulted rooms. We could look out through its arched door into the hot daylight to the defile of the Naina Rud, and beyond and above to villages in two green islands on the slope, and to the stony reaches of Gavan Kuh, which lead to the Caspian.

Another man soon dropped in from nowhere at all, and, sitting down in the friendly Eastern fashion, began to give at a great rate more information than we wanted. He told us that beyond those villages, in the lonely parts of the hills, is the *Imamzadeh* of Nur-Rashid, to which people make pilgrimages. These solitary shrines, now far from any habitation, usually point to localities once much more populous than now, and they are useful guides to the wandering historian.

Very little indeed is known about this country and there are many unidentified, sites to be discovered in its recesses. The Daylamites were as strange as the Highlanders in their day to the more settled people of the plain. Their hostility, says Mustawfi, who must have heard a good deal about them, dates from those Sassanian days when Shapur had to bribe them to keep away from his city of Qazvin, which he was then beautifying. In Ommeyad times, Muhammad, the son of Hajjaj, the famous governor, marched into the hills against them. From Daylam came the Buwayid princes who ruled the Muslim East during the tenth century. Their capital was called Rudbar and the residence of the governors was called the Shahristan, and it is a reasonable conjecture that the name of Shahristan in the district of Rudbar may be the legacy of those times. I leave it to experts like Professor Minorsky to judge of these matters; but the modern Shahristan certainly holds a central position in the fertile valley, two days' journey from Qazvin, and with a great feeling of age about it and its castle.

When the Isma'ili propaganda grew powerful and the Assassins established themselves in this country, they seem to have collected the Buwayid heritage and to have carried on the old feud against the Seljuks, making use no doubt of the tenacious loyalty of the hills. While the whole of the East was being devastated under the heel of the Mongols, while the cities of Merv and Balkh, Tus and Ray and Nishapur were so soaked in blood that they have never recovered, and the desert now lies on their sown fields, the men of Rudbar still held this slanting hilltop, and looked out for months over the heads of their enemies to the walnut trees of Shahristan and the Shah Rud in its valley beyond.

We left it and rode back across the rice-fields and shallow downs to our *Imamzadeh*, and there found the headman of Shahristan and his Mirza waiting to call upon me. They were an amusing pair: one, a jovial middle-aged man of the world, rather loud in manner, and made more so in his appearance by two bright red curls sticking straight out over each ear, while the hair on the top of his head retained its natural black; together with his very up-to-date European suit and watch and chain, this made him look more rakish than he intended. The Mirza was an ascetic – one of those sad-faced Persians with tired eyes and gentle manners, pathetically thin, who spend their lives meditating inaccurately on abstruse subjects, and are roused to mild enthusiasm over beautiful and harmless things like calligraphy. Seated on the poor carpet in the hut, with the peasants at a respectful distance round, they cross-questioned me, the Squire doing the talking, but the Mirza, the Man of Learning, nodding his head over my answers and evidently giving the verdict as to whether my historical pretexts for travelling were to be taken as valid or not. The result was in my favour, and I have promised to visit the Squire of Shahristan again.

But I now had trouble with Ismail. He had taken my guide aside and privately begged him to mention no more castles, even if he knew of them, in the district of the Shah Rud and its mosqui-toes. He would find me castles higher up, said he. I naturally resented this interference, but that night, lying out in the field under my mosquito net, I began to feel very ill. Providence was on the side of Ismail; it seemed wiser to travel up towards Alamut and leave the river valley for a healthier season.

V

The Throne of Solomon

Sitt Zeinabar's Tomb

A story has it that King Solomon, having married the Queen of Sheba, could in no wise make her love him. He was old and she was young. He tried every inducement in vain, and at last he sent out the birds of the air and charged them to discover for him the coldest place in the world. Next morning at dawn all returned except the hoopoe, who remained absent all day. As the dusk was falling he too flew back and bowed before the king, and told him the cause of his delay. He had found a summit so cold that, when he alighted, his wings were frozen to the ground, and only the midday sun had been able to thaw them: and he had hastened to give the news to the king.

On the top of this mountain, Solomon built his bed, and took Belkeis the queen, and when the cold of night descended, she could not bear it, but crept into her husband's tent. In the morning, King Solomon touched the rocky slope, and a warm spring gushed out for her to bathe in. And it remains to this day.

This is the story, and the mountain is still called the Throne of Solomon, Takht-i-Suleiman, and stands south of the Caspian and north-east of Elburz, the highest Persian summit west of Demavend, and the third highest summit of Persia. As I rode down from Salambar to the sea, after visiting the Assassins' Rock of Alamut, in 1930, I saw it glistening in the solitude of its snows at the head of an unmapped valley, and I decided to climb again into these mountains and see it more closely if I could on some later day.

In August, 1931, I spent a week of discomfort among noise, dust and mosquitoes in the Qazvin hotel, waiting for my old muleteer 'Aziz to emerge from that blue skyline which hides the Assassin valleys from the plain. A message finally did materialize, brought by Ismail his servant, the most loutish, clumsy, incurably stupid type of stable-hand that Persia ever produced, whose ancient bits of cotton clothes hung about him with so accidental an air that one could not help wondering what system of relativity kept them there together at all. He, fumbling among amulets in small leather cases, produced a scrap of paper to say that 'Aziz could not leave his little sick son, but would wait for me in Alamut, whose ways I knew from the year before, and whither Ismail with his two mules would take me.

I thought I would ride up the fortress valley of the Assassins, and out at its eastern end, and make farther eastward still for the Throne of Solomon: and after that I would either descend north, into the almost completely unvisited jungle country, or keep along the watershed and examine at leisure the headwaters of the Shah Rud.

But a chance rumour postponed these plans. In the Qazvin Grand Hotel, over glasses of 'dug', or sour milk and water, after dinner, the local notables told me of Lamiasar, and of how it was one of the most important of the Assassin fortresses, and one of the only two which stood long sieges before their final destruction by the Mongol armies of Hulagu Khan. It was there, said they, somewhere in the mountains of Rudbar west of my route. Its site had never yet been identified by historians. Though the data I had to go upon was more than vague, and though the climate of the lower Shah Rud was most unhealthy at this time of the year, I then decided to search for the lost stronghold.

How, on our first evening, we opened up the mountains of Rudbar and saw Lamiasar there in the last light, faintly visible on a hill across the valley, a two days' journey away; how we reached and examined the castle, and how Ismail, terrified by the heat and sickness, tried to persuade the people of the country to conceal all further ruins so that my steps might be turned as hastily as possible back to the hills: this is another story which has nothing to do with the Throne of Solomon and which has been told in the previous chapter. But the fact that I fell ill in the valley did have an influence on my subsequent journey, and so I will begin my tale when, feeling sickness already upon me and hoping to stave it off by the delayed ascent to Alamut, I fell in with Ismail's perfidious diplomacy, renounced all further ruins in Rudbar for the time being, and started to ride eastward again along the banks of the Shah Rud.

Ismail, delighted to have been so successful, rode on the baggage mule behind me, indulging for my benefit in a sort of rhapsody on all the delights that awaited us in the hills. The path was narrow and red, eaten away at its riverside edge by floods and rains, unless it broadened out into swampy rice-fields, that quivered with mosquitoes and heat. Shut in by its mountain range from the Qazvin plain, the fertile and beautiful valley lay like a world of its own. Blue hills, ever fainter, settled to its shallow horizon on the west. Eastward, we were penetrating into the salty stretches of Rudbar on our left hand, a country uninhabited and lifeless as the moon. The Ma'dan Rud, a stream bitter as Acheron, fell before us from salt marshes through waste land. We crossed it, and came to a part of the track so narrow that Ismail had to unload the baggage and coax the mules one at a time round the corner telling them the most distressing things about their parentage, punctuated with a stick from behind. I, meanwhile, sat with my head in my hands, looked at the flooded river below, and wondered at what was going on inside me to make me feel so ill.

We saw ahead of us the first red pinnacles of the Alamut gorge, naked rock piled in chaos and rounded by weather, without a blade of grass upon it. Most of the bridges were washed away, but we found one, sagging in the middle but still fairly solid, and crossed to the south bank of the Shah Rud below a village called Kandichal.

Here there was no salt in the ground, and a kinder nature appeared; we rode along an overhanging cliff, high above the brown snow-water. But here I felt too ill to continue. We came to a small solitary corrie where a whitewashed shrine or *Imamzadeh* slept peacefully in front of a sloping field or two of corn. A brook and a few tangled fruit trees were on one side of it in a hollow. A grey-bearded priest, dressed in blue peasant garb and black skull cap, gave permission to stay; and Ismail put up my bed in the open, under a pear and *sanjid* tree overgrown with vines near the brook.

For nearly a week I lay there, not expecting to recover, and gazed through empty days at the barren Rudbar hills across the river, where shadows of the clouds threw patterns, the only moving things in that silent land. To look on its nakedness was in itself a preparation for the greater nakedness of death, so that gradually the mind was calmed of fear and filled with austerity and peace.

I lived on white of egg and sour milk, and had barley cooked in my water so that the taste might tell me if it were boiled, since the little stream running from the village on the hill was probably not as pure as it looked. It was an incredible effort to organize oneself for illness with only Ismail to rely on and the women of Kandichal, whose dialect was incomprehensible. One of them, called Zora, used to look after me for fourpence a day. With her rags, which hung in strips about her, she had the most beautiful and saddest face I have ever seen. She would sit on the grass by my bedside with her knees drawn up, silent by the hour, looking out with her heavy-lidded eyes to the valley below and the far slopes where the shadows travelled, like some saint whose Eternity is darkened by the remote voice of sorrow in the world. I used to wonder what she thought, but was too weak to ask, and slipped from coma to coma, waking to see rows of women squatting round my bed with their children in their arms, hopeful of quinine.

The whole Shah Rud valley is riddled with malaria and desperately poor, with no doctor. Even soap was an unknown luxury. A man of Kandichal once brought a wife from Qazvin, who remained a year before she fled back to civilization, and left a memory of soap as one among the marvels of her trousseau. But the women brought me eggs and curds in blue bowls from Hamadan to pay for my doctoring, and looked at me pityingly as they sat round in their long eastern silences. Behind us rose the mountains which cut us off from Qazvin and motor roads and posts: they were ten hours' ride away, as inaccessible as if they had been in another world, as indeed they were.

A little way off, under another patch of trees, the two mules browsed, and Ismail sat through the day smoking discontented pipes and anxious to be off. There the old Seyid used to join him, with his sickle under his arm, for it was harvest time. He would pause as he passed my bed, and with his back carefully turned out of a sense of propriety, would ask how I did and tell me that Sitt Zeinabar, the patroness of the shrine, was good for cures. He was a fine old man, descended from a venerable Seyid Tahir, and evidently much looked up to round about. Sitt Zeinabar, he said, was a daughter of the Imam Musa of Kadhimain in Iraq. I was pleased to have happened upon a female saint – so rare in these lands – and I promised her Seyid the sacrifice of a black kid if I recovered under her auspices. Her little well of water, which they called the Spring of Healing, sounded clean and pure: I made a vow to use none other for my food or drink or washing, and Zora, favourably impressed, would toil every evening across the fields with a two-handled jar, from which she poured handfuls over my face and arms, murmuring blessings in her unknown speech.

As the dusk fell, the old priest would come in from his harvests, lay down his sickle, and sit and smoke a pipe beside Ismail, while he told of his difficulties with his flock – how they had tried to take this land away from him, and Sitt Zeinabar had punished them, sending the Shah Rud down in flood for two successive years, so that their low-lying rice-fields were carried away – until they repented and gave him back his land. As it grew dark, he would get up to light his little oil wick in the shrine, which always burned the whole night through, and would borrow my matches for the purpose in the place of his flint.

By the third day I was no better, and my heart began to give trouble. I decided to send Ismail and one of the mules across the mountain range to get a prescription from some doctor in Qazvin. This he did, and came back on the afternoon of the next day with a bottle of digitalis and a letter in good English from some unknown well-wisher who 'hoped that I now realized the gravity of my situation and would abandon this foolish idea of wandering unprotected over Persia.' I had, as a matter of fact, very nearly abandoned any idea of wandering altogether, and was envisaging eternity under the shadow of Sitt Zeinabar's tomb. But on the fifth day my temperature dropped, the pain ceased: I had long ago abandoned the thought of King Solomon's Throne; but I thought I could now make shift to be carried over the mountain range and find a car next evening to take me to a Teheran hospital.

In spite of myriads of mosquitoes I slept peacefully that night, soothed by the fact of having been able to decide on something. I woke now and then, and looked at Cassiopeia between the pear leaves and the vine, and finally roused myself in the gentle light of the dawn because Ismail was already packing the saddle-bags. He made a smooth platform on the mule's back, and spread my quilt on top of the luggage so that I could ride half reclining. A few early reapers and Zora and the old Seyid came to wish us good-bye. And then in the morning light I looked up at the mountains. I had not been able to see them all the days of my illness: and now they appeared beyond Alamut in the east as a vision ethereal and clean. If only I could get up among them, I thought, in the good hill air away from these mosquitoes, I would get well. Suddenly I decided not to make for hospital, but to trust myself to the hills and try to reach Solomon's Throne after all. I was already mounted by this time; all Ismail had to do was to turn the mules round and start in the opposite direction.

A Doctor in Alamut

When I reached Alamut the year before the stream was in flood, and we penetrated into the valley by a mule track above the cliff and defile of Shirkuh. This was now beyond my strength and was luckily not necessary. It was August, and the water low enough for fording, so that we could follow zig-zagging from bank to bank the defile through which the Alamut River pours itself into the Shah Rud.

Cliffs pile themselves on either hand and make a cool winding passage hardly touched by the sun. On the left, red precipices such as I had looked on through my illness; on the right, black and grey granite where the mass of Shirkuh, or Bidalan, as this part of the promontory is called, tumbles in stony ribs hundreds of feet to the water. Somewhere at the top is the Assassin castle of Durovon.

But I had enough to do without thinking of Assassins. Even on the level ground it took us three hours to reach the far side of the defile from Kandichal, and when we had done so, I lay on my quilt, injected camphor to steady my troublesome heart, and fed myself on white of egg and brandy, the only food I dared risk. We were in the last of the shadow cast by the defile, where it was filled with the pleasantness of running water that travelled there like light. The boulders by the river were covered with mauve flowers belonging to some creeping plant, and in the damper crevices a scented, milky-leaved shrub about five feet high, with bell clusters of pink flowers veined with red, swayed in the breeze of the river, and filled the place with a secret loveliness.

Having rested here, we rode for another two hours along the first hot stretch of the Alamut valley until the open lands of Shahrak appeared, green with walnuts and poplars and meadows. Under the shadow of trees, people were harvesting. The black oxen trod in a slow circle round heaps of corn, pressing out the grain with heavy wooden rollers.

'The years, like great black oxen, tread the world.'

At a little distance, where the young men worked with forks, hillocks of chaff were rising, tossed and carried to one side by the wind as the heavier grain dropped down.

We dismounted and I lay under the walnut trees in the grass.

Here, too, as at Sitt Zeinabar, I found myself under female juris-diction, for the squire of Shahrak is a woman, though possibly not a saint. One of the villagers soon came to ask me to call on her; but this I was unable to do, and lay with closed eyes while the hill-women gathered round, their bright clothes and air of prosperity noticeable in comparison to the poverty outside the valley, a thing I remembered observing the year before. They were full of pity, and sat fanning the flies from my face, while a young girl, seizing my head in her two palms, pressed the temples gently and firmly, with a slowly increasing pressure, amazingly restful, that seemed to transfer her youthful strength to me.

We left again at three-thirty, hoping to reach the head of the valley and 'Aziz my guide before nightfall, in a district free of mosquitoes. It was not to be, however. The hot sandstone reaches were almost unbearable in the afternoon. I was tortured with thirst. Water seemed to draw me as if I were bewitched: I thought of Ulysses and the Sirens: it was all I could do not to slide down and lie in the streams as we waded through them. Towards five o'clock we saw the trees of the village of Shutur Khan appearing round a bend, and I decided to stop there with my friends of last year, and go no farther that night.

The first man to greet us was the owner of a little melon patch outside the village. From his small platform, a thing perched on four poles to be out of reach of mosquitoes (a fond idea), he came running to welcome us.

They were all expecting me, said he. We turned the corner, and saw the Assassin fortress, the Rock of Alamut, in the sunset, shining from its northern valley, and the Squire of Shutur Khan, owner of the Rock, standing with all his family to greet me on his doorstep.

All were very kind, and nothing had changed from the year before, except that the baby had died and a new one was coming, and the pretty daughter whose husband had deserted her was wasting away with a strange disease due, they said, to her having swallowed the shell of a nut by mistake. The two boys were as jolly as ever, and the wife had a new blue bow to her hair. As I crept to my bed on the terrace, she, with that Persian insight into beauty which redeems so many faults, told one of the servants to turn the brook into the little garden below, so that its murmur might soothe me through the night.

I was, as a matter of fact, too tired to sleep, and lay enjoying the quiet noise of the poplar leaves that moved one against the other in the moonlight. In spite of the long day, no pain or fever had returned. I felt wonderfully happy to be out of the deathly Shah Rud, and up again in the hills. The stillness of the mountain valley lay like an empty theatre round our village and its waters; the night was full of peace; when suddenly a new and strange crisis seized me: every ounce of life seemed to be sucked away; I was shrivelled up with a withering dryness, soon succeeded by floods of perspiration; and I knew by a slight unpleasant shiver that this must be malaria.

This added complication was the last straw, and made it impossible to leave again next morning. I lay gloomily in bed, while various village acquaintances came to greet me, among them 'Aziz, my good guide, with pleasure and concern all over his face and with the surprising news that a Persian doctor from the Caspian shore was spending a summer holiday in a village only five hours' ride away. He had not brought him because it would be so expensive, said 'Aziz. The doctor refused to ride for ten hours during his holiday for less than five tomans (10s.). But 'Health is more than gold,' said I, or words to that effect, and sent Ismail off at once to fetch him.

He returned in the dusk with a young man neatly dressed in European fashion, all but a collar and the shoes, which were white cotton Persian *givas*. He had a pleasant, big-nosed face, with one wall eye, over which a shock of hair continually came drooping, and a mouth which seemed always on the edge of a smile in some secret amusement of its own. He questioned me capably, and diagnosed malaria and dysentery; 'diseases we are used to,' he remarked.

'To-morrow, I will take you to my village, and get you well in a week,' said he, while injecting camphor, emetine, and quinine in rapid succession, and in the most surprising quantities. 'Now would you like a morphia injection to make you sleep?'

His ideas on quinine ran to three times the maximum marked in my medical guide, and I thought that a similar experiment with morphia might have too permanent an effect altogether. I refused, and turned my attention to a bowl of a soup called *harira*, made of rice, almonds and milk.

'Almonds,' said the doctor, who had specially ordered this delicacy for me, 'are most excellent for dysentery. They scrub one out like soap. Pepper is good also.'

He caught a dubious look, and begged me to have confidence.

'We know more than your doctors do about these diseases,' he said again.

Supper was now brought and laid on a round mat on the floor by the head of my bed, where my host and the doctor sat down to it in the light of a small oil lamp. Having dispatched it, they settled to the business of opium, handing the pipe to and fro over a small charcoal brazier, a scene of dissipation in the flickering light that made me think of the 'Rake's Progress', which I used to wonder over at Madame Tussaud's in my childhood. Here it was all in action, so to say, and I myself, rather surprisingly, in the picture, with the opium smokers squatting at my bedside in the Assassins' valley.

'I can see that you disapprove,' said the doctor, looking up suddenly with one of his whimsical smiles. 'I disapprove myself, but I do it all the same.'

'It will make you die young,' said I.

He shrugged his shoulders with the melancholy fatalism which is all that the East promises to retain in the absence of religion.

I was so weak that next morning I could scarcely walk across the terrace to my room, and did not think myself fit to go away. To dress and pack my few things was difficult. I fainted twice on to the saddle-bags, and finally emerged for the five hours' ride feeling anything but confident. But the doctor was cheerful if I was not. He hoisted me on to my mule, my sunshade was put in my hand, the kind people of Shutur Khan waved good-bye, and I was led, drooping and passive, up the valley, which is barren and hot for some way above the village.

We crossed and kept to the southern bank of the Alamut stream, and looked at last year's path on the other side, wondering at its extreme narrowness as it clung to red, slanting cliffs. But I was unable to notice much, and lay half reclined on my jogging platform, seeing little except the doctor in the immediate foreground who, with feet dangling below his saddle and the *Pahlevi* hat at a rakish angle over a handkerchief draped against the sun, was humming Persian love songs, and swinging a stick, while the long ears of his mule bobbed up and down before him.

After about three hours we came again to green parts of the valley, and to Zavarak, its loveliest village, in the shade of trees. It is the largest village of all Alamut, and the brother of Nasir-ud-Din Shah seized on it as a royal gift, built a castle, and held it for twenty-five years, in spite of protests from the peasants who had never had an overlord since the days of the Assassins. When the late Shah was dethroned, the men of Zavarak took and razed the castle and returned to their independence. They are, as may be imagined, staunch supporters of the new *régime*.

They were all out now in the meadows, threshing and winnowing – a scene of prosperity in Arcadia.

Here they lifted me down and laid me on felt *Mazanderani* mats in a small room. They gave me glasses of tea, injected more camphor, and threw a cloth over me to keep away the flies, while the doctor chatted to the family and heard the village news. After three hours or so, we started again.

We climbed now southward, up the face of the Elburz range, which here hangs out an immense terrace, running parallel with the valley but about 1,000 feet above, and intersected at more or less regular intervals by wide, deep, and nearly perpendicular gullies. On this terrace are three villages, Painrud, Balarud, Verkh, each cut off from its neighbours by these gullies, each with the shoulders of Elburz behind it, and with Alamut and all the eastern hills, even to the Throne of Solomon himself supreme on the skyline, spread in a semicircle before it.

We climbed for one and a half hours, first zig-zagging up the wall from the Alamut valley and then making at a gentler but still very steep gradient over the stubble-fields of the shelf, till we reached Balarud, tilted towards the north among fenced gardens, with a brook running through its scattered houses, and every sort of fruit tree, walnut, cherry, apple, pear, medlar, and poplars and willows, throwing shade upon it.

'Aziz, who had abandoned his affairs in his village of Garmrud to attend to me, now spurred up his mule.

'Which house would you like?' said he.

I selected a high cottage with two rooms on the roof and open spaces on three sides of it. 'Aziz went to turn out the inhabitants.

With the unquestioning hospitality of the East, they cleared away most of their belongings in fifteen minutes, swept the reed matting on the floor with an inadequate brush of leaves, and allowed me to install myself while they settled in what looked like a hen-house down below. And while 'Aziz and Ismail busied themselves with the furnishing, I stood at the window and looked at King Solomon's Throne, its black arms high and sharp in the distant sky, but nearer than I had ever thought again to see it.

Life in the Village

Here I spent a week convalescing.

I had a good room, with two doors and a window, and little niches scooped all round it in the mud and straw walls. The ceiling was made of poplar trunks, with other logs crosswise above them, and above these a layer of thorns to support the mud of the roof. On the reed mats of the floor they laid felt *Mazanderani* rugs in brown, red, blue and grey patterns. The niches in the walls had garlands of dried roses hung above them. They were also decorated with embroidered mats to which the usual absence of soap in the village had long ago given a dingy colour. There was a photograph on the wall. These efforts at European elegance came from the fact that the two sons-in-law keep an eating-house at Shahsavar on the coast in winter, leaving their wives and an old mother at Balarud. In one corner of all this luxury I erected my bed, behind whose mosquito net I could withdraw when the village circle squatting on the floor, or 'Aziz and his little son noisily eating their midday meal near the door, became too much for me.

The doctor visited me two or three times a day to inject quinine. A hundred grains daily for three days definitely frightened away the malaria. He would then sit and chat over his opium, holding a glowing charcoal delicately with a pair of small brass tongs to the hole in the porcelain pipe where the brown paste is pressed down to bubble and liquefy, with the most nauseating smell. When the opium failed to console, a pocket flask of *arak* was propped up in front of the doctor. Loneliness, which strains all but the strongest natures, was slowly demoralizing this amiable young man: he was going to seed merely from the want of someone of his own kind to talk to. He had taken a degree in Teheran, and now spent his life on the Caspian shore, dividing himself between typhoid, dysentery and malaria in a region so deadly that Lord Curzon declared: 'There is not in the same parallel of latitude a more unhealthy strip of country in the world,' and Sir John Chardin relates that when a governor was sent there by Shah Abbas, the courtiers would ask: 'Has he killed or robbed anybody, that he is sent Governor of Gilan?'

The doctor's baby girl, who was teething, had begun to fade away in that damp heat, and this was the cause that brought him to his mother's village in the mountains for the first time since his student days, at so providential a moment.

I was not the first English citizen he had rescued. A young man travelling to buy silks along the Caspian had been caught by illness years ago and fled like me for refuge to the hills. There in a village of the jungle my doctor found him, delirious with typhoid, unable to say a word to his Persian servant, and weeping quietly into his pillow – a proceeding which under the circumstances anyone who has ever been in such a predicament may understand. He was still strong enough to fight violently when put into a cold bath, and eventually recovered.

'The truth is,' said the doctor, 'that we know more about these illnesses than you do, for we deal with nothing else all our lives.'

He had many difficulties to struggle against, the first being the complication and cost of getting stores from Europe, and the second the backwardness of the people. My friend, the squire of Shutur Khan, who spends his winters in the enlightenment of Qazvin city and ought to know better, refused the chance of saving his dying daughter when the doctor came, because she could on no account be seen by so improper a creature as a man: all that he had been allowed to do was to send her a dose of Epsom salts by her father. As for the village people, they usually brought their cases in the last and hopeless stages. And his rates were not exorbitant, even for these poor folk. When I left, after a week of constant injections and care of every kind, and – with strenuous protests from 'Aziz – offered him twenty shillings, he could hardly be prevailed upon to accept so large a sum.

These days were very pleasant in the village of Balarud. It was pleasant to think that we were not marked on any map; that, so far as the great world went, we were non-existent; and yet here we were, harvesting our corn, living and dying and marrying as busily as elsewhere. We could look across to right and left to the villages of Verkh and Painrud, apparently quite near, but in reality separated from us by the deep canyons on either hand; and across the drop of the Alamut valley we could look out to the Rock of the Assassins and the hills of Haudegan and Syalan, and the fair uplifted line of the Throne of Solomon, our eventual goal: and watch how on their flanks and buttresses the hours of the day were marked in sun and shadow.

At the end of the village, on a sort of terrace overhanging the canyon, the business of the harvest was going on. The old men sat in the sun, guiding the spiky wooden roller round over the corn. Great yellow heaps and humped black oxen stood out against empty spaces of valley far below. Above us, where the rocks of

Siahsang already belong to Elburz, a little triangle of dirty snow showed the birthplace of the torrent in the gully.

Looking down into the gully, I could see a kite flying surprisingly small in its deceptive depth. A very steep path descended, and there was a little mill by a trickle of water in the bottom, where the village ground its corn. An ibex last spring, shot at the canyon's lip, fell straight to the water's edge, so steep was the slope. Here at the top, when the rains came and washed the earth away, graves had been laid bare with ancient bronzes inside them. The place had probably been inhabited for innumerable centuries, and still lives its life very much as it always has done since the beginning. Its little mosque has a wooden colonnade before it: the pillars, roughly carved, are designed somewhat like the stone pillars of Persepolis, with flattened double capitals one above the other, and bear out the theory that the particular architecture of the Achæmenian kings came to Persia from the wooden houses of Mazanderan.

'Why do you not plough more land?' I asked the villagers, for about a third of the area of the shelf is never cultivated.

'We have enough corn as it is,' said they.

'But you could sell what is left over.'

'To whom could we sell? All the villages of Alamut have corn enough for themselves.'

'You could sell it in Qazvin or on the coast.'

'We have never sold corn,' said they.

They sell their surplus walnuts, and so buy tea, sugar, paraffin, and the few oddments which the village is unable to provide of itself. Three-quarters of all the produce belongs to the Arbab, the owner of the village; the remaining quarter goes to the peasant. On the hard ground in front of their doors the women weave rugs, drawing the thread over two poles, and using a kind of steel hand to bang the warp into place. They either keep them for furnishing, or sell them for ten tomans or so after a month's labour upon them. The felt rugs, made of wool, soap, and water, kneaded together and rolled over and over on the floor until it becomes the right shape and consistency, are much cheaper: I bought one for six shillings and used it for the rest of my journey.

On the second day of my stay the owner of the village came with the doctor to see me. He was an officer stationed in Tabriz, a very trim good-looking man in gaiters and khaki, with a gold tooth and pleasant manners, and many apologies for the simplicity of his village, together with a pride in it which came out as soon as I told him how much I liked its high air and quietness. We would shoot ibex as soon as I was stronger, said he.

He was staying in the place to arrange his daughter's wedding, and as soon as I was able to negotiate the steep hillside, I climbed to the other end of the village and called both on him and on the doctor's wife. The latter was a pretty woman neatly dressed in the city fashion, with a white veil pinned under her chin, and evidently on very good terms with her young husband. Two ragged but healthy boys, Gustarz and Darius, were running about, and the baby Raushana, or Roxana (after the Persian wife of Alexander), whose teething had so providentially brought the party up here, was gurgling on her father's knee while, as best he could, he pounded medicines for me in a mortar on the floor, and told me that Alexander the Great had been a Persian.

The other household was not nearly so pleasant, for the Arbab had no wish to show me his daughter, of whom he was ashamed, and she herself shared the feeling so thoroughly that she could hardly be induced to speak at all. Her father had never seen her or troubled about her since he departed in her infancy, collected another wife somewhere else, and left his village *ménage* to grow up among the peasants. He was now going to settle her with some farmer, and that would be the end of his responsibilities. Agreeable as his manners were, he was no better than most of the absentee Persian landlords: a thin smattering of civilization, sufficient to make them despise the country things from which they draw their income, and a complete unconsciousness of the fact that some duties might be attached to their position, make a type such as one recognizes in French memoirs of the eighteenth century. Meeting it in the flesh, one realizes what ideas could rouse a revolution in 1789.

I found this state of things only where the head of the village was 'civilized' and lived in a city; in the more primitive places, where he stayed on his land and was one among the other farmers, there seemed to be complete contentment all round.

Day by day I grew stronger in that good air. Day after day I strolled out in the morning and looked across to the mountains, where the Caspian sea cloud, drifting up to the watershed from the north, poured itself like a wave over the edge of our valley, to be dried away and melt in our hot sun.

My doctor's doses of quinine were now reduced from 100 grains to fifty a day, and I could walk about without resting at every other step. 'Aziz was anxious to be off. I nearly lost him, for he was wanted by government to answer for a carpet which he was said to have bought in Qazvin: to buy a carpet for someone else turns you into a merchant liable to taxes – the charge must be disproved. But I was not going to let 'Aziz out of my sight, and I marooned in the Assassins' valley. Government could wait; they could not get at us anyway until we emerged into more accessible country; and meanwhile I would pull myself together so as to make a start from Garmrud. I was the more inspired to do this as a colony of bugs had invaded my mosquito net, almost the only ones I came upon in Mazanderan.

So we left next morning. I sat in the porch of the little mosque and waited for my mules. The Throne of Solomon shone faintly, like a transparent flame in the white summer sky. 'Aziz and his small son had gone ahead to prepare the welcome in Garmrud, and Ismail was to take me across the valley to see an old castle on our way.

'Do not forget me,' said the doctor, as he came to see us off. 'We shall never meet again.' He waved his hand with my clock in it, which I had left as a legacy, and watched us as we jingled down over the stubble.

Three Weddings

We climbed from our shelf down to the Alamut by Zavarak, rested a minute at the house under the trees, and then made straight up the other side of the valley towards a little village called Ilan, where an Assassin tower was said to guard the way from Syalan and the Caspian.

The tracks from the old stronghold of Alamut go by Atun and Ilan, over many Sialan passes, down on to the Do and Seh Hizar Rivers in the north. It is natural that there should have been fortifications to overlook them, and it is not the existence so much as the character of the ruin of Ilan that is unexpected. The place is on the very top of an immense boulder about 100 feet high, and steep on every side as a 'gendarme' in the Alps. It is made of a sort of pudding stone, and has rolled down in a desolate wilderness of rocks of the same kind where, as one descends, one may think of Dante climbing from one infernal circle to the other. In the over-hanging pock-marked cliffs wild bees have made their nests; I tried some of their honey at the end of a stick, and thought it sweeter than any honey I had ever tasted.

An old man watching his goats on the hillside above consented to guide us, and we were soon joined by villagers from Ilan, who showed us a narrow ledge which just gave foothold to creep round the edge of the boulder and led to a crack where we could lever ourselves up with both arms against the sides. A last steep bit of pudding stone destroyed Ismail's morale completely. At the top of all this inaccessibility are the remains of five small compartments cut in the stone itself, with a water-tank about 3 by 12 feet, evidently cut out by hand below: no trace of mortar, no shards of pottery, nor any sign of habitation. It must have been a look-out and nothing more, and the village of Ilan, a poor place with but few scanty trees, is visible in a triangle of the landscape to the north.

Disappointed and very exhausted, I came away and returned down red ridges to Zavarak, and in the late afternoon started up the valley track of last year, through green glens with fruit trees and mistletoe, the river on our right hand, and on our left the precipitous sides of Nevisar Shah. In the dusk we came to Garmrud, which leans against the cliffs that close the valley.

'Aziz's wife was out to meet us with many of the village women, dressed in reds and yellows, a pretty sight among the poplar trees and boulders of the stream. She ran out to hold the bridle rein, and led me in triumph, while the people on the roofs of their houses bade me welcome. There was a general air of holiday, for three weddings were to be celebrated on the morrow, one being, so to say, an international affair between our village and that of Pichiban on the way to the pass.

Under these circumstances, the Throne of Solomon must again wait for nothing would drag 'Aziz away before the festivities.

'Aziz's wife was as pretty as ever, but disunion now rent the little household. 'Aziz had married again, and spent most of his time with the new bride, who lived across the stream. I will say in his defence that things were not made too pleasant for him when he did come to his old home. The eagle-faced old lady, his mother, stood up for him staunchly, but the offended wife would not hear of compromise. Like Medea, and many lesser ladies, she held up to him with tactless reiteration the mirror of the past with all his faults recorded, ever since their wedding sixteen years before, when she was fourteen and he sixteen. Even the best of men could not be expected to enjoy this, but the poor woman's grief was so deep that it was useless to point out how much worse she made the matter by railing. Love, like broken porcelain, should be wept over and buried, for nothing but a miracle will resuscitate it: but who in this world has not for some wild moments thought to recall the irrecoverable with words?

'Aziz enjoyed the situation in a shamefaced sort of way, being teased for a gay dog by his friends, and being no little in love with the new lady, a determined sort of beauty with black hair and iron muscles who could crush the little man to powder with one hand, and will no doubt be doing so one of these days.

'What do *you* feel about it?' he asked me in confidence, and looked rather glum when I remarked that, in my opinion, a man's days of peace are over when he has married two wives simultaneously.

Everyone joined in bearing with my pretty friend in the old house, listening to her outbursts with compassion, as to a regrettable but natural disease – a sad episode to be expected in woman's life of sorrow in this world. But when she became too violent in her remarks, her father, a mild old man who sat in a corner over his long pipe, would pull her up, reminding her that she had nothing out of the way to complain about, for the general opinion naturally gave 'Aziz a perfect right to a second wife if he wanted one. At such times, the only comfort one could think of was a mention of the little son, Muhammad, whom she embraced with passionate sobs, to which he submitted with an air of bored masculine condescension, remarkable and alarming in one so young.

Muhammad, at the age of eight, was just engaged to a little playmate of five, a red-haired, blue-eyed minx whom everyone spoiled, and who made the most of her short years of sovereignty as if she knew how transitory they were. Little Muhammad enjoyed the mention of his *Namzadeh*, and took great pride in her, and it was pretty to see the two children playing together, growing up in the village freedom which Persian townswomen might envy.

The next day was that of the triple wedding, and the village was already buzzing with it by the time I got up.

A visit to the bride was the first ceremony. My hostess arranged a tray for me, with nuts, raisins, *nuhud*, and a cone of sugar in the middle, to be borne ahead of us as an offering when we went to call. We followed, in our best: my hostess in a very starched chintz ballet skirt over black trousers, a yellow damask shirt, striped velvet waistcoat, and white lace coif fastened under the chin with a dangling ornament of cowrie shells. She had four bracelets and an amber necklace with silver coins, turquoises, and many little odds and ends attached to it: an amulet was fastened on her right arm. Her mother-in-law was even gayer, with a yellow silk shirt, green waistcoat with gold buttons, and one white kerchief with a red one above it tied into a point over the forehead.

We climbed up among houses till we came into a room crowded with women, in a confused twilight lighted from the middle of the ceiling by a small round hole. The dower chest was being filled: an affair of gilt and coloured tin with three locks, and all the *lathes* were helping with the packing. The whole female part of the village was passing in and out, bearing gifts, looking over the bride's trousseau, rushing into an inner room to give a hand with the *pilau*, and talking in high excited voices.

Ladies [margin handwritten annotation]

In one corner, apart from it all and completely hidden under a pale blue *chadur*, or veil, stood the bride. She stands motionless for hour after hour, while the stream of guests goes by, unable to sit down unless the chief guest asks her to do so, and taking no part in the general gaiety. I went up and lifted the veil to greet her, and was horrified to see large tears rolling down her painted cheeks. The palms of her hands and her finger-nails were dyed with henna; her hair was crimped with cheap green celluloid combs stuck into it: she wore a pink machine-embroidered shirt in atrocious taste, and a green velvet waistcoat brought specially from Qazvin; and all this splendour, covered away under the blue *chadur*, was weeping with fright and fatigue, thinking who knows what thoughts while it stood there like a veiled image at the feast. She was not to appear in public again for twenty-one days after the wedding, they told me.

The male relatives of the bride sat round the guest room floor in a quieter and more dignified manner. They were being provided with food, and I was soon taken in to join them and given bowls of soup coloured with saffron, with pieces of chicken floating about it. When this was cleared away, and when the women had also eaten in their noisier part of the establishment, we began to enjoy ourselves. Two copper trays were brought to use as drums; the bride's aunt, a lady with as many chains and bangles as an Indian idol, sat crosslegged to beat the time, and one after another the women danced to the clapping of hands. They held up a handkerchief which, at intervals, they threw to one or another of the company, who would wrap it round a piece of silver and toss it back. They danced with remarkable abandon, cracking their finger-joints and leaping into the air with both feet close together.

In the corner the bride still stood, her face completely hidden. But it was soon time for her to start: already various messengers had come to say that the young men were on their way. The friends of the bridegroom would come to fetch her: they would be repulsed three or four times, to show that there was no indecent eagerness about the affair: but finally they would succeed and escort her to the new home.

When we stepped out into the village, the young men were already galloping wildly up and down. Their mules, delighted to have no packs on their backs, and very gay under household carpets that covered them, were kicking their heels and tearing up and down the narrow beehive streets.

Two weddings were now in progress. The bride from Pichiban was expected at any moment. She had a three hours' ride down the precipitous track from Salambar to negotiate under her *chadur*. She was coming: a beating of wooden sticks and drums announced her; '*Chub chini ham Iaria. Chub chini ham Iaria,*' the boys cried, dancing round her. A vague and helpless look of discomfort made itself felt from under the *chadur* which hid the lady on her mule, all except her elastic-sided boots. Two uncles, one on each side, kept her steady on the extremely bumpy path. So, in complete blindness, the modest female is expected to venture into matrimony. The village seethed around, waiting. The lady approached, riding her mule like a galleon in a labouring sea. At a few yards from the door she was lifted down: a lighted candle was put into either hand: in front of her on trays they carried her mirror, her Quran and corn and coloured rice in little saucers, with lighted candles: these were all borne into her new home, but she herself paused on the threshold with her two lights held up in white cotton-gloved hands; and her bridegroom from the roof above took small coins and corn and coloured rice, and flung it all over her as she stood. The little boys of Garmrud were on the look out: a great scrum ensued for the pennies: the bride, unable to see what was going on and with the responsibility of the candles, which must not blow out, in her hands, swayed about, pushed hither and thither, and only sustained by the buttressing uncles: it is as well to have relatives at such moments.

With a great heave the threshold was transcended: in the shelter of her new home the lady unveiled, while the bridegroom, paying her not the slightest attention now he had got her, devoted himself to our reception.

The bridegroom also has to stand at the end of the room till one of the guests takes pity on him, and asks him to sit down. This young man, however – he was just fifteen – bore it with more cheerfulness than his fiancée. His new boots and orange tie – for he was dressed as a *Ferangi* in honour of the occasion – were sufficiently glorious in themselves to make up for any other discomforts of matrimony.

We had more dancing and a village idiot to come and tie himself into knots on the floor for our amusement; a revolting spectacle. And then, leaving the Pichiban bride to settle into her new house, we returned to our own show, which was just now reaching the dramatic moment of the meeting between bride and groom at the outskirts of the village.

After three or four attempts, and as many gallops up and down the open space by the torrent, the young men of her family had induced the bride to leave the shelter of the paternal home.

Accompanied by seven female friends the little procession encircled the village and was now coming back to it across the cornfields on the west. The bridegroom, climbing his roof, saw his bride in the distance, flung himself on to his mule, and with his friends behind him dashed to meet her. The two little cavalcades came together just where the valley slopes down into a peaceful distance of trees and river and figures threshing their harvests far away: against this background, the gay dresses of the little crowd, the coloured rugs on the mules' backs, the blue veiled figure of the bride on her steed, looked right and significant, an old ceremonial that expressed the meaning of life here where it is still so simply lived.

The bride and groom now parted again after the meeting, and came to his house by separate ways. The dower chest was brought staggering after, and various treasures such as lamps and *samovars* carried separately on people's heads. From the flat roofs under the cliff wall that closes in Garmrud from north and east, the bride's new neighbours gathered to welcome her, and joined in the *Hymen io-Hymenee*, or its Persian equivalent. Here she came to live her new life – to be a part of the village in a sense which we who make so much to do over the community and our share in it – but can leave it whenever we wish – may hardly conceive.

The village in these remote mountains is the one unit by which all else is measured, the censor from whom no one who belongs to it will ever escape. It is the focus for all loyalty, the standard for all judgment. You are happy or unhappy, according to what the village thinks of you: and even your virtue is practised chiefly because the village expects it. A week or two later I came to one of these little communities and enquired for some potatoes; the man I asked shrugged his shoulders.

THE VALLEYS OF THE ASSASSINS

'We do not grow potatoes,' said he. He pointed to the next group of houses, scarce a mile away. 'They grow them there,' he added: 'but our village has never grown them. It is not our custom.'

In the face of this innate conservative instinct of the human animal, the force that yet makes us do new things in spite of all is very amazing, an energy for exploration whose power must truly be incalculable when we consider what a mass of inertia it is always attacking. And let us not think too strangely of the village where potatoes were not grown. Any civilized British community would provide half a dozen things and more that are either 'done' or 'not done' with just so small a show of reason.

The day after the wedding is devoted to a feast, and every guest brings an offering of cash and presents it when he sits down to the *pilau*. I, however, was growing more and more impatient for my mountains. I presented my contribution on the day of the wedding itself, and decided to start next morning for the Salambar, in spite of 'Aziz's reluctance, torn from the arms of his bride. I was afraid that, if once I allowed him to settle down, he would never be induced to start at all.

He had now got his servant from the year before, Hujjat Allah, The Refuge of Allah, a tall, handsome, simple creature who would walk with the mule's halter in his hand from 3 a.m. to midnight, and still be ready to perform every sort of service. 'Aziz gave him eighty shillings a year and his food, and treated him like an equal, for he was a distant cousin. And during nearly a month which I now spent with these two, I never had a word of complaint to make to either of them.

We had decided – but we did not get away till eight-thirty next morning, and then it was by a great effort, and half the forgotten necessities for our journey were carried along after us by panting relatives, and slung about the packs as we moved along.

'Keep him away a long time,' 'Aziz's wife murmured as she said good-bye. 'I do not want to see him back at that house across the river.'

The Master of Flocks

Through the eastern defile of the Assassins' valley, under the precipice of Nevisar Shah, we left the river track and began to climb as we had done the year before for the Salambar Pass. It is steeper than the way to the Hornli hut from Zermatt, a wild granite country. There were fewer people than the year before, for spring and autumn are the busy times over the Caspian passes, and this was August 23. Fewer flowers too: but we came, nevertheless, to borage and many sorts of dianthus, mallows, jasmine, mignonette, a scented pink thistle, and a shrub covered with white and faint pink bracts like sunlit snow, *Atraphaxis spinosa*. As I rode under a waterfall, about 8,000 feet up by my aneroid, I saw *Gentiana septemfida* in the damp earth, and felt a sudden gladness, as over a meeting with friends in a strange land.

At a small *chaikhana*, a low hut with brushwood roof and long earthen hearth on which one sat, we rested, and discovered that in the agitation of good-byes someone had forgotten to shoe the mules. The Refuge of Allah now proceeded to do so with shoes which the *chaikhana* kept ready suspended from the roof by a string and with a crooked nail or two which he produced like a conjurer from somewhere in his shirt.

We sat in the hut and drank tea, and listened to the gipsy-eyed housewife, who had made the pilgrimage to Meshed in Khorasan last year with 'Aziz's mother. Her husband was still down at the wedding in Garmrud, so that we were first to tell the news about it.

An hour after noon we came to the huts of Pichiban. We were on the shelf which lies north of the upper Alamut valley, and were climbing the watershed of which Solomon's Throne is the culminating point. Here was undulating pasture with brooks tunnelling through it, and damp grass and gentians at their edge. The mass of Elburz across the valley seemed smaller now than under its winter snows, but a tiny semiglacier still hung in each of its two pockets. On Mount Sāt, to the east of it, snow still lay. A line of white strata running in a jagged zig-zag across the uninhabited eastern landscape is tailed Abraham's Path, where, travelling quite unhistorically with his ewes before him, their milky dripping udders are said to have left this enduring sign.

Here the air was thin, the distances were clearer: we were truly in the hills at last.

In a hollow strewn with boulders, where two or three springs bubbled out of the ground, we found a master of flocks and his people, living in summer huts whose low roofs were made of poplars from Narmirud in the valley below, covered with faggots and turf, and whose wall was the hillside itself, which pushed thick shelves of rock into the rooms. Three walls of stones loosely piled were built out to make each dwelling: a boulder made the table, a bit of flat earth the hearth: and little stone pens surrounded the huts, filled with trodden sheep dung whose acrid smell, mingled with that of smoke from household fires, comes not unpleasantly to the nostril of a mountaineer.

These people lived at Verkh through the winter, and on the slopes of Chala in the spring. Here to their summer pastures they brought only the bare necessities of life, and chief among them the tall four-handled jars of earthenware in which milk, gently tilted from side to side, is turned with time and patience into butter. 'Dug', or curds, were drying in sacks on the roofs, which, being not more than about four feet off the ground, were used as tables from the outside. Dogs and children and cooking-pots surrounded the little camp, where everyone stopped, their various activities suspended, to look with suspicious surprise at our approach.

While 'Aziz fulfilled one of his most important unofficial duties, which was that of explaining me to the inhabitants as we went along, I sat by the hearth in the chief hut and enjoyed the play of light from the door on four jars which nearly filled the interior against a cavern-like background. A cradle took up what space was left over, and in it a wizened baby doomed to die was being fed on milk and *chupattis*, a sodden diet which must account for tens of thousands of infantile deaths every year. In the warmth of the fire the slabs of hillside which formed the inner wall were completely blackened by flies, petrified in an innocuous coma.

Only the Alpine air can make light of these discomforts. By five-thirty I was glad of my coat; the sun rays had lost their power and in the keen evening one seemed to breathe health and strength with the mountain coldness. Out in the sunset the homing flocks poured like honey down the hillside with their shepherds behind them; beyond the cries and greetings, the barking and noises of the camp, lay the silence of uninhabited mountains, a high and lonely peace.

The master of flocks and 'Aziz had a lot to say to each other, being old friends. The former was a wealthy man, with a habit of authority no doubt fostered by three wives, and he apologized for the simplicity of his mountain life, passing it over lightly, as a man of breeding.

I soon left them to their gossip, and found my way into one of the little pens, where my bed was put up in the moonlight. Elburz, under the pale spaces of the sky, stood in majestic folds, as if wrapped in some royal garment of light: the moon swam above, barely higher than our high sleeping-place she seemed. When I awoke, some hours later, she looked scarcely to have moved in those distances of sky. I was roused by a large black figure snuffling close to my pillow, moving about among my soap and toilet things; for a paralysed moment I thought it human. I nerved myself to look, and saw a black calf, very much interested in my belongings, and full of indignant snortings when I shooed it out.

By eight-thirty next morning we reached the Salambar. There, one and a half hours from Pichiban, one tops the skyline, leaves the red southern world and looks on the northern green. I walked up so as to pick flowers and accustom my weakened muscles to exercise, but there were few plants on this side, as the water comes to the surface lower down near Pichiban, and the dryness produced little but abundant spiky cushions with pink blossoms, dry and crackly as paper. At the top of the pass, the *chaikhana*, still in use the year before, was now deserted and ruined, the little domes of its roof broken down by the winter's weight of snow.

There in sunlit solitude, with the Seh Hizar valley below winding to the Caspian jungle and with Elburz at our back, I sat for three hours taking compass bearings and trying to make out heights with an Abney level, which of all small instruments must be the most exasperating and captious. To propose to a wayward beauty can be as nothing compared with the difficulty of keeping the spirit-level for one second in the place where it is wanted; the slightest suspicion of a quiver sends the elusive one out of sight altogether or down with a bump groundwards: and who can keep a steady hand on Persian passes buffeted by winds?

'Spite of the world, the flesh, the Devil,
He strove to keep his spirit level.'

Many, many times have I thought of this engineering epitaph, and many, many curses have I lavished on the Abney level: nor, when I pull out my small set of instruments, do I ever regard its angular surfaces with that affection which my compass receives, whose round face, placid and reliable, is that of a friend.

While I wrote in my notebook, 'Aziz and the Refuge of Allah buried the aluminium water-bottle to the neck in lighted tussocks of thorn and boiled tea. And then I took a last look over the landscape: the Assassins' valley westward to its vaporous defile where, only ten days ago, I toiled up doubtful of living; Balarud on its ledge, like a toy far below; and, hiding the Rock of Alamut, Haudegan with a clean edge against the sky. I wondered if I should ever see them again, and did not much care: for were they not mine for ever? And then I ran down the northern slopes with 'Aziz behind me, among little springs of water, lavender-like *Nepeta*, campanulas, an aromatic sage-like plant they call genetically *Benj*, and flowerless plants of iris. I pulled one up for its roots.

'Why do you want that?' said 'Aziz, who was a snob in flowers. 'It is not a narcissus.'

And I discovered the name of the iris, which they call *Sirish*.

Still three hours down our old route to Maran, along a narrow valley walled by the Salamhar, green on its northern side. Steep fields appeared with cocks of hay made black by constant mists. The river rolled below us in a bed made by its own millenniums of effort; it dug itself a canyon, and wound like a worm in its earth hole. As we crossed high over this abyss by a tributary waterfall, I found Grass of Parnassus, another Alpine friend. The flowers here were different from those of the southern slope, and less Alpine; scabious white and blue, wormwood, vetches, and white and yellow marguerites.

At Maran the pastoral upper valleys end, and thickets with hawthorn and roses begin the Caspian jungle. The Seh Hizar flows down between wooded mountains where I had followed to the sea the year before. With the afternoon sun against us, the flat roofs and poplar trees round the village were lit by a kind of halo against dark silhouettes of promontories, tier after tier beyond them and below.

Here we left our old route, descended steeply to the ford, climbed a slope of sunlit fields facing west, and then among thickets where violet leaves and a speckly thing like foxglove brought English woods to mind, we turned a corner and saw the Darijan valley running from east to west, flat like a map in sunlight.

An old keep called Qal'a Marvan, now only a mound of stones, stands at the turn of the valley, with a view down the Seh Hizar as well as into Darijan. From here our path descended easily, and brought us in dusk across the stream to Sern (about ten houses), and in fifteen minutes or so after to Shahristan (twenty houses). Here one of the older villagers, sitting over an evening pipe on his threshold as we came riding up, asked us to halt for the night.

The Watering Resort

It does not do in this crowded world ever to suppose that one is first anywhere, and the Emir Sipahsalar of Tunakabun, who committed suicide at the age of eighty, owing to an inconvenient exhibition of royal curiosity in his financial affairs, and who used to own a shooting box beyond Darijan, is said once to have brought a party of Englishmen up this valley. Apart from this we heard that a Hungarian engineer with a Greek wife, one of twenty, who, as a direct consequence of the suicide, were plotting out and preparing to develop the region for its new master the Shah, was installed in the last village.

The people of Shahristan, however, might have been South Sea Islanders before the days of Captain Cook so little were they influenced by these contacts with civilization. They rushed to me as if I were a circus. Twenty times or more I was asked to stand up on a roof to show myself full length to new audiences. Only the Elders, ardent Shi'as with a Dervish among them, withdrew and cast self-conscious glances from a distance, ashamed to show interest in so negligible an object.

It is a remarkable thing, when one comes to consider it, that indifference should be so generally considered a sign of superiority the world over; dignity or age, it is implied, so fill the mind with matter that other people's indiscriminate affairs glide unperceived off that profound abstraction: that at any rate is the impression given not only by village *mullas*, but by ministers, bishops, dowagers and well-bred people all over the world, and the village of Shahristan was no exception, except that the assembled dignitaries found it more difficult to conceal the strain which a total absence of curiosity entails.

'Aziz was never deterred by this sort of convention, and used to come up bravely to attend to me and my wants with a respectfulness which the villagers thought more peculiar than anything else about me. He arrived presently thoroughly disgrunded, and informed me that, though chicken and eggs were to be had, they were only to be given with the one hand when money was seized with the other, a want of hospitable feeling which, as he said emphatically several times over, we had never encountered in his own valley of Alamut.

I myself thought – rightly as it proved – that civilization in the shape of the Greek wife of the Hungarian engineer must be to blame and merely said to 'Aziz with pain in my voice that this village must be very different from any other we had ever stayed in. This aspersion was received by the men in the audience with obvious shame; they would evidently have handed over hens and chickens and all if it were not for the firmness of their womenfolk, who were not going to let abstract convention endanger house-keeping. We bowed to the more resolute sex. Indeed, we did not mind paying for our food as we got it, but our nicer feelings were hurt at this lowering into the realm of commerce of what should have been left on the higher plane of gifts offered and returned. When the ladies saw with what a ready grace we parted with sixpence in exchange for a hen, they too began to feel remorse, and murmured apologies on the score of poverty.

They were indeed poor, dressed in rags, half of the mountain sort and half of the jungle. The men wore moccasins on their feet, and sheepskin caps that gave them a Struwelpeter appearance, and square capes of felt they call *shaulars*, tied in two shoulder knots or with comic stumps of dummy sleeves. In this tortoise-like casing, the Caspian rain is kept off for hours.

I longed for solitude and peace, and made the most of the recent argument and my justifiable displeasure to obtain it.

'Women,' I said, addressing the landscape in general during a pause brought about by the payment of our sixpence, 'women are ignorant creatures.'

The assembled men, delighted to see the argument shift from household economics to the so much more obvious field of masculine superiority, unanimously rushed at the ladies and shooed them with insults off the roof into their proper kitchens below.

The valley was now full of loveliness. A last faint sense of daylight lingered in its lower reaches, beyond the village houses whose flat roofs, interspersed with trees, climb one above the other up the slope. Behind the great mountain at our back the moon was rising, not visible yet, but flooding the sky with gentle waves of light ever increasing, far, far above our heads. Here was more than beauty. We were remote, as in a place closed by high barriers from the world. No map had yet printed its name for the eyes of strangers. A sense of quiet life, unchanging, centuries old and forgotten, held our pilgrim souls in its peace.

Here in the moonlight shadow of the mountain itself, I heard the legend of King Solomon and his Throne; and an alternative version which has it that the prophet, burdened with more wives than even he could stand, sent there for a different one every night, and left her in the morning, frozen to death by the mountain air. The men of Shahristan sat round me in a circle, smoking their long straight pipes and twinkling slowly over the thought of how King Solomon managed his wives; bits of wood and iron nails from his bed still lay scattered, they told me, on the mountain-top. But when it came to a closer enquiry, none, it appeared, had ever been up there except a hairy old mountaineer with wrinkled face, the village shikari for ibex, who seemed loath to describe the matter in detail, but said he would take us up either to the summit or to the pass below it.

We decided first to go up the little valley where the warm stream gushes out that was made for the Queen of Sheba, and whither people still ride a three or four days' journey from all the lands around to be healed. And from there we would climb the walls of the Throne, and perhaps its very summit, but at any rate we would cross its great buttress and make our way into an engagingly blank bit of country on its eastern side.

This great buttress wall runs unbroken and only dipping slightly from the Throne itself to a pass above the Seh Hizar which leads to Daku in the jungle, and between these two points there is only one high col a little north of the mountain, which is possible though difficult for mules. 'Aziz and The Refuge of Allah denied its existence, having no wish to go east of their own country; but one is not bred in hills for nothing, and the shikari disclosed the pass of Kalau just where I expected to find it. Here, then, after our visit to the watering resort, we would go and take the shikari to guide; and we set out again at seven next morning. In fifteen minutes we reached Darijan, the last village, which has forty houses and a *mulla*, and a bath whose little domes of mud, enlivened by flat green bottles inserted as skylights, were shining in the morning sun.

I had spoken nothing but Persian for three weeks, and I felt I could not let the chance go by of meeting another European woman, whatever my forebodings might be as to the Greco-Hungarian. So I banged on a low door in Darijan behind which they told me were the engineer and his wife: and sure enough, after a long interval, an angular, dishevelled lady appeared, so apologetic for not being up at seven in the morning that my own apologies for so early a call had no chance even to begin. She also, she said, was going to the hot springs of Ab-i-Garm, the Queen of Sheba's bath, and I promised to wait for her there.

We now rode up the valley towards Mian Rud, or the Place between Rivers, where two streams meet that encircle the western and northern flanks of Takht-i-Suleiman, and together descend as the Darijan water. Here, they say, was an old town buried, and a vague look of human handiwork still seems to lift the hollows of the ground. A little higher up, above the meeting waters, the shooting box of the dead Emir is also falling to decay, soon to add one more ruin to this cemetery of a world on which we play: its garden outlines are lost already, though a roofless line of buildings and mangers for horses still stand on a grassy knoll under the morning shadow of the mountain. An immense and solitary cherry tree was waving its leaves near-by in the draught of the valley. There was no village, but only a peasant's house, and the two streams meet below it, foaming at the foot of slopes of hay. We followed the right-hand water up a long and narrow valley, uninhabited, but visited by haymakers and shepherds, and with a hut of boughs where a hermit lives in its midst.

The water ran brown and white over rocks, and a strange crimson poppy grew in the boulders of its bed. We crossed and recrossed, while our valley, embracing the western peak of Solomon as with an arm, held on in a single groove with only one small tributary from the west. It was open and cheerful, treeless and inclined to pasture where the mountain did not press in buttresses and towers down to the water's edge. The western slope was gentler; a limestone ridge lay white against the sky, and thorn trees, well grown and spaced as in a park, showed on a nearer ridge against it. We left the torrent at last, and looked down on it in a canyon below, where it dropped in blue pools like a necklace of sapphires in the sun. And turning a corner, two hours from Darijan, we saw our watering resort before us.

Even at Balarud, and farther off still in the Shah Rud valley, I had heard of this place as a populous centre for people from all parts of the country, a sort of Karlsbad of the mountain: and though I have learned to doubt Persian description in general, I had not expected quite such an Alpine solitude as we now looked down upon. The river ran through its stony valley with not a tree to shade it; and, close above it on the slope, were two small caves fronted by a tiny enclosure of loose stones, and showing by discoloured yellow streaks which oozed from them down the face of the rock that here were the mineral springs.

Perhaps a dozen people, men and women, were in the valley, sitting on boulders while their mules wandered at will up the hillside, a row of small bells arranged, most inconveniently, one would think, round their hindquarters, so that they can be heard at night as they roam untethered near their sleeping muleteers. On the flat ground near the river bed a few large rocks had been surrounded by stones to the height of a couple of feet, as enclosures for the visitors to lodge in.

We made a tour of inspection, and having selected the most promising of these abodes, with a big boulder to shelter it from the south, we rigged up my little tent for shade, spread the quilt on the ground, and settled down to the making of tea and the discussion with our fellow-pilgrims of what the waters do to one's inside, as it might have been Aix-les-Bains or Baden.

On the whole it was a more cheerful place than these, made so by the very simplicity of things: rock and grass and air and water were all the ingredients of the landscape, so light and pure that the very thought of sickness was hard to entertain. And the people were pleasant mountain folk from Talaghan and Kalar Dasht, out for a holiday and ready to make friends with all the world. I thought I had little enough luggage with me, but when I saw how these travelled, riding two days from their houses into the mountain solitude with nothing but a little bread and cheese in a handkerchief and a *samovar* for tea, I felt ashamed of all the paraphernalia spread about me on the ground.

Here I first saw the headdress the young women wear in Kalar Dasht, a circlet made of small silver leaves sewn on to a band, with perhaps a turquoise at the centre, worn at a rakish angle over one temple under the kerchief. I bargained for one of them and had almost got it, when The Refuge of Allah, a silent but outraged witness of the negotiations, remarked that two shillings was a monstrous price for such a bauble, took it from my unwilling hands and flung it back to the lady, telling her to our mutual chagrin that the matter was closed.

By this time the sun was straight overhead; not a cranny in the valley was hidden from its rays except the small space under my tent.

Up over the brow of the hill, sitting apparently on masses of luggage and with a parasol to shade her, the Hungarian-Greek lady appeared, giving the last touch of fashion to our gathering.

'*Quelles horribles gens*,' said she, as my assembly, having got up to greet her, squatted down again at about two yards' distance. She shooed them away with her parasol. 'Madame,' said she, 'I would never have thought it possible to live in such a savage place. Every night I lie and weep.'

'Dear me,' I remarked. 'They all seem harmless enough.'

'How can one tell?' said she. 'The houses are not safe. There is a hole in every roof for light, and always I expect to see a strange man letting himself down into my room. My husband is away all day. All the time I think he has fallen over the edge. Not a path here but, if you fall off it, you are dead.'

This seemed unreasonable. Why should anyone fall off a path? But the lady hardly paused: she had so many woes to pour out.

'Nearly all our luggage,' she said, 'we lost in a torrent in the dark, coming up here through these forests. The bridge gave way and all our cognac went.'

This was, indeed, a tragedy. But why come up through the jungle in the dark?

'It was because they made us late in starting.' I could sympathize with the poor lady over that. 'You have no idea, Madame, what a terrible life it is here. The people hate us. I have grown old since I came three weeks ago.'

Her husband, it appeared, was away all day surveying. He had gone in for commerce in gramophones and, having lost his money there, now hoped to recover it by engineering for the Shah: but the royal salaries, she said, were anything but regular. The Shah intended to develop all his new estate, which stretches from the coast at Khurramabad and Shahsavar up to the watershed, over all the Seh Hizar. Shahsavar is to be the port, and the timber and mineral wealth of the mountains are all to be exploited. Rashly, as it proved, I said that I was interested in maps and would like to see those of her husband, to get some idea from him as to the heights, for my own aneroid, which only reaches 10,000 feet, was going to be useless above Mian Rud.

We now went to bathe in the green twilit cave, with 'Aziz on guard before it. The water was warm and dim, with small ferns at the edge, the cave just big enough for two people to move in comfortably, about three feet in depth. It was so pleasant, being the first real bath for three weeks, that I stayed in much too long, and felt rather ill for the rest of the day, for the water is evidently full of sulphur and iron.

The lady continued her woes through lunch and after; in the light of her fears the peace of the little valley was shattered. When the sun got low she mounted her mule and departed. She felt towards me as a sister, said she, and pressed a sheepskin waistcoat on me regardless of protest. She was going south again next day and, *Dieu merci*, would need it no more. Hardly had she rounded the corner of the valley, than the despised inhabitants returned, pulled out their bags of tobacco, filled their long pipes, and settled down for a comfortable chat.

It was getting dark much more quickly than in the open mountains of the night before. A dank feeling fell upon the air, and suddenly, noiseless and insidious, a white mist that had crept up the valley lay with its snout pushed along the river towards us. In another minute it had enveloped us, drizzling gently.

My tent is an affair made of two pieces of canvas which button together, but of which I had brought only one so as to travel more lightly. This, when erected, reached about halfway down the poles and just covered my bed, keeping off water though not dampness, and giving me a useful shelter for dressing when no other was available.

'Aziz and the Refuge now arranged it as snugly as possible for the night, while I sat with my collar turned up in the rain, wondering why on earth I was there when I had a comfortable home of my own. I remembered my godfather who, being asked by some enthusiast what his thoughts were during lonely nights in the beauty of the mountains answered: 'I usually think: Why the devil did I come?'

Presently a fire was enticed into life in our enclosure.

There was no wind, only a gentle dropping of water which fell harmlessly on the men's *shaulars*, as they moved about attending to the straying mules in the dusk. They looked scarcely human in those stiff felt things in the gathering night. Having warmed myself with hot tea I undressed quickly, put my clothes under my pillow to keep them dry, slipped into a loose fur lining and felt happy again. As for 'Aziz and the Refuge, they wrapped themselves in a *shaular* and a *Mazanderani* carpet respectively, and were asleep on the ground in no time.

The Throne of Solomon

Next morning a rim of big drops hung from the suspended edge of my tent like a fringe and, peering out from beneath it, I looked on to a grey world apparently dead. A few motionless heaps of greyness among the stones was all one saw of the visitors to the watering resort. Presently a faint stir began among them. The women, their cotton rags and ballet skirts very limp after the wet night, began to move about and seek the stream of water. A slight morning breeze brought life into the air. And when the sun rose over the mountain-side, the Caspian sea mist broke and vanished. It comes up, they told me, nearly every evening, and leaves only the actual mountain summits unsubmerged.

At seven-thirty we departed. After so many delays, we were to climb the ramparts of Solomon's Throne at last. I thought longingly, indeed, of the summit itself, and spoke of it to the shikari, who seemed much more reserved than he had been in Shahristan. The matter was left for the time being, and meanwhile we descended to Mian Rud by yesterday's track, meeting haymakers on the way under loads of thyme-scented grasses. There we left the Darijan route and turned up the other stream, which encircles the northern side of the great Throne.

Here a first hitch became manifest.

Our shikari, elated by the fact that he was being given sixpence a day and a holiday as well, had volunteered at daybreak to bring us an ibex from the hills. 'Aziz, in an access of generosity over which he did not consult me, lent him my field-glasses for the occasion, with the result that we saw no more of either him or them for the rest of the day, and soon after Mian Rud discovered that we were guideless and lost.

At first this did not matter. All we had to do was to walk up grassy slopes eastward, keeping the river in a narrow valley below us on our right, where the central pyramid of the Throne rose on the other side in massive ledges with string courses of grass here and there, black as a dungeon keep in the shadow. The difficulties began when the encircling stream turned up into the centre of things, rising through a ruinous and apparently unrideable valley towards the high summit of the Throne itself. Our path, on the other hand, such as it was, appeared to continue straight over a wall of rock some thousands of feet high which, the peasants of Mian Rud told us, formed the pass of Kalau, or Chertek as some prefer to call it from the name of the pastures at its feet.

Before we reached the point where this insoluble problem would have to be tackled, our minds were distracted by the arrival, panting behind us, of the Hungarian-Greek lady's deaf village maid, who handed me a note, evidently compiled after a heart-to-heart scene with the engineer, asking apologetically for the sheepskin that had been forced upon me the day before, and suggesting that her husband would like to see my maps.

This was impossible, for our faces were turned eastward and not to Darijan; and having signified as much to the deaf one by signs, we watched and waited while she descended to a spring near the river's edge, and brought up her mistress's and our waterbottles filled with a sparkling delicious mineral water which the Municipal Laboratoire in Paris declares in printed French and Persian to contain the following ingredients per litre:

	Silice	gr.	0·0275
	Albuine	"	0·0002
	Oxide ferr.	"	0·00628
	Soude	"	0·184
A l'etat de bicarbonate	Chaux	"	0·5064
	Magnesie	"	0·985
	Potasse	"	0·926
	Chlore	"	0·1204
	Acide sulf.	"	0·1201

This spring of water goes by the name of Shelef, and is known at Khurramabad on the coast, but is at present too inaccessible to be exploited.

We now stood on an edge and looked along the desolate valley to the peak of the Throne of Solomon. The massif we had been skirting ever since we left our camping-place at Ab-i-Garm was the most western of the three summits of which the group is composed. I think it is called the Orfan's mountain, Iatim Kuh, though I have only the shikari's word for it. The central summit, with precipitous sides and flattened top like a natural keep, recognizable from its peculiar shape far away in the Shah Rud country, now appeared between the other two over a long shoulder of snowfield, and justified by contrasting blackness its name of Siah Kaman, the Black Carder's Bow. On the left and nearer to us, the Throne itself rose to a gentle point, a pyramid shape like the Weisshorn, most beautiful of mountains, only not detached as that is from the landscape around it, since the great wall we had to climb runs up and joins it by a north-eastern spur.

The desolate valley led towards this peak, and drew its waters from the snowfield or glacier which fills the deep corrie between the Throne and the Black Carder. Though there appeared no difficulty for an able-bodied mountaineer it was a depressing sight as far as I was concerned, still weak from my illness.

It meant first a steep descent and long march up the valley, where no path appeared for a mule to follow: and then, instead of a crest, there was nothing to climb but the dreary black face of the mountain, an endless grind of scree till one comes to the actual rocky peak. Looking it over, I judged the thing to be a ten hours' effort. Mian Rud, the last place where my aneroid could prove itself useful, was 9,300 feet: the valley below us I judged to be anything over 10,000, and the Throne itself, after much weighing of evidence and very doubtfully, I estimated at about 15,300. Six thousand feet, mostly over scree, was not a thing even the most optimistic of convalescents could contemplate: I still hoped, however, that the shikari, when tired of hunting with my field-glasses, might reveal a way for mules along the valley or an alternative way round the mountain from the south-east. Meanwhile there was nothing for it but to put up the tent in a grassy corrie where a few cows wandered round an empty hut, and to admire the beauties of Nature while waiting for the shikari and his ibex.

Here we sat for a good many hours, in a place with grey boulders in long grass, and *Nepeta* flowers and iris roots about. 'Aziz, stricken with remorse over the field-glasses, would shout at intervals across the valley towards the unresponsive mass of Iatim Kuh, amid whose black precipices the oblivious shikari must, we presumed, be wandering.

As the afternoon advanced, action of some sort became imperative. To go up towards Kalau seemed better than to descend in the mere hope of an invisible path in the valley, and it would be easier to retrieve a mistake by retracing our way downhill rather than up. So we climbed the first step in the ascent of the barrier; and after an hour's struggle, so steep that the mules took it in short scrambles, scattering stones and pausing every few minutes in the obvious hope of some mulish miracle to make us change our minds, we reached another and larger corrie called Chertek, a great lap between the knees of two hills, at the head of which our barrier still towered higher than ever, red rock with a turret-like point against the sky, deceptively near and clear in the high air.

At the far end of the corrie, showing its size by their smallness, were flocks of sheep browsing on the scree or standing with their heads together in the sun. The Refuge and I went to find the shepherd, and scattered as we walked crowds of partridges with their young families, who ran about the rocks calling their liquid cry.

The shepherd was far up the hillside, but the Refuge of Allah had no thought of toiling after him. The wayfarer in Persia has every privilege; to direct him is no mere act of easy courtesy: you leave whatever you may be doing to come when he calls and tell him what he wants to know, however far off you may be at the time of asking. We were just within hailing distance, but not near enough for conversation, and the shepherd showed some natural reluctance, which outraged the Refuge of Allah. It would take him half an hour to get back to his sheep again from where we stood: after several shouted messages, however, he came towards us at last; he stepped from boulder to boulder with the easy balance of the hills. He was a young lad, in a khaki tunic and blue cotton trousers, with a shock of henna'd hair under a curly black sheep-skin cap; his eyes were green, and he held a staff in his hand. 'No mule can go along the valley down there,' said he. The only track in this region was that of Kalau, on which we were. We returned to 'Aziz, who had already unloaded the mules in a sheep-pen of loose stones, close to the corrie's edge.

It was cold after sundown with a delicious Alpine coldness, and plenty of thorny stuff to burn grew among the iris roots in the corrie. And as the two men sat over the fire, and I had already got into my sleeping-sack for warmth, 'Aziz was justified, a voice hailed in the dark, and the shikari, with field-glasses and three eggs from the farm of Mian Rud, appeared in our circle.

No ibex was slung over his shoulder, but he had been seeing them all day through the glasses, said he, 'as if one could touch them with the hand', and appeared to think that this delightful occupation should be as much a cause of joyous excitement to us as it was to him. Without wasting more words, he settled down to bread and cheese. He was a shy and simple soul – one of the few dwellers in the valley who spent the whole year there or wintered on the coast: and so he had never spoken to a European in his life, or seen one before the arrival of the Hungarian engineer. But as he found that I liked to hear about the paths and wildernesses of the hills, and saw me eat and drink like any ordinary creature, and especially now being exhilarated by the glorious day with the glasses, he became less reserved and began to talk about his hunter's stock of knowledge, more familiar with the ways of animals and storms and seasons than with those of men.

High in our corrie that night was full of peace. From behind the peak of Solomon the moonlight spread, opening like a fan, while we were held in shadow. The air was still, with the warmth of a summer night untouched by wind, cooled by the nearness of the snow and scented with hay. From the valley, through rifts in a wind that blew there, a sound of water came intermittent, puffing like a distant train. And far away through distances of moonlight we looked out upon Salambar and the Alamut mountains dissolving in dimnesses of sky.

Next morning we started early to climb the great wall, and found the sheep already out, browsing this time on the north-eastern slope, whence the shepherds shouted a greeting as we passed.

Of that climb, which lasted four and a half hours, I have only a vague distressing memory. The way soon became too steep for riding and zig-zagged fly-like with scarce a respite. The height of the pass I calculate to be about 14,000 feet, judging partly by my Abney level, partly by the lowness of Salambar far away (which is 11,290 feet, and the only altitude in this landscape marked on the

Survey of India map), and partly by the fatigue of my men, who found it hard to breathe.

I was not yet fit for any strenuous exertion under the best of circumstances, and felt the height for the first time in my life. It caused a cold clamminess at the back of my neck, and a blackness over my eyes which hid the world at intervals. The two men lifted me on to a mule whenever any slight easing of the gradient made it possible: but this route is only practicable for very lightly laden animals, and the latter part had to be walked. I crawled along, resting every fifty paces or so with a leaden feeling of nightmare upon me – and at last, after a final unspeakable bit of scree to finish off with, emerged upon the ridge.

This was the top of the great buttress, and here we stood on the threshold of our desires: we could see its broad backbone running north-westward, more or less evenly, with rounded curves like smooth waves one hiding the other. It hems in the Darijan valley and then, leaving a westward spur to run to the Seh Hizar, a long main ridge encloses Daku and the Iza Rud in unexplored jungle country to the north: this at least is what the Refuge of Allah told me, who has once been to Daku. On the south, the ridge rose to the very point of Solomon's Throne, now deceptively near, a lovely pyramid with snow on its northern face. North-east of it between us, and not so high, another peak showed, called Barir. The world lay spread around. Small, as through the wrong end of a telescope behind us, Salambar with the Alamut hills, Rudbar and Elburz; and Narghiz Kuh and Syalan, which I had looked up to from Balarud – they stood high on their own range, but far below us, washed to a gentle colour by distance. In front of us, eastward, at right angles, ran a deep valley some way off, hidden by intervening spurs of our own system: on the farther side were saw-edged ridges with wooded slopes.

'That,' said the shikari, 'is the valley of the Sardab Rud. It comes from the direction of Talaghan, out of sight there to the south across the pass of the Thousand Hollows, the Hazarchal. And it flows to the plain of Kalar Dasht, of which you see one corner there in the north-east.'

There the hills became lower and rounder, covered with forest, until the Caspian sea mist hid them. Beyond them, eastward, were other ranges, their names unknown to my companions, the mountains of Kujur. And farthest of all, incredibly high, among white cumuli of cloud, smooth and serene above all earthly visible things, shone Demavend, striped with snow, seen only for a moment.

But though there are few instants in themselves better than those when, from an escaladed ridge, one looks upon new country, the joy of complete achievement was not ours: and if this were a story with a plot instead of being merely the matter-of-fact diary it is, the Hungarian engineer would certainly figure as the villain. It was he, though we did not know it at the time, who robbed us of our triumph. He who, in the Arcadian peace of Darijan, took our shikari apart and told him that if the foreign lady climbed the Throne of Solomon where no *Ferangi* had ever been before, the whole of the government and Shah Riza himself would come along with punishments on all who helped her: he himself had not climbed – why should anyone else do so? No doubt he reasoned thus in the blackness of his soul. And our shikari said nothing, but instead of leading on from Ab-i-Garm, where an easy mule track would have led us within possible distance of the summit, he brought us here, a Peri's jump from Paradise, and showed us the obviously impossible with an air of regretful, religious resignation. We learned nothing of all this till the morning after. Takht-i-Suleiman still remains, so far as I know, for a

European climber to conquer: and I curse the engineer in my heart, wishing him that his wife may never cease from talking and his angles be perpetually inaccurate.*

Shepherds from the Jungle

On the pass we sat and enjoyed the rewards of our toil, the mules especially, whose packs were laid upon the ground. 'Aziz and The Refuge had long ago resigned themselves to my love for passes, places which they look upon as unreasonable, waterless, wind-swept, unprovided with fodder for animals, and unkind to human beings. They knew, however, that argument was useless, and settled to sleep in the shelter of the packs as best they could, while I struggled with the imaginations of my map and, reality spread for comparison before me, tried to spot out a route for my return.

The map (Survey of India, four miles to the inch) left much to be desired. The Sardab Rud valley and Hazarchal Pass were marked in a dotted red line; so was the Salambar and Seh Hizar. But between these two parallels why was Takht-i-Suleiman, the high-est object west of Demavend, left out entirely? The only moun-tains marked were in the wrong place, and after trying over and over again to induce my compass to bring them into harmony, I came sadly to the conclusion that the Indian Survey had filled this bit of country in by hearsay – a melancholy fact, since it made me uncertain of my triangulation points at starting.

---

* Since writing the above, Mr. Busk, of the British Legation in Teheran, has climbed the central peak – Siah Kaman; and discovered that it is the highest of the three, and about 15,500 feet. See his account in the *Alpine Journal*, November, 1933.

Where, too, was the blue dotted river which, said the map, flowed eastward into the Sardab Rud? There was no visible place for it in the landscape, and the shikari denied its existence positively. I had hoped to introduce the name of this river into the world of geography, so that it was extremely annoying to find it non-existent.

The wind felt as I did about my map and nearly buffeted it to pieces. It shook even the steady nerves of the compass and caused the Abney level to behave like a lunatic. How different from the sheltered peace of Mr. Reeves's study in Kensington: I sent him an affectionate thought across whatever continents lay between us, and began to wonder which summits he would recommend in the landscape before me as objects for my amateur practices. As soon as one descends from a pass all the peaks and heights which there seemed so conspicuous vanish behind unimportant foregrounds – even as the Philosopher is obscured by the Politician – not to reappear until, after miles and days or hours, they have altered their shape and – like the above Philosopher's principles – become unrecognizable. From the valleys, also, one hardly ever sees the actual top; some inferior hump or shoulder usurps the skyline and puts out the geographer.

And here was a third difficulty. Nearly all that lay before us – the sea-like forest country and the hills, the far horizon ranges and nearer system descending with sharp crests to the Sardab Rud – were nameless as far as we were concerned. Except for the valley below and Kalar Dasht in the distance, neither my map nor the shikari knew anything about any one of them.

After three hours of struggle with all these problems I felt excessively weary. But I made one more effort and climbed about 100 feet higher, over a scrag heap of rust-coloured slabs, to a small rise on the ridge, so as to look over its broad back towards the jungle. There was little to see. That unknown country wraps itself in a double mystery of trees and mists, and is as difficult to look at as to visit. J. B. Fraser describes its almost impenetrable tangles which, except for a small strip along the coast, have remained unaltered since his day; and Major Noel, in *The Royal Geographical Society's Journal* of June, 1921, speaks of the 'virgin forests . . . where the villagers are almost as wild as the forest itself; and where the tigers lurk in the boxwood thickets in the daytime, and stroll about openly on the beach in the night-time . . .' though this habit, no doubt, the new motor road has interrupted.

My idea had first been, after visiting the Throne of Solomon, to descend into this obscure region and discover something about the men who inhabit it – a primitive people, I had been told, who live in houses built in trees and are unfriendly to travellers. These were the men who gave much trouble to the British towards the end of the war, stirred on by a local leader called Kuchek Khan. Later they helped the Russian revolutionaries, or rather undertook independent raiding and looting in combination with them, and came to be known as Bolsheviks by the quiet inhabitants of the land. Khurramabad had been a kind of headquarters to Kuchek Khan, and the Emir Sipahsalar – the man of the shooting box at Mian Rud – had been friendly to him and allowed him to set up a toll station at Maran, to advance up into Darijan, and to charge one toman for every load of rice that went over the Salambar. About eight years ago, his 'Bolshevik' successors tried the same game. They penetrated into Alamut and looted as far as Balarud, until government troops drove them out again over Syalan while the Emir Sipahsalar, who had been friendly at first, helped in their eviction. Darijan had been robbed, but the more eastern lands of Kalar Dasht were never reached by these troubles, though they too at that time were full of robbers of a more ordinary kind, as were also the passes north of Qazvin.

'Nowhere,' said 'Aziz, 'could we *charvardars* go without paying toll to this man and that man on every pass of the hills. May Allah bless this Shah Riza, who has made the country safe'.

This praise one hears everywhere from the poor in Persia, and it may be set off against the complaints of the wealthier landowners and merchants in the towns.

To return, however, to the dwellers in the jungle. As we travelled along its mountain fringe, looking down upon it from one height or another and hearing more about it, I began to wonder if it is indeed inhabited by any particular and special race, or if there is not rather a mixture of people from the villages who become Jungalis only at certain seasons of the year. Kuchek Khan himself was a jungle man, they told me, from the neighbourhood of Resht, with long hair and beard such as the Daylamites wore in the Middle Ages: and when he was pursued they never caught him, but chased him up into his fastnesses, where he died of cold in the hills.

But his two chief friends and lieutenants, Hala Qurban and Hishmet, were not of the forest at all, the latter being a man from Talaghan: the Refuge of Allah knew him, and saw him at the last, handcuffed, and with his feet tied together under a mule, being taken as a prisoner to Teheran. And as for the later 'Bolsheviks', they were practically all Alamutis, Talaghanis, and riff-raff from the coast, with a few 'foreigners' sprinkled among them.

It is useless, they told me, to travel in the jungle in summer, for it is empty, deserted by its inhabitants for the hills; and the higher forest villages such as Daku, which is a large place, though not on the maps, are summer resorts for the coast-dwellers. In that wide belt of forest between the mountains and the sea there seemed to be no fixed population, but a continual passing to and fro from the coastal to the Alpine villages, who all have their appointed stations and grazing grounds for the various seasons of the year. But what there may be apart from these known villages I could not discover. There are long uninhabited stretches, a day or two days' march at a time, and whether the shepherds and wood-cutters who wander there are a race apart, or whether, as I think more probable, they are the sort of people I was meeting and living with, only more shy because of their more solitary life and rarer dwelling in the social village centre, I do not know. Nor could I, on this occasion, hope to solve their mystery: the high summits and the malarial lowlands were alike beyond my powers. I decided to follow the summer custom of the country and keep to the Alpine pastures; and as the map seemed to say so little about them, I thought I would examine at leisure the rivers that descend from Solomon's Throne, and finally, after following the Shah Rud to the engaging blankness of its headwaters, drop over one of the passes on to the Teheran road some hundred miles or so east of where I had left it.

So I decided; and looked once more over the outspread world from this, the highest point of my journey, before turning regret-fully back with The Refuge of Allah. He, too, had climbed the little height. However tired (and he always walked when we rode) he felt himself bound never to let me wander up a hill unpro-tected, but would follow silently, carrying the camera and glasses, and keeping at a sufficient distance to prevent his iron nails and odds and ends from interfering with my compass. When told he need not come, he would merely answer: 'To see the world is good', and would then sit with his pipe, gazing unblinkingly over new lands, wearing an air of serenity which economists might find hard to reconcile with an income of ₤.4 a year.

On the eastern side of the pass we found no iris but quantities of *Nepeta* along the edge of a snowdrift down which we now slid easily, and followed its muffled waters by a rocky valley very different from the open face of our ascent. After two hours the sun set. Far up his light still shone on yellowing pastures above the cliffs which shut us in: a flock was grazing there. The shikari, who knew this region, suddenly turned left off the path, over rocks, to a semi-circle of loose stones laid against a perpendicular cliff – the home of the shepherds. We were still far above the region of villages.

The shelter, if it can be called such, for the wall was barely two feet high, contained four sacks of wool, a goatskin or two, a rug, shearing scissors, and half the carcase of a goat or sheep, which was evidently being eaten joint by joint by the shepherds. Beside these things we camped, while in the gathering darkness the flock returned, and filled the narrow couloir above us, indistinctly bleating and pattering as the shepherds milked it – a friendly sound in that austere place.

The night was very cold. My aneroid had not yet reached a level low enough for its activities, so that we must have slept at well over 10,000 feet. The gully was too narrow for moonlight: it shone on the rocks above; in the darkness below the flock slept with little shufflings now and then, and a cold still wind crept over the ground.

Next morning we started at seven and parted with our shikari. He had apologized for asking as much as sixpence a day, and was crushed with dumb gratitude when I paid him his time back to Darijan and a small present over. And it was after this moment of emotion that we heard of the iniquity of Takht-i-Suleiman and the engineer.

As we now descended, streams began to come into our valley from the right – foaming waters called Barir, which is the name of all this region. One of the chief difficulties in mountain geography is that peaks actually hardly ever have a name: passes have names, and grazing grounds have a minute variety of names, but the summits, being of no use to anyone, are not bothered about unless they are as striking as the Matterhorn. The result is that a new mountain will be introduced in three or four different ways, according to the side from which it is approached, for the shepherds will refer to it everywhere by the name of the last grazing ground on their own side. This demands a great nicety of discrimination from the enquirer.

Barir was also the name of the first and only hut in this wild valley. It was merely a large stable for shelter, half buried with slat roof almost level with the ground, and surrounded in the pleasant morning sun by sheep and goats ready for their pastures. They would soon leave the grazing, the shepherds told us, and go to their winter lands on the coast.

Here walking down, for it was still too difficult to ride, I saw a trap for stone-martens, of which there are quantities all over these hills. It was a simple affair – a forked branch put with the fork downwards in a hole in the ground, and with a few sticks laid over: on top of these were three or four heavy stones. The marten walks under the fork, catches in it with his shoulders, and pushing it along brings the sticks and stones on top of him and is crushed in the *débris*. The skins are kept for wandering merchants who come up these valleys for this purpose, and will give as much as twenty shillings for a good one.

At last, after about two and a half hours, we came out into the main valley and met the Sardab Rud, white and green, sweeping round from the south-west. One could ride again now, to my relief, for I felt ill after the strain of the day before and wondered if here, five days' ride from Teheran, and at the farthest point of my journey, I was going to collapse after all, when the nearest road for anything on wheels was three days away. I recovered, however, as the day wore on, and we soon came into country lovely enough in itself to make mind and body forget.

Kalar Dasht

Sardab Rud means the River of Cold Water. It pours down from the south-east slope of Solomon's Throne, and flows beneath the pass of the Thousand Hollows, and has no villages for a long day's journey, nor buildings of any kind except one *chaikhana* hut below its meeting with Barir in a grassy flat space called Vanderaban. A track runs by the water's edge, and as many as a hundred people will pass along it from Kalar Dasht or Talaghan in the day, for it is one of the thoroughfares of the hills. We must have met about thirty, all in the morning hours, who had slept in the woods and would make their southern valley in the evening. They were mostly carrying loads of charcoal, and greeted us, since Talaghan and Alamut are neighbours and 'Aziz knew many of their homes.

Our river soon turned due north and little glens came into it with water from the right. On the left also a glen came in, water-less except in winter. After that, there were no side valleys for hours: the blue dotted river of my map, which, if anywhere, should have appeared somewhere about here from the left, proved to be a mere work of fancy, as we had concluded before.

This most beautiful of valleys is in the jungle. Through glades and leafy waves, reddish mountains break into it like hulls of ships, high in the sky. The trees – thorn, beech, ash, sycamore, 'divar', medlar, pear – spread there as in a park, great in height and girth; and the river stumbles over their roots in shining eddies.

Over all is a virgin sense of freedom, a solitary joyousness, a gentle bustle made by stream and sunlight and the warm light wind, independent of the life of man.

Herds of humped black cattle inhabit the valley in summer. The herdsman's boy, a light-haired Gilaki lad with small features, fair skin, and beautifully shaped Nordic head, appeared out of the seemingly uninhabited solitude to look at us as we lunched under a thorn tree. In his hand he carried a hatchet engraved with a running scroll from Khurramabad on the coast. It is a remarkable fact that the people who do things by hand still find time to add to their work some elaboration of mere beauty which makes it a joy to look on, while our machine-made tools, which could do so at much less cost, are too utilitarian to afford any ornament. It used to give me daily pleasure in Teheran to see the sacks in which refuse is carried off the streets woven with a blue and red decorative pattern: but can one imagine a borough council in Leeds or Birmingham expressing a delicate fancy of this kind? Beauty, according to these, is what one buys for the museum: pots and pans, taps and door-handles, though one has to look at them twenty times a day, have no call to be beautiful. So we impoverish our souls and keep our lovely things for rare occasions, even as our lovely thoughts – wasting the most of life in pondering domestic molehills or the Stock Exchange, among objects as ugly as the less attractive forms of sin.

The Gilaki lad, like all the jungle dwellers I had met so far, spent his winters on the coast, when the cold up here would be so severe that 'not even a crow could fly'. I asked him about Daku in the jungle, and he told me that it was a two days' journey by a valley opening out close to Kalar Dasht – a streamless valley which led west to a pass called Mazigasar, and thence on the second day to Daku, with not a village or any inhabitants on the way. About

4 p.m. we came to the opening of this valley, or rather to two of them, Kulud Qal'a and Rashak, one going west and the other north-west, both without streams and both leading to Daku, and together opening out into the plain of Kalar Dasht into which we now emerged.

Captain L. S. Fortescue and Major J. B. L. Noel have both visited this place, and mention that Kalar Dasht used to be the favourite hunting-ground of Nasir-ud-Din Shah, who built a mule track hither so that his harem and all his court could follow him on his yearly holiday. It is a rich plain, about twenty miles across: our valley opened into it gently, with foothills to the right, ploughed on their lower slopes and wooded above, while on the left along the river the mountain wall continued, low but steep. Small hamlets folded in greenery, Mujil and Ujabey, were visible in the cornland, and Rudbarek in front of us on the river. Before reaching it, I sat on a stone and took bearings on Takht-i-Suleiman and the Black Carder and the point of Barir west of them, all visible again and as lovely, rising in distance from the forest valley, as they had ever been. Villagers, coming along with herds, seemed friendly; but we had all enjoyed our recent solitary nights of peace, and decided not to ask for hospitality, but to camp outside the village if we could.

This was the first and last time we tried to do anything so impossible. We found a pleasant place with boulders to support our fire where the River of Cold Water ran strong and green in the twilight, our fellow-traveller of the day: but scarcely had we spread our sacks on the ground and started a flame, when a procession became visible, making like a black caterpillar towards us from under the trees. The vanguard was more or less plebeian, with so large a mixture of children that one was inclined to sympathize with 'Aziz who, when I lamented over the mortality which had killed practically all the babies I knew in Alamut the year before, answered that 'it was as well most babies died the first year, or one could not have any more the second.' In Rudbarek evidently they had not died when they should, and came pressing round, friendly but overwhelming. The parents followed: the circle widened: another circle formed itself outside: still we resisted all invitations to the village. Presently a wave of respectful agitation swept over the gathering: everyone rose, and the Agha, a fat blustering bully of a Kurd with three layers of neck and goggle eyes, came and sat on the carpet opposite me.

'What papers have you to allow you to be here?' said he truculently, without even the decency of a greeting.

I had half risen out of politeness, but hastily changed my mind under this unusual attack. 'My passport is in order,' I said languidly. 'My servant will find it.'

The Refuge of Allah obediently got up to hunt among the saddle-bags: the way a Persian flattens out before a bully in authority is always the most depressing sight. The fat man, disregarding my existence and evidently waiting for sensational depths of imposture to disclose themselves in the passport, sat as if every second of delay were adding guilt to a score already almost beyond official patience. He had the sort of head whose shape I dislike. I determined not to sit and be trampled upon without an effort at some kind of an offensive.

'Happy has been your coming,' I lied, with the little half inclination that accompanies the courtesy.

'Your amiability is excessive,' he was bound to reply, since one formula calls for another. 'The pass—?'

'The condition of your health, how is it?' I continued, refusing to be checked. And if he did not know the things one says to a stranger, I did, and he was going to get them all.

'Thanks be to God,' he murmured, and finished the formula with an indistinctness which did not sound as cordial as it might. 'The pass—' he began again.

But there are about fifteen polite things one can say at meeting, each requiring a little bow, each demanding their appropriate answer, with an answering bow from the person addressed. I knew about half, and the Kurdish Agha had the full benefit of them. By the time we reached the end of my repertoire I had him tamed. He did not ask for the passport when I stopped. After a decent interval to let the rules of politeness sink in, I took it from The Refuge and handed it to my adversary, who was now fortified by the presence of most of the magnates of Rudbarek, sitting in a crescent shape over against me, with his fat bulk as centre.

The passport as a matter of fact was quite adequate, and if it had not been, no one would have discovered the deficiency.

'What is that?' they asked me, pointing to the Baghdad consular signature.

'That,' said I, now completely above any sort of scruple; 'that is the signature of our king's vizier. All peoples are expected to help and befriend me when they have read this paragraph,' and I proceeded to translate Lord Curzon's remarks on the first page as to 'passing without let or hindrance'.

The Agha, his Mirza, and the various Elders there assembled listened, visibly impressed.

'Are we friends with the English?' said the Agha at last, making with laudable perspicacity for the centre of the argument.

I satisfied them on this point, but as a matter of fact the battle was won already. What we were now to suffer from was excess of hospitality. There was no question of a night of peaceful solitude: the Agha would entertain me.

Seeing that resistance was vain, I left my two men to pack up, while I followed near the van of the procession, which now made for its village in the dusk.

It is sad to relate that I spoilt the dignity of my victory by falling into a stream. There are no bridges over anything less important than the Sardab Rud, and as I jumped in the half light a slippery boulder betrayed me. The procession behind was delighted; the Agha himself, who preceded, barely turned his head and, seeing me emerge safely though wet, continued at a rapid pace until, through lanes that might have been in Devonshire, we reached his house, a two-storied building roofed like a chalet with wooden slats, with a fenced garden full of vegetables, scarlet runners, pumpkins, and sunflowers in front of it.

Some of the Darijan bouses, with wooden balconies, had already been an improvement on those of Alamut and the southern side of the watershed in general. But here in Kalar Dasht one really comes into the tradition of an old prosperity and finds buildings designed for ornament as well as comfort, as good as many a country cottage in the Alps. There are balconies and outjutting eaves; ceilings fashioned in little wooden squares reminiscent of Italy and the Renaissance; open fireplaces, niches worked in stucco, and rough ornaments in relief, cocks, flower-baskets and geometric figures, which evidently belonged to a day when Kalar was a flourishing city, as I hope to show.

The Agha's house was not the best in Rudbarek, being eclipsed by that of his brother, a long-faced Kurd with gay, easy, and irresponsible manners often found among the tribesmen. Passport or no passport, it did not trouble him: he looked at me with frank admiration for having come so far, and began to tell me, as we sat waiting for dinner in an upper room, about an English captain who had stayed with him twice, and whose Persian had impressed them all with its forcefulness if not with its variety, consisting, as he told me, chiefly of the two sentences: 'The ibex has escaped', and 'Son of a burnt father', the most energetic of Persian epithets, which the captain apparently had frequent reason to employ.

Sport in this country must be excellent. The river has trout, the hills have deer and ibex and pig; the climate is perfect and the people are pleasant and peaceful. Nothing but its remoteness from any high road can have kept it so long almost unvisited.

As we sat waiting for dinner and discussing religion, our first hostile impressions were gradually smoothed away. I recited the opening chapter of the Quran and proved myself less ignorant than had been supposed: a translation of the Lord's Prayer established the essential unity of religion, to the satisfaction even of the thin little Mirza from Medina: and a short discussion on history produced out of the bottom of a chest a Persian translation of Sir John Malcolm's *History of Persia,* which the Agha studies on winter evenings.

One will not come to a village in these mountains where the old legends are not familiar to one or two at least of the inhabitants, and a copy of Firdausi will usually be pulled down from some shelf. Among the Kurds of Kalar Dasht these classics seemed to nourish a rather aggressive spirit of patriotism, and the Agha was slightly ruffled when, having asked me who would win in the event of a war between our nations, I told him that *we* should, without any doubt at all.

'If *we* fight, every one of us is a Rustum,' said he, swelling his already portly form and placing both hands on the sash where evidently a dagger or two should be.

'We have as many Rustums,' I remarked, 'and more guns.' Whereupon the brother laughed, having a sense of humour and a disposition to like me, and I guided the talk into less delicate channels by reminding my host that, at present, all the Rustums on both sides were at peace and amity.

I found these Khwajavends, who were originally Kurds from Ardalan and Garu settled by Agha Muhammad Khan Qajar in many villages of Kalar Dasht, most useful and intelligent with historical information. They were the first to tell me of the Mound of Kalar, a few hours' ride away, whose name alone would rouse the interest of any historical student of the region.

The Site of Kalar

Although a good many references can be gleaned here and there in history about Tabaristan, the mountain country of Mazanderan, they are mostly so meagre and disconnected that it is difficult to weave them into anything like a picture of what the life of these highlands must have been before the armies of Timur Leng sacked them in the fourteenth century.

The earliest Persian legends have their home here, and probably represent a blurred outline of events long handed down by word of mouth alone. The battle between Sohrab and Rustum was said to have been fought, in spite of Matthew Arnold, at a place called Likash in the country of Ruyan. The land was full of magic and portents, a sort of Broceliande where the figures of heroes move, seeking adventure: on the coast, the White Jinn, the Div-i-Safid, was supposed to have built the castle of Ispi Rud: Minuchihr, the king, took refuge at Chalandar. He found a marshy plain, drained it by removing some boulders which are still pointed to at the mouth of the Chalus River, and built, they say, the town of Ruyan which later became the capital of the mountain district. This town is placed by Mr. Rabino, in his book on Mazanderan, in the region of Kujur, which adjoins Kalar Dasht on the east.

The medieval geographers mention Ruyan as a flourishing city with fine buildings and gardens. Close to it were the region and city called Kalar. In Kalar Dasht I was told that a mound, still known by the name of Kalar, existed, and I hoped not only to identify it as the old city, but to confirm by the help of its location a point in the medieval history of this region – namely the eastern boundary of the Daylamites, a robber people of the hills who inspired constant terror and lived in more or less perpetual warfare with their neighbours until the Assassins began to take over their lands and much of their reputation in the twelfth century.

The connection between Kalar and the Daylamites is given by the fact that the geographer Yaqut describes the town as being at one day's march from Chalus on the coast; two days from Ray (near Teheran); three from Amul on the east; and *one day from the Daylamite frontier*. From the plain of Kalar the only probable dividing line to fulfil these conditions is that of the Hazarchal Pass: Darijan – the other valley – could never be considered a day's ride, and all north of it – i.e. west or north-west of Kalar – is thick jungle until one reaches Daku, a two days' journey. The Hazarchal leads to the upper Talaghan valley, which is mentioned in the tenth century as part of the Daylam country, and Kalar would naturally be described as being at one day's distance from that fertile region: it would be equally accurately described as being close to the Daylamite fastnesses of the western jungle: in either case the site of Kalar fits the geographical requirements, and answers also to numerous references made by the historians of those times.

Yaqut also mentions the little town of Sa'idabad as close to Kalar, on the way between Hasankeif and Laktar, which latter village still exists in Kujur. Hasankeif, though not marked on the maps, is now the capital of Kalar Dasht, almost in sight of

Rudbarek. The track from Kalar to Ruyan would also be the track from Hasankeif to Laktar, along the Pul Rud valley, where Sa'idabad must be looked for.

I have gone into these references because they form the basis for the geography of Kalar.* But at the time, I had no books packed in my saddle-bags. All I remembered was the importance of Kalar in connection with the Daylamites, for if this were really the site of the old city, then we had probably crossed the Daylam border on our way down from Barir along the Sardab Rud.

I spent a happy night in Rudbarek in an upper room with three windows, in which a cooking-pot full of hot water and the unusual luxury of privacy to wash in made me feel at peace with the world. The morning looked out on gentle slopes of stubble. Humped oxen were ploughing against a wooded background and a brook beyond the fenced kitchen garden ran with murmurs in the early sun. After the mountain solitude here was a sense of relaxation and ease. How delightful these villages would be, if only they did not so constantly entertain one! To eat, rest, write, read or meditate with fifty or even a hundred people watching, though it became almost habitual by the end of my journey, never ceased to be a strain.

The Khwajavends had all the free and gay conviviality of the Luristan tribesmen to whom they belong, and came after breakfast in a body to lead me across the Sardab Rud, which runs through the village under high walnut trees, to a handsome two-storied house with overhanging eaves and wooden balconies, approached through a courtyard from the back. This was the brother's house, and had sheltered Captain Fortescue on both his

---

* For a more detailed study see my article; 'The Site of Kalar' in the *Royal Geographical Society Journal* for March, 1934.

visits, and I was brought here to see the loot of an ancient grave laid bare by floods ten years before. The brother was a charming host, with manners something between those of a cavalier and a highwayman: he was a bachelor, and ready at a moment's notice to offer his hand and heart – temporarily I rather suspect and, like an Elizabethan hero, without attaching too great importance to the proceeding. He showed me all his treasures, including five champagne glasses and a gilt fruit dish, with an air of:

'if these delights your heart may move'

and sat contemplating me in a meditative manner through his long eyelashes while I turned over in my hands two pots and a bronze spear-head from the grave.

These were obviously very ancient, and people who are good at dating such objects have since told me that they probably belonged to somewhere about 1500 B.C., and that they are similar to other objects found near the south-west corner of the Caspian. The two pots were made of grey earthenware, with a decoration of lines and small circles scratched upon them, and very good in shape. The spear-head was bronze, the tip broken off, probably for ritualistic purposes: it had been found lying on the breast of the skeleton, while the pottery stood at its head. Other graves, they said, might probably be found in the same place – the valley of Rashak we had passed the day before, some way from where it opens into the plain. There was no getting them to dig, however, as the laws on this point have become very stringent in Persia.

An hour or so went over the bargaining, interspersed with glasses of tea. When the two principals appeared to reach a deadlock, friends and retainers took up the controversy and set the negotiations going again. I finally parted with two tomans (4s.), and a procession formed to carry the objects in triumph to my room.

After this I managed to escape and was allowed to wander through that most delightful of villages whose houses are all embowered in walnut and fruit trees, and whose main street is but a narrow earth track beside the rippling loveliness of the river. Blotches of sunlight filtered through shade almost as green as the leafy canopies that caused it; a green luxuriance flung itself over the fences of the little gardens; and the bright colours and many beads and bangles which the Kurdish women love made them to look as gay as butterflies against their whitewashed walls, where they sat spinning on benches built to run along the outside of the houses, in the manner of old Italian palaces.

At about three-thirty, I decided to move east across the plain so as to be nearer the Mound of Kalar, which I meant to examine next day. I took leave of the Agha's two wives, both friendly to me, but frank enough to mention in each other's presence how very little use they had for each other. This the Agha himself corroborated, declaring that a wife at a time is as much as a man can deal with comfortably.

'I think one is enough,' said the younger bride, whose position was secure, with something as near a toss of her head as her voluminous head-dress would allow. But a look of great anxiety crept into the eyes of the older and less beloved one.

'I am thinking of divorcing her soon,' the Agha remarked to the party in general.

And I felt it was not the moment to stand up for monogamy.

Two young women, visiting in Rudbarek, now offered to escort us across the plain to their home at Lahu for the night. We set off with them in the pleasant afternoon and, emerging from the last low undulations of the hills, stepped out into the openness of Kalar Dasht.

Hasankeif on the river, the same that Yaqut mentions in the tenth century, is the capital of the plain, where the police stay whenever any happen to be up here. But Kurdichal on the eastern hill and Lahu in the south-east are the two biggest villages, counting about 200 houses each, and inhabited by the Khwajavend, mixed – in Lahu at any rate – with a number of Ali Ilahis who live at daggers drawn with the Kurds.

As we approached this village we were in rich country out of the mountains. Corn and hemp were grown. Ricks stood on platforms raised above the ground, dark against the distance of the western valley, where the peaks of Solomon and Barir and Qabran floated like smoke above the forest green. A little stream, the Dakulad, came out from the south-west, where a forest-clad ridge ends this part of the Sardab Rud valley and holds in its recesses the *Imamzadeh* of Shahre Zamin, a place of pilgrimage.

South of the ridge, eastward, is a lower rim of hills, dividing Kalar Dasht from the Chalus, and called Bashm (or Bash). The city of Kalar probably lay near that low, easy col. It is still, as when Yaqut wrote about it, a three days' ride from Qazvin. In sight below lies the Pul Rud valley, which led to the neighbouring city of Ruyan, known also as Shahristan, and mentioned as being sixteen leagues from Qazvin on a pass.

In verifying the old geographers, it is a great advantage to be using the same methods of transport as they did, and I was able to gauge fairly accurately what the league or *farsah* meant to a medieval traveller; it is roughly supposed to be four miles, but when travelling with local guides I usually found it to be more. 'Aziz, for instance, always told me that eight *farsahs* were a full day's travel: but even our longest stretch, six and a half hours along a more or less level valley track, not counting halts, only covered three *farsahs* by local estimates. When the distances are reckoned in daily stages, they are far more accurate, and Yaqut's one day from Chalus and three from Amul are perfectly reasonable for the col of Bashm today: a modern traveller would probably do the latter in only two days, but there is now a good coast road, whereas at that time the track turned inland at Natil, climbed the watershed by Ruyan, and came west along the Pul Rud valley.

The weak point in Yaqut's distances, as far as the col of Bashm is concerned, are the two days to Ray (Teheran). This route can have altered little during the centuries. I have never been over it myself, and it may be possible, though not easy, to do it in two days; and Mr. Rabino, who is the best authority for this country, mentions it as feasible. There are two watersheds to cross, and a day's journey in mountain country is very often determined by the watershed: people will get up early and do a long day to get over a pass: or conversely will limit themselves to a short day if two passes are near together, so as to avoid a night out of range of the villages: and a traveller in Yaqut's time would have the less cause to dally on this bit of his journey if the lawless Daylamites held the upper Talaghan valley, as we have inferred from the position of Kalar. That city and Chalus were both fortresses against the Daylamites, and the neighbourhood of this robber people in itself would probably cause the western routes across the mountains to be less used than others by tourists of the time, so that accurate information might have been more difficult to obtain: the wildness, difficulty, and natural dangers of the Mazanderan tracks are commented on in every century from their earliest mention to the present day. The fact remains, however, that two days is little to allow between Bashm and Ray.

The site of Bashm, however, fulfils all the other conditions left by the old geographers for Kalar, and the probability of the locality is further strengthened by the fact that traces of old extensive habitation spread all down the slope towards the Chalus valley. Here next day I was to find carved tombstones evidently of a very early date; to be told of traces of walls and masonry discovered here and there when the fields are tilled: and to learn that the rumour of a great vanished city still clings to this hillside. The Mound of Kalar itself, below the col of Bashm in the plain, was possibly, as Mr. Rabino suggests, once the palace of the governor. And another point further supports the general identification of these sites. The great causeway of Shah Abbas, built by that monarch in the sixteenth century to open up the Caspian shore, turns inland only once, and that is precisely in this region of the Chalus valley: a piece of it about twenty miles long was reported to Mr. Rabino as being still in existence near Pishembur, which is a village on the northern edge of Kalar Dasht where cross tracks still take off for Daku and the jungle. Owing to my having no books of reference with me I neglected Pishembur, and merely looked at it across the plain instead of going to investigate: but the fact remains that, if the king's causeway came so far inland over hilly country instead of sticking to the easy coastline, there must have been something of sufficient importance in the plain of Kalar to justify the extra trouble. Shah Abbas probably built his causeway on the line of the old track which ran from Amul (the capital of the plain) to Ruyan (the mountain capital), and thence by Banafshe (which still exists under the name of Banafshade just below Bashm) to Kalar and on into Daylam.

Apart from statistics, however, there is a remarkable feeling of old and prosperous civilization in the plain of Kalar Dasht. The buildings especially make one think that the people there are still doing in an incomplete way what once they knew how to do much better. The stucco ornaments and careful ceilings and pleasant wooden porticoes all speak of a 'decayed gentility'; and before I left Lahu, a woman brought me a piece of blue lustre tile, thirteenth century or so, which she had found by the mound, but which – as she thought it worth its weight in gold – I was unable to buy.

Labu

Our hosts were of the poorer sort, and our coming to their house was no end of an event. No sooner had we reached it than the younger woman volunteered to show me the view south of the village, where the Dakulad comes out of a forest bay, as it were, into the plain: this was merely so as to show me off to the inhabitants, as I soon discovered, for after wandering a long way through the ups and downs of Lahu – which is another lovely community half buried in dim shade – when we finally reached the last house and looked over open country with no one to observe us, she lost interest and began to entice me back again as fast as she could to call on various important people she thought I ought to know – just as the distinguished visitor in an English village may be taken to call on people who will be 'so interested to meet him', regardless of his feelings.

There was in all this a lot of drama which I missed. I noticed that while I was induced to linger in some places with an obvious effort to make me show off nicely, I was hurried past others inhabited, as I learnt that evening, by Ali Ilahis, whom the Kurds consider unbelievers. One would think that in a prosperous district full of villages, it would be possible so to arrange things that one would not have to live door to door with one's enemies; the mere discomfort of lifelong hatred would be too much for our weaker European nerves. The East does not feel this, or perhaps looks on the excitement of a next-door enemy as something to enliven life: you will find people in one place for generations and centuries, closely united as oil and vinegar in one cruet, and as incapable of mixing.

When we got back to the house, I found that a cloud had fallen over the geniality of the party. It was the fascination of either 'Aziz or The Refuge of Allah that was to blame. The master of the house had been asking his wife what she meant by inviting strange men. He would have nothing to do with us, and my escort, with very black brows, were preparing to camp in the courtyard. The blot of inhospitality was threatening our host, and through him the whole village, and perturbed Elders went to and fro between the parties, trying to save the name of Lahu in the mouths of strangers.

I sat aloof, on a sort of raised dais in the living-room, counting the family belongings hung from rafters in the ceiling and watching the women, now thoroughly cowed and flustered, as they held up bits of chicken for my supper against the flame of an open fire. At the other end of the room, where there was another dais for the men, the peace overtures were being made. 'Aziz was accepting them with a haughty condescension quite remarkable in the mild little good-natured man. The room had no windows, but round holes about a foot in diameter here and there: glass is not known in these hills. The inner room, into which the family retire when the winter cold really begins, had no window at all, but an earthenware oven let down below the level of the floor, which they fill with embers and cover with a quilt and sit there with their legs tucked into the warmth and nothing to do but talk the winter through.

In spite of various dark sayings about the danger from Ali Ilahis, I refused to sleep indoors, and had my bed put up near the cows and mules in the moonlight. There I retired, after an evening of conversation with an old man called Said Ibrahim, who came to distract my attention from the discourtesy of our host and to discuss Persian history. He told me that the plain of Kalar still belongs to its peasant owners, and is more contented than the lands of Kujur and Khurramabad east and west, whose lord is the Shah. He was a charming old man, with that interest in life and affairs which distinguishes the hillman or tribesman from the peasant, and learning was to him a real divinity, however small may have been the crumbs thereof which could be gathered in Kalar Dasht. If I were asked to enumerate the pleasures of travel, this would be one of the greatest among them – that so often and so unexpectedly you meet the best in human nature, and seeing it so by surprise and often with a most improbable background, you come, with a sense of pleasant thankfulness, to realize how widely scattered in the world are goodness and courtesy and the love of immaterial things, fair blossoms found in every climate, on every soil.

We were made late next morning by my anxiety to buy *golapish,* one of the silver coronets the young women wear, and some silver buttons in the bazaar. The ladies of Kalar wear also little silver pendants all round the edges of their short coatees, but there were none in stock, and the bazaar – a row of nine or ten huts – was not properly open, reserving its activities for two days in the week. To have a bazaar and four baths turned Lahu almost into a town, although its grass-grown hilly lane, with a water and ducks meandering down it, and the houses dotted about accidentally, some whitewashed, some neatly caulked of wood and mud, and some just logs one on the other, made it look more than ever like a Devonshire village that had got itself mixed up with Swiss chalets, and been filled with inhabitants whose taste in dress was not yet spoilt by the industrial age.

Here too, however, as at Rudbarek, the feeling of an old and civilized prosperity still lingered. It must have had many centuries of unbroken tradition behind it from very early times. The town of Kalar was destroyed by the Mongols in the early thirteenth century, but rebuilt and walled in A.D. 1346, and continued under its native rulers – a family called Padhusban – from the end of the seventh century until A.D. 1595, when Shah Abbas finally did away with them. Islam came here slowly, with no shock of war, spread by the proselytizing of 'Alid refugees. The Arab governors could only rule in harmony and conjunction with the native lords; and as late as the tenth century these mountain people were still 'partly idolaters and partly Magians'. In the bazaar of Lahu I bought a silver coin belonging to one of these native princes of the eighth century, with a Zoroastrian fire-altar on the reverse side.

We now visited the Mound of Kalar, which is barely half an hour from Lahu in a north-easterly direction. It stands in the open plain with nothing near it except another small mound called Golegombé, and is about thirty feet high and 550 or so in diameter. On it I found a few shards of shiny black earthen-ware and much of the common red ware – but nothing like the woman's bit of glazed tile or the coloured pottery of the Assassin castles. It is a fine mound, waiting for the excavator. The view from it was full of a prosperous peace, with corn-lands and their platformed ricks in the foreground, long woodland spurs rising westward to the mountains of Solomon at the far valley head, and lower wooded ridges on the north where, through a defile, the Sardab Rud leaves Kalar and travels a day's journey through jungle to the sea.

Night in the Chalus Valley

The Chalus is a big narrow valley, with Nasir-ud-Din's easy level track along it, now arranged for motors to meet the new Karaj road from Teheran, but still untouched when we travelled there.

We made for it down easy slopes across the col of Bashm, passing Banafshade on our left, Sangesarek, Shahri, and Kiviter. Leaving Kiviter with protests from 'Aziz, who hated to reject villages offered by Providence at lunch-time, I rode off the track down to the left across cornfields to a small *Imamzadeh* of Muhammad, hidden in a grove of beech trees.

This was a solitary place; by some obscure message it must have called across the cornfields, for there was nothing from far off to promise so much beauty. The beech glade grew within a low wall of boulders, round a whitewashed chapel mellowed by ages of sunlight, with door of wooden lattice work. Around it lay the carved tombs of the city on the pass. There were numbers of them, crooked and half sunken in the ground; moss and lichen had eaten into their scrolls and ornaments of stone. Each grave was made of four slabs, two short ones at head and feet and two long ones or sometimes more down the sides, with earth in the middle; there was no Arabic or script of any kind on any one of them, but a running or geometric pattern, and often the slabs at head and feet rose in their centre to a stone hump, evidently typical of this region, since I came across the same thing later at Joistan in Talaghan. New graves too were here, for the place is still used, and a box of Qurans for the congregation stood in the porch of the chapel: but we found no inhabitants except the birds, who felt themselves at home, and three Kurdish lads who presently materialized out of nowhere to look through my glasses, and took me a few hundred yards over the stubble to where another carved tomb lay out in the open. The hillside is covered with them over a great area, including Shahri and Kiviter, and the ridge north of it which they call Ikane; and there are remains of walls, now indistinguishable heaps, but once, the village people say, a great city rising up towards the ridge. Not a single tomb seen by them, the lads told me, had any script upon it.

The elder of these boys could read and write: there was a *mulla* in Kiviter who taught him, and he had been for a short visit to Teheran. He would like to learn English, he said: did I think he could do so in six months? This keen adventurous Kurdish mind is a pleasure to meet, so different from the peasant's apathy of the plains. Truly the world belongs to the hillmen.

Rather late in the afternoon, though the exact time is uncertain since my watch now went on strike altogether, we left our sanctuary and continued downhill over wide natural terraces scattered with thorny bushes till we came into the valley: then crossing a little ravine full of acacia thickets we climbed in dusk to the village of Baude, where we hoped to spend the night.

Silence met us even before we entered among its dozen or so of houses. Not a soul was to be seen. In the last daylight the fenced gardens shone with a careless luxuriance, tossing untended shoots of scarlet runners and pumpkin out across our path. We called and called without answer. A cat came at last, and rubbed itself against the wooden uninhabited colonnade. Grape vines trailed everywhere, and unripe figs hung over the path. A solitary donkey, round and sleek, with evidently no *arrière-pensée* of toil, came browsing about, picking out a green morsel from the gardens here and there. And round the village, fields of *arzan*, which seems to be a sort of millet, stood waving almost ready for the harvest, with not a soul to gather them.

We abandoned Baude and went on southward by a wide track almost good enough for cars, with the river running against us in a cliff bed far below. Its voice grew louder as the darkness fell; everywhere else the same inhuman stillness lay.

Mosquitoes began to hum in the twilight, explaining the valley's solitude, for these unhealthy lowlands are left in summer, while the population lives in mountain *yailaghs* a few hours' climb above.

Down by the water, a half-dozen houses and a bridge, reached by a steep path, is Barazan. We looked at it intently from the top of the cliff, and seeing no movement there, concluded that it, too, must be deserted, and walked on – the Milky Way in a straight line above us in the narrow valley. The darkness grew so thick that gradually even the mules' ears were lost to sight. 'Aziz sang. He sang of the young tribesman who, with gun slung on his shoulder, went to the fair of Tunakabun and there saw Zerengis.

'Thou hast a tent in the summer, *ai* Zerengis.
Thy short coatee is made of velvet, *ai* Zerengis.
My breast is full of trouble, *ai* Zerengis.
Fearing that thou hast loved another, *ai* Zerengis.
Thy love turns towards me, *ai* Zerengis.'

The refrain came with a lowering of the voice to great depth at the end of each verse, giving the ballad a strange poignancy.

But the parents of Zerengis would not hear of her marriage with the young man with the gun, and how it all ended I never heard, for now in the darkness and silence of the valley a light appeared shining dimly from what turned out to be the ruins of the burnt *chaikhana* of Masal. We rode up hopefully, intrigued by the total absence of sound: not even a barking dog to meet us. And as we turned into the court of the *chaikhana*, we saw that the light came from a lantern standing on the ground, at the head of a man wrapped in a *shaular*, apparently sleeping. There was no other human being anywhere about.

The man neither rose nor answered our greeting. 'Aziz and The Refuge went up to him and spoke in low voices, dragging monosyllables out of him as he lay. They came back after a minute or two, said briefly that this was no place for us that night, and turned the mules round; it was only after we had ridden on again some way that I thought of asking why the master of the *chaikhana* had received us so strangely.

'He was not the master,' said 'Aziz. 'The *chaikhana* was burned down the day before yesterday, and that was just a traveller walking to Teheran, too sick to continue on his road.'

'What?' said I. 'Do you mean to say he was lying there ill and we gave him no help?'

'One cannot help everyone one meets,' said 'Aziz, who gives his pennies to any rogue of a beggar whenever he sees one. 'He was probably dying. He is too poor to have even a donkey to ride. He does not come from our part of the country.'

I was for turning the mules round again, but the suggestion roused a protest even in the silent submissive Refuge of Allah. I realized that it would be difficult to make the two tired men retrace their steps, and my own fatigue no doubt took a good deal out of the active spirit of charity. We compromised, and decided to send help from the next *chaikhana*, or to return down the road after our own supper if no *chaikhana* appeared; and I rode on sadly in the darkness, weighed down by the cruelty of Asia in its vast spaces of solitude, where the name of enemy and stranger are almost synonymous.

How friendly are the Alps, their villages and small church towers climbing to the very lips of the glaciers: no one, lying there by the side of the path, would want some helping hand stretched out. But here was 'Aziz, the kindest and gentlest little man, thinking me a fool for being concerned about someone 'who does not come from our part of the country'. The great religious leaders have all come from Asia: it is the more spiritual continent, we are fond of saying. But perhaps it is also because the woes of mankind are here so much more evident; the need for reliance on something more universal than human charity is so much greater; and the deep and tender hearts of the prophets are more inevitably awakened by the sight of human suffering. The Ages of Darkness produced saints: perhaps their relative scarcity at the present day is the result of a higher standard in ordinary comfort and kindness.

The next *chaikhana*, when it did appear as a dim silhouette in the night, turned out also to have been burned down. We seemed, indeed, to be in a valley of Death. Its little stream of water could be heard, however, dripping across the path in the night, and we decided to stay there and put up my bed by the light of the lantern. 'Aziz and The Refuge were happy anywhere because they lived on nothing but cheese and *chupattis*; it was always necessary to bring to their minds that I needed something more varied. We had eggs, however, and the last tin of sardines, and as we sat finishing them up, steps were heard striding down the road, and it turned out to be the companion of the sick traveller, who was not quite alone in the world after all: the man had gone to look for food along the road. We provided him with what we could, including quinine, and retired to sleep with a more cheerful feeling about the world in general. The Milky Way, the 'Road of God,' lay like a lid to our box of a valley, with stars thick as a field of daisies round it. Mosquitoes hummed in the sticky warmth. I decided to leave the Chalus as soon as I could next morning, and find a healthier and less depressing way home across higher ground.

The Squire of Bijeno

We found the first sign of habitation at Tuvir next morning, after one hour's ride in the dawn.

A roadside *chaikhana* was giving breakfast to travellers, our own sick friend of the night before having passed along there in the earliest hours. We took in a new store of bread and turned westward uphill towards Tuvir village, which is well above the road in groves of trees. We climbed up by a rough path where steps had been laid here and there, made of carved slabs from graves such as those seen round the *Imamzadeh* the day before.

The Chalus here is one of those steep sunken valleys which open to comparatively flat ledges high up, where villages and fields spread themselves out of sight of the world below. The path we now took led us from one to the other of these villages along the western side, through woody lanes of beech and oak and thorn, with hidden brooks that might have been in England; and a trailing wet mist came down upon us, hiding the distance, but giving more than ever a pleasant homelike feeling to the brambles and drooping wet grasses among the boulders. The villages that we passed were inhabited almost exclusively by women, the men having gone higher up with the flocks. Tuvir, Qutir, Meres, we passed: from here there is Kandichal, the way over the ridge, westward into the Sardab Rud valley. We next came to Pishkur, a large village, with one well-built stone house among its wooden chalets, where I was unexpectedly greeted by a Bahai from Tunakabun whom I had met the year before. We refused to stop, however; trusting to the map and the probabilities of the landscape, we were making for Delir, which must have been visited by Europeans since it was more or less correctly placed, but which neither of my men had ever heard of; they could not get over their surprise at finding these villages really in existence when we came to them.

After Pishkur the rain came down and the landscape was blotted out completely. 'Aziz paused beside some men who were winnowing in the downpour, and enquired the name of the owner of Bijeno village which we were coming to. We soon turned down a steep and slippery sheet of mud between houses, came to a chalet with carved wooden pillars, removed a sheep that was blocking the entrance to the squire's reception room, and found the owner of Bijeno, a young man, sitting on the floor with a pocket mirror and comb beside him, smoking his pipe of opium.

The Squire of Bijeno was more than cordial, he was delighted to see new arrivals on a wet day. He had a fire in the hearth in no time, while I sat on the carpet and dried myself. The mist came trailing in wisps at the open doorway; the black sheep settled down again among our shoes; the squire's wife, a handsome lady, imperious and benevolent, who had been called in from the next room, sat cross-legged before the *samovar*, while four daughters, ranging upwards from seven years, crouched round in a circle and caressed a white cat called Mahmal, decorated with streaks of henna.

In a far corner of the room an ascetic, long-faced servant with two curls sticking out over the ears under his black felt cap, cut up a newly flayed sheep with a pocket-knife borrowed from one of the daughters, and managed the operation with remarkable neatness, in a manner suitable to the drawing-room.

I spent the day in this family atmosphere while the squire told me about the Bolsheviks who came up as far as Bijeno in 1920, and murdered his brother and carried off 150 sheep. These were really the local marauders we had been hearing of before, but the name covers a multitude of sins and, in all this country, Bolsheviks are still spoken of with intense hatred; much propaganda will be necessary before they are looked upon with any kindness. These raids were the last events of any importance in the district apart from the Sipahsalar's suicide, and they have remained fixed in the minds of the people, for now that the country is at peace, village life has become complete stagnation as far as the small *seigneurs* are concerned. They have not yet learned to take any real trouble over their estates; the habit of opium saps their energy and prevents even the effort of hunting in the mountains; all they do is to sit in their rooms receiving visitors, talking endlessly, and hearing bits of news from far around. In the next room, their female household also sits in idleness, waiting upon any stray command: and when the winter closes down, they retire to the windowless refuge of the interior, bring out the *kursi* over the central sunken fireplace, and continue to talk till the snow melts again.

The squire of Bijeno was a reader. We spent the evening over the history of Alexander and over *Memoirs of the Boxer Rising*, translated into Persian from the French – a strange waif of a book that I came upon again in a wild part of Luristan, amusing the leisure hours of a tribal chief. But the history of Alexander is appropriate enough anywhere between the Nile and the Indus, where that unique and undefeated conqueror passed in a trail of splendour that has not yet abandoned his memory. His legend, together with that of Firdausi's heroes, are familiar to most of the village lords. One is sorry in a way that they can now only read about war while its practice is abandoned, since that alone might keep them, it seems, from going to pieces altogether under their village boredom.

The squire and his family did not tire of telling me about the comfort and splendour of the bath of Bijeno. A clear stream, said they, renewed every day, ran from a mountain spring into a tank where, being heated, it received the ablutions of the squire's lady and her friends before any villagers were allowed in: I should have it all to myself if I liked.

The mist was still creeping in at our door in a dark and cheerless way; the rain dripped outside: the prospect of a hot bath in limpid water sounded alluring; against my better judgment I consented. I went out in a dressing-gown into the mist; two daughters and a maid preceded me with a lantern down a narrow muddy lane, out into fields, in again among houses, and finally down steps to a subterranean catacomb littered with *débris* and egg-shells, where five or six elderly Maenads with nothing on to hide the repulsiveness of their bodies welcomed me with exclamations of joy. I felt as if I were to be initiated among witches into worlds of darkness. Through two low doorways of stone I saw the water, a torpid brew which looked many weeks old already: the toothless naked ones saw me hesitate, and invited me with shrieks of delight. But my courage failed. Though I knew that it meant an insult to Bijeno and all its inhabitants, I could not face it: I gathered up my dressing-gown and fled.

When I returned to the family circle, the squire's musician was with him, a wizened little man in a felt suit much too big for him, gathered into a tight belt which made him look like musical comedy. He was playing on a pipe that Theocritus might have handled, made of the Chalus reeds and decorated with patterns burnt into it, fish, camel, ibex, and geometrical designs among them, all done in delicate primitive lines. The pipe was about two feet long, with four stops close together and one separate. The piper sat playing the folding tune for sheep, which the animals know and, hearing it, will gather from the hillside of their own accord: and as I listened, I thought of the Italian mountains in my childhood, when an old man would walk through the village every morning with a horn; and as he blew on his instrument, all the goats stepped out from the low doorways of their stables and followed him. We sat a long time over the music, the squire join-ing now and then with sad monotonous tones, while I discovered an unsuspected talent and sang German songs remembered from the nursery.

The whole of next day was swathed in mist, and spent over maps in the squire's drawing-room, where I also slept with the family, six in the same room, but luckily with the door open. It was a good room, with niches all round in the usual fashion, but a touch of originality was added by a narrow channel filled with running water, built round the base of the wall for bugs to drop into and get drowned: not many seemed to get across, for they are not among the most adventurous insects and have none of the *élan* of the common flea.

The Pass of Siolis into Talaghan

On the third day a gleam of sunlight suddenly revealed an unsus-pected hillside opposite, and we started off immediately, for we were anxious now to reach the Talaghan valley, our last bit of exploring on the way home.

The mist still hung on our flanks like Cossacks round a retreat-ing army: out of its softness, as we rode up along the banks of the Halis stream which waters Bijeno, came a sound of drums. It was a column of pilgrims, some fifty souls, as it might have been in the days of Chaucer, setting out on their way to Meshed in Khorasan. The most of them were old people, some few on donkeys, others walking along with staffs; a good many women among them, and no one apparently with more luggage than would be tied up in a striped handkerchief. The two large shallow drums that made the noise were carried by a couple of young men in the rear. They all greeted us. 'God give you strength,' said we as we passed, which is the correct thing to say; and they were lost again in the mist.

The clouds lifted a moment to show us Natil, a large village on a grass slope, and a young Kurdish merchant from Kurdichal in Kalar Dasht strolling down it behind his two donkeys laden with wares. Out of one of his saddle-bags he produced tea, and weighed it out in a pair of scales with two stones in the other, while 'Aziz haggled for the price. He came here to buy marten skins off the mountain people in winter, and now travelled over the region with these few wares in his pack which the villagers could not supply out of their own resources.

Beyond Natil the mist sank round us again as we climbed over grass to the Michilisera Pass, with high hidden rocks on our right hand. A gleam of crest would appear now and then like some goddess shoulder turned in flight: a wayfarer or two loomed out of the whiteness and vanished – one man, a fine sight in red trousers patched with blue. The bells of our mules seemed to tinkle in a wadded silence; and in the absence of all else, our attention was concentrated on the small flora at our feet, gentians, linum, wild snapdragon, iris plants, and sempervivum and violet leaves in the cracks of the boulders. The gentians seem widespread at anything over 8,000 feet; they had a starry brilliance, with drops of moisture in the hairy rim of their chalices.

South of the Michilisera is Delir, a big place of about 150 houses at the head of a shallow plain suspended, as it were, between two passes, the Michilisera by which we came and the Anguran out of sight to the south, the most frequented of the ways between Chalus and Talaghan. Behind it the mountains rise ever higher and rockier to the Throne of Solomon, by wild and barren valleys: but eastward is a flat stretch of cultivation for some miles, where a river meanders to another small village called Ilat, and then drops off the plateau as off a ledge, into the unseen Chalus far below.

The sun came out, and we strode down on this landscape with great strides, inflicting a shock on the children of Delir, who were playing by the roadside. They gave me a long look, burst into tears, and fled screaming: this was the effect of my *terai*, which invariably demoralizes all *Mazanderani* babies. The grown-up population of Delir were not much more self-restrained than its children, and far more troublesome, for about two hundred women turned out, crowding the roofs, surging round me in the narrow streets, venturing close up to touch my garments to see if I was real, and very nearly suffocating me among them. They were brightly dressed, with their silver coronets saucily tilted over one eye, and many silver ornaments hanging round the edge of their short jackets. Men, just as interested, but with their dignity to consider, were interspersed here and there, and to this more reasonable portion of humanity 'Aziz turned in despair, and procured me a little momentary breathing space by shooing the women away, and likening them to wild beasts of the forest.

Our idea of lunch in a cottage here was soon abandoned: one might as well have lunched in a tornado. But presently, questions and answers having been exchanged, a man from Talaghan emerged and took matters in hand. Talaghan is next door to Alamut and therefore, in 'Aziz's estimation, capable of containing a few good men: the two fraternized over the wickedness of everywhere else, shepherded me, with a tumultuous crowd behind, out of the village streets, and walked along for half an hour or so up the valley, till only the stronger-minded pursuers followed. The Refuge of Allah stayed behind to collect food.

The ridge behind Delir rises up gradually to the Hazarchal, the Pass of the Thousand Hollows and its peaks, which lead like lesser notes of music to the grand chord of Solomon's Throne, out of sight. We sat at the opening of the valley, enjoying tranquillity, and looking at the new peaks behind shifting clouds through my glasses, until The Refuge appeared with five eggs in his hand and a crowing cock under his arm, whose throat he proceeded to cut with a pocket-knife, in a silent spasm of viciousness evidently intended for the uncivilized population of Delir. Little trailing processions of inhabitants, visible far away across the fields, disturbed the end of our meal, and drove me farther up the valley, not before a Mirza's daughter, a tiresome girl who would have been a bluestocking in a town, cross-questioned me in religion amid a circle of her female friends. There are no Kurds or Turks in this part of the country. The people are dark-eyed and fanatical; the name of Armenian, indiscriminately applied to any Christian, rouses dislike. But I found that what knowledge I had of the Quran, and the ordinary politeness of mentioning the Muslim saints and prophets with the titles of respect to which the people are accustomed, would make them friendly very soon.

The river of Delir is considered locally to be the Chalus River, and we followed it to where it swirls round a corner from its source in the valley of Seven Springs. Here we decided to camp for the night. Shepherds had built a semicircular enclosure against a cliff by the stream, and there we made our fire: there were two small plots of *arzan* behind walls across the river, and otherwise nothing but rock and short grass and grey water, with thorny bushes higher up for fuel. A man with a long-handled axe, and black hair, lank at the back on his neck, turned up from nowhere to be a guide: we kept him because of his pleasant smile, and he reappeared after an interval with a cooking-pot and gun. An old trapper then joined us, a shepherd from Kujur, a cousin, said he, of Riza Shah, who came from that country. With a jolly manner, and a staff over his shoulder, and the smallest of skull caps on his head, he sat and asked me for medicines which would give him children, and talked about the trapping of animals in the hills.

The evening cleared to a limpid sky with small clouds floating: swallows flew under the cliff. The water made its pleasant noise, and so did our *pilau*, sizzling in the pot. And as we sat there on the boulders, little groups of visitors came walking up to see us from Delir, talked of this and that in their good-mannered way, and slowly worked round to the subject of medicines, for which Teheran, a three days' ride, was their nearest source of supply. They had fine faces, much lined and wrinkled, framed like fourteenth-century portraits in their long hair: and the medieval likeness went further than the mere external – it was the same life that created a recognizable type.

A touching couple came – two middle-aged people with a small sick baby, dying obviously of starvation. The woman carried the child, while the father had six eggs in a handkerchief as a fee, which he put down on the ground beside me with a pathetic humility. All their children had died, and if this one also died, said the woman, she would be too old to have another: they had no doubt as to my being able to cure it, but only as to my willingness in view of the insignificance of the six eggs. I gave them a tin of Ovaltine, hoping for the best, and filling them with a joy which wrung one's heart.

The Pass of Siolis is not so difficult as the Kalau, though it is nearly as high, and only open for the summer months of the year. It is chiefly used for the transport of salt from the south, while charcoal and heavier merchandise go round by the lower and easier Anguran. From our camp at 8,000 feet it took us five and a half hours to get up to the top, climbing steadily, first through oak scrub, then in and out of rock with patches of snow. I was still incapable of bearing the height, and rode nearly all the way, with twinges of remorse on behalf of the mules.

'The perfume of the hills seizes one's heart,' said 'Aziz, who also hoisted himself on to a mule whenever I did so, with no similar excuse. The Refuge of Allah had been bullied out of his breakfast because I insisted on an early start, but walked on without a sign of weakness, as steadfast as the landscape around him: no work was ever too much for him. But as for 'Aziz, he carried my field-glasses and my stick, trying to look as if they belonged to him, and limited himself in the matter of work to a general amiability with passers-by.

This Siolis track was more beautiful than that of Kalau, for below us on our right we had a wild, uninhabited valley running up to Lashkarek, a conical peak near the Thousand Hollows Pass, and the black rocks of a mountain called Siahkulu faced us like a castle rampart across the fosse of the valley. And on our left were green tiers of corries of the valley of Seven Springs, where the Chalus River begins in waterfalls.

We were refreshed on the way up by meeting mules with panniers of small apples from Talaghan: but it was a weary pull, and the pass itself a wearisome, sand-coloured distension, leading one on and on towards an elusive skyline, one of those passes that have a world of their own of small bumps and hollows at the top. From the little height of Saraban, which makes one of the horns of the pass, as it were, a beautiful high world spread itself around us. There, led up to by the ridge of the Thousand Hollows, whose nearer peaks rose at our feet, we saw again the Throne of Solomon and all its sisters, with a snow wreath curling round it in a semi-circle, from which the River of Cold Water, our Sardab Rud, takes birth. Round it and lower, the hills lay like tumbled folds of blanket. The gradual southern slopes of Elburz and his peers, hitherto invisible, showed in the farther west, and below them, coming eastward towards us, a broad, populous valley, the bed of the Shah Rud of Talaghan. A blue serrated edge of hills with many passes, all more or less on a level, bounded its farther side; beyond it, out of sight, was the Qazvin-Teheran plain, the world of motor-cars; the Survey of India had looked up from that civilized flatness and reached the skyline from the southern side, locating the points and giving me at last, after my weeks of travel, an identifiable object to use as a base.

We descended by a rough way towards the Narian stream, meeting tributaries as they poured in, for the ridges spread like fishbones, making many little uninhabited valleys before they break in precipices and defiles on to the Shah Rud below. Above the defiles are villages, situated in the middle parts of these side valleys, on a line more or less parallel to the main stream but much higher, with a track connecting them which leads straight from the Anguran Pass in the east.

As we came down in the evening towards the water, the hillsides grew more steep and stony; we looked around for a sheltered place, with grass for our animals, to eat and sleep. Just as we came upon it, a little rocky semicircle by the stream, 'Aziz sneezed. Nothing would induce him to stop after so sinister an omen: reluctant but docile, we followed him, and found no other space to camp in until, in darkness, we reached the meadows of Narian and unloaded the packs in a stubble-field surrounded by willows, filled with chirping crickets and small watercourses that ran through the tilled earth, a comfortable sound after the mountain silence.

The Upper Shah Rud

I now meant to make straight for Teheran, sketching out the more or less unmapped eastern Shah Rud as I went – but the problem of the Daylamite frontier made me decide first on a western detour by Joistan in case any medieval traces might be visible at the southern opening of the Hazarchal track.

Joistan, however, which we reached through a dreary land of red earth by Dizan and Mehran, turned out to be a large, prosperous village with some of the old humped tombstones (called *shutur* – or camel), and with carved stuccos and lattice work in the houses – but no trace of fortifications. West of it, the Shah Rud runs in an open populous valley filled with villages, with the chief place and centre of government visible in green groves at Shahrak, some hours' ride away. North-west of it is Elburz, not impressive from this its gentler side, masked from the lower ground by a world of folds and outworks.

On the opposite side of the valley, the slope rises gradually to the passes on the skyline, with a fair number of villages, and many tracks over the edge to the Qazvin plain. One comes here into reddish earth like that of Alamut, and this, and the softer lines of the landscape, give to the lower Talaghan a mild and smiling aspect after the dark granite and high severity of Takht-i-Suleiman.

I did not rest long at Joistan, which is at the opening into this milder land, for I heard of a fortress some hours' ride away on this side of the Hazarchal Pass near Parachan. In spite of the heat, in spite of the extra fatigue involved by the moral effort of retracing one's steps, in spite of 'Aziz's remonstrance and The Refuge of Allah's eloquent silent resignation, I decided to go to Parachan and return; the mules' loads and 'Aziz were left behind; and in the very hottest hour of the afternoon, The Refuge and I started off again up the Hazarchal valley.

Our ride had no incident except that turning a corner above Dizan, we met a young lad walking carefully with an egg in each hand; irrelevant curiosity prompted me to ask what the eggs were for, since the place seemed inappropriate for omelettes.

'They are to cure a sick mule,' said the lad. Verses of the Quran had been written on them by the village *mulla*, and now they were to be broken over the mule's forehead as it lay in convulsions down below in a meadow.

'If God wills, it will be cured,' said we, in the best manner of the Delphic oracle, and hurrying on, for twilight was falling, crossed another bridge into Parachan. Here we were again in the mountains: the stream was narrow, with bushes of brier at its edge; the village climbed beside it.

The first thing that met our sight was a street of hayricks far bigger than the houses. They stood close together, rough grass with thistle tangled in it: it was all winter fodder, since Parachan, the last village before the pass, is under snow for four months of the year. During all that time, the people told me, the only paths made are those which lead from the water or the ricks to stables and house: a village down the valley is as inaccessible as a foreign land, and if anyone is sick, he must carry on as best he can till the snow melts, or die. (In any case there is no doctor in all the Talaghan valley, so it makes little odds.) The winter's food supply for humans is stacked in large grain sacks in their inner room, together with a sufficient quantity of tea, sugar, and paraffin to last through the snow. Sometimes the young men venture out after ibex, which they encompass in a circle made by ten or twelve of their number and, converging upon it, seize it on the mountain-side where the snow impedes its flight. One would have thought that, with so many idle winters behind them, the people of these mountain villages might have invented some means of locomotion like skis or snowshoes to break their prison; but nothing of the kind has been done, and I spent the evening trying, in very inadequate Persian, to describe the elements of winter sports.

The Philosopher who runs Parachan was an old man with a venerable dignity and an ample dark blue turban, which he wore as a member of the sect of Huseini, an ultra-Shi'a confraternity fairly widespread in all this country. He lived in a tiny house raised high on a mud floor off the steep street, and littered about with female objects, cradles, distaff, and white flocks of wool for the spinning. His daughter-in-law, called Flowering Bud, ran the house for him, a fresh and buxom bride pleasant to look on and very friendly, though her language was of no use for conversation, being a local dialect. The Philosopher too was cordial, as much so and a little more so than he felt he should be to anyone so dangerous to religious prestige as a member of the female sex. The disabilities of my position were brought home to me, for having come with hardly any luggage, I relied on my host for things like bowls and basins, and found that though he would stretch a point and let me drink out of the household vessels, he did not feel he could risk his salvation by letting me wash.

I resigned myself to dirtiness with a good grace and an understanding of these nicer points which evidently gained his heart, for he soon invited me from the inferior society of the harem to a seat on the tea-carpet among the Elders, where we discussed the politics of Parachan while the whole village population passed in queues before the open door, taking a look in turns. They had never seen a European woman, they told me, nor did they remember a man, though Captain Fortescue must have passed through here on his way to the pass above us. The Philosopher, as headman, had the onus of gathering taxes: he was expected to pay so much to government, and to collect it as he thought best. I have never seen any dissatisfaction with this arrangement, and the leaving of the matter entirely in the hands of a local Elder, who has his own popularity among his people to think of, is probably much more satisfactory than direct collection by a Persian government official. The Parachan headman had the added advantage of holiness to endear him to his folk; he did, indeed, seem a kind and just man, and his voice in the darkness as he said the last prayer of the day floated over the heads of his sleeping flock – dim, shrouded forms on the flat roofs under the stars. Through the night, Orion swung above the village street; and still in starlit darkness, the young men of the village rose, gathered their sickles, and started off to cut hay in the hills. We left when daylight came and, with the headman beside us, climbed to the so-called tower, known as Ahmad Raje, about an hour's walk above us on a western spur.

Nothing at all was left above ground except a few nondescript potsherds, and there can never have been anything here but a small look-out or guard tower to dominate the way from the pass. But a storm was sweeping across the Hazarchal; Solomon's Throne towered among the clouds, and I was glad to have almost encircled that Unattained One, and to see it in magnificence from the south as well as from the other three points of the compass. When rain and hail came pouring from the ridge towards us, we descended hastily to Joistan by a shorter way, down barren hillsides for sheep along the Shirbash stream, which burrows down the valley through a canyon. There is a track here to Ab-i-Garm, our hot springs of the Darijan valley, which can be reached in a day; and a venerated *Imamzadeh* shows high above it, white among the rocks of Mounts Sāt and Avater. We were seeing all our familiar landmarks from the other side.

Next day we travelled from Joistan to the last of the Shah Rud villages, riding between uncultivated and uninhabited valley walls into which defiles opened at intervals from higher tracks, invisible on right and left. There was plenty of traffic – chiefly charcoal, coming by the Hard Rud tributary from the Anguran Pass into our valley – and in the afternoon we came again into pastoral meadows by Gatideh, and to grassy slopes that run by Garab, the last village, to the gentle Asalek Pass.

We, however, camped on the open slope, and next morning, following the early trains of mules that carry charcoal to the tree-less southern plain, climbed up to where, on the northern side of the Sirbash Pass between two smooth hills, the Maiden's Castle – Dohtar Qal'a – stands in a sweep of solitude, a small irregular pentagon with round buttress at one corner. It is a rather disappointing place, being comparatively modern, built of small stones, more tidily constructed than the older ruins I had seen in Alamut and the lower Shah Rud: it had walls three feet thick and a sort of shaft in the middle of the building, now filled with earth and stones. At one time a village must have scrambled below its walls down to a cuplike hollow, and a graveyard on the opposite rim of the cup suggested with its modern tombstones that the place was quite recently inhabited. One or two of the gravestones go back to the seventeenth century: they were cut in a pale green limestone which does not exist in the neighbourhood, and which puzzled me until next day, when I came upon the boulders which produced it far down in the southern valley: to have carried it up so toil-somely meant a good deal of traffic and a fair standard of well-being on the upland; it was probably once far more inhabited than now, for an old conduit still runs along the hillside, built, they say, by Malik Shah, the Seljuk. We were on the line of the higher track, which runs along these solitudes from the Asalek

Pass east of us, through empty pastures to Kochiré at the head of the valley of that name, and probably much farther along, from village to village.

Such as it was, the Maiden's Castle had the inestimable advantage over many antiquities of being above and not under the ground. Only the real expert has eyes to see as in a vision what is buried: for the rest of us, the dust of great persons' graves is speechless.

'King Pandion, he is dead,
All his friends are lapped in lead.'

One likes to have a visible peg or two on which to hang one's imagining. And Dohtar Qal'a provided this in an eminent degree, as journalists say, whatever that may mean. The Shah Rud valley lay below it, far below, and the mass of Takht-i-Suleiman rose on the other side across six ranges, borne as a hero on the shoulders of the crowd, with spurs and lesser ridges radiating outwards like spider's legs. He alone had snow upon his sides. Around him, in diminishing galaxies, were mountains. We saw the long cleft of the Hard Rud water outlined in a spiky fin of rock, and Zarine Kuh behind it, opposite us, above the grassy shoulders of the Anguran Pass, where the caravan route runs by Dehdar.

No human building was visible in this solitude except the old fort and a tea hut buried nearly to its roof in the hillside against wind and snow. Here I slept shivering at a height of nearly 10,000 feet until The Refuge crept up in the coldest of the night and spread his own carpet over my unconscious body, while he lay on the hillside thorns in his *shaular*.

To the Teheran Road

By seven o'clock next morning we were up on the neck of the pass, and even then the wind was so bitter that the two men made a big fire of thorns to sit by while I took my bearings with numbed fingers. This was an important point, as this southern watershed of the Shah Rud is properly mapped, and I hoped that these last bearings on Takht-i-Suleiman and Elburz would help me to get an approximately correct result for all the rest.

We now descended southward, with that melancholy feeling of turning one's back to the hills, down a narrow gully of a valley with only one waterfall to enliven it, towards the district of Arenge. After a while our path rose again and led us along heights over the river that wound in rocks below, so that one's feet seemed to hang over it as they stuck out beyond the pack-saddle. And then we came down to the first small village, with mulberry trees to shade it, hot at its lower level of only 5,600 feet.

At Arian, the second village, we lunched. The women were busy making jam out of small red and yellow plums and apples of the woods. They cook them without sugar and leave them in the sun to dry to powder, and use them to flavour soup. Ground grape-stones are used also in this way for flavouring. But besides this sort of preserve, they had some excellent real jam which they eat together with the *shiré* or sweet mulberry syrup known all over Persia.

Our valley grew wild and beautiful. High limestone cliffs encompassed it, built in fantastic battlements, regular as masonry. Here the green boulders of the tombstones lay scattered, washed by the jade-green stream. At Pulab, the Laurà River comes in from the left, and we found the first survey pegs for the Shah's road, now built and finished, but then looking still like a titanic impossible labour. Old carved tombstones here and there show that this was an ancient, well-trodden way; they were being used for the new road, and there are probably none left in sight by now.

We got tired of rocks upon rocks; they rose in chaos from the very water's lip where our path cut its way on narrow ledges; only here and there, in some widening amphitheatre of the river bed, small villages crowded with their trees. Their ripe white mulberries were sweet for the picking as we passed, not pausing.

This barren landscape grew wilder as the daylight faded; piled up like a discordant orchestra in fierce confusion, it had none of the mighty serenity of the higher hills. But at last, with dusk falling, we opened out on a wide bend, and saw Varian in groves of trees and orchards through which the river flowed unconstricted, catching last sunset gleams.

We asked for lodging, and were taken to a garden full of fruit trees and a small house with three good rooms raised on a terrace, where carpets were soon spread. A dish of grapes and pears was brought me, first fruits of the warmer plains, and we were told that our last stage next day would be made along the level surface of the new motor road.

Some way up the valley, at a village famous for its weavers, we had stopped to bargain for one of the woollen covers they call *jajims*. 'Aziz had shouted casually over a garden wall, and the thing was produced, its many-coloured stripes and close texture approved of after expert handling by the men, and the negotiations carried on half-way down to Varian, with various refusings, handings back and re-takings of the object, and returns of its owner back to his village and down again after us. Now the cover, of which I was very proud, was produced for the approval of the assembled ladies of Varian, who had gathered to call on me. They instantly rose and departed, and soon brought along a far more engaging *jajim*, with all sorts of geometric fancies woven on its stripes. Another series of negotiations started.

If I had paid ten shillings for the plainer one, how much more must I not give for this superior specimen, said they.

If I had paid too much for one, how much the more reason for not doing so with another also, said I.

The lady who had woven it, a merry black-eyed bride, was not anxious to sell, said she. The *jajim* had taken her a long time to make; its wools were spun, its colours dyed, and its pattern invented, all by herself.

True, said I, and I would not wish to deprive her of anything so valued: but why should I get another *jajim* when I had one already, except as an unnecessary extra if the price were truly reasonable? and I handed it back to her for the night, while the friends of both sides took up the chorus, 'Aziz and The Refuge with a strict eye upon me, knowing my weakness towards the latter stages of such long-drawn-out battles.

They were quite right. Next morning, after the night's meditation, the *jajim* was handed to us from a doorway as we passed.

This was the last night of my adventure, and in the stuffy lower air by the splashing fountain of the little garden, over-arched by unfamiliar branches of trees after the open hills, I could not sleep. I roused 'Aziz early, but failed to make him move: and when at last we started down the valley, two thousand workmen were already on the road, and we had to pass by nearly all of them.

'God give you strength, God give you strength,' The Refuge continued to say politely as we passed each shift. They were sturdy, pleasant-looking countrymen with little of the navvy look of such people in Europe. They got, I was told, three krans [6*d*.] a day, and came from the villages around. They had already done all the level bits as far as Varian, and were now tackling the rocky intervals, which had been left like islands; where we came upon such places, we had to abandon the new smooth surface and take to the old track, which appeared more precipitous than ever by contrast and had all sorts of surprises in the way of dynamite and men with instruments along it.

One of these nearly cost me and my mule our lives as we rode near an edge of cliff above the river. A navvy came along with two iron bars under his arm, and as they were long and not well under control, the point of one of them prodded my animal as we passed. Shikar the mule had already been showing a doubtful attitude towards the blessings of civilization as exhibited in modern road-making; this unprovoked attack demoralized him altogether; he turned at a gallop down the small strip of scree which separated us and the river, three hundred feet or so below. No one is more helpless than a rider on a pack-saddle: seated as on a platform, without either rein or stirrup, suicidal mania in his mount is a contingency not provided for. But luckily The Refuge of Allah happened at the moment to be walking ahead with the halter in his hand. He pulled with all his might and said soothing things at the same time: the mule paused; I slipped off, and rescued my camera which had got caught at the very lip of the abyss.

'Thank God it is not broken,' said I, with the single-mindedness of the photographer. The Refuge of Allah said nothing for a long time.

'If you had got killed,' he remarked at last in a reproachful tone, 'what should we have said when we got to Teheran without you?'

After this, Shikar the mule showed a natural dislike for anyone who was carrying anything, and tried to shy on every narrow place we came to, so that we were glad when finally we saw the last of the two thousand workmen, and trudged along a level surface where red flat reaches of the plain run up between the hills.

A mud-walled obsolete fort holds the opening of the valley, and beyond this, in the hottest of the afternoon, we came to Karaj on the main road. Here we left The Refuge and the mules to trudge on through the day and night to Teheran, while 'Aziz and I took to the miseries and discomforts of Persian cars. Many delays there were and breakdowns in very sight of the capital, but finally we did arrive that evening, and in a flowering garden amid the refinements of life, said good-bye to each other with hands upon our breasts.

JOURNEYS

Other books in the series: